THE HISTORY OF
MEDIEVAL
EUROPE

*from the mid-eighth to the
mid-thirteenth century*

BRIAN PULLAN

Fellow of Queens' College, Cambridge

BASIL BLACKWELL · OXFORD
1971

ISBN 0 631 09630 2

First Printed 1966
Reprinted
with corrections
1971

PRINTED IN GREAT BRITAIN BY COMPTON PRINTING LTD
LONDON AND AYLESBURY
AND BOUND AT THE KEMP HALL BINDERY

To My Parents

with affection and gratitude

B. S. P.

PREFACE

This collection of translations is principally aimed at students of medieval European history—especially undergraduates—who would like to see something of the raw material on which the writing of that history ultimately depends. Most people feel some curiosity about the raw material: but, unless there is some manageable selection from it available, they may find access to it very difficult. This book has been compiled in the hope of helping such people.

There is little need to point out the inevitable limitations of the book. Selections of documents are not really 'primary sources'—they reflect the special interests and prejudices of their makers as much as do 'secondary works'. The smaller the selection the more arbitrary it must be; and the selection must be small to be manageable. No translator can exactly convey the meaning or flavour of the original or produce an impartial translation of a highly controversial document.

The documents translated here are mainly concerned with the history of law and government in the Church, the Empire and the great secular kingdoms of medieval Europe: with the theories behind such law and government, with feudal and Roman law, and with the relationship between clerical and lay power. The book has been confined chiefly to these themes to prevent it from becoming too much of a miscellany. I have made the selection in the belief that these branches of history are the ones whose study most immediately gains from documentary illustration; sometimes, indeed, they are incomprehensible without it. My selection of documents is not intended to imply that these are the only branches of medieval history which matter. The documents are chosen for their power to illustrate within a fairly narrow space the themes mentioned above.

The commentary on the documents is intended only, where necessary, to describe the circumstances which surrounded the issue of each document or to say something, very briefly, about its author. Sometimes there are rough hints about what to look for in the document, but apart from these I have avoided expressing personal opinions about its interpretation. Many of the documents have been the subject of much controversy—some of them were chosen for that reason. It has seemed to me that the only fair way of coping with this is to draw attention to books and articles which either discuss the document concerned or deal with subjects closely related to it. Accordingly a short bibliography has been attached to each document or group of documents. These bibliographies do not claim to be complete: only to provide a lead for those who are particularly interested in a particular document. Some apparatus has been provided for those who wish to use it. It would be dishonest to imply that I have personally absorbed the contents of all or even of a large proportion of the books and articles listed, that the commentaries in this book summarize all their views or that the translations necessarily take account of these. This book is not the work of a professional medievalist. My part is confined to certifying that the books and articles listed discuss the documents concerned or subjects related to them. I have, however, found many useful suggestions on the translation of certain documents in some of the authorities listed.

Like most anthologies, this one owes much to its predecessors, and especially to the following: C. Mirbt, *Quellen zur Geschichte des Papsttums und des römischen Katholizismus* (4th edition, Tübingen, 1924); E. F. Henderson, *Select historical documents of the middle ages*, in various editions; R. G. D. Laffan, *Select documents of European history* (London, 1930); and Joseph Calmette's volumes of *Textes et documents* in the Clio series (Paris, 1937-). Among recent discussions of sources, it is worth drawing attention to van Caenegem, *Kurze Quellenkunde des Westeuropäischen Mittelalters* (1964).

It only remains to me to thank those who inspired this book and advised me during its preparation. Dr. Walter Ullmann, my supervisor as an undergraduate, originally suggested it to me, has given me invaluable help and encouragement, and has made many suggestions for the bibliographies. My debt to him is very great. Mr. R. F. Bennett, who read an earlier draft of part of the book, has with great kindness advised me both on the selection and on the arrangement of documents. When the book was in its early stages, Dr. Michael Wilks made a number of very useful suggestions. Dr. David Knowles and Dr. R. C. Smail have also given up precious time to advise me. I owe many thanks to Dr. Karl Leyser for his generous help in correcting a number of errors in the first impression of this book and for his advice on certain questions relating to German history.

I am greatly indebted to Mrs. T. R. Maltby for her assistance in preparing the typescript and for her criticisms of my 'translator's English'. My wife has helped me very much and has been enduringly patient.

B. S. P.

ABBREVIATIONS

A. ABBREVIATIONS USED IN CITING SOURCES
AND IN FOOTNOTES

C.S.E.L.	*Corpus scriptorum ecclesiasticorum latinorum*
Du Cange	Du Cange, *Glossarium mediae et infimae latinitatis*
Mansi, *Concilia*	J. D. Mansi, *Conciliorum nova et amplissima collectio*
M.G.H.	*Monumenta Germaniae historica*
Cap.	*Capitularia Regum Francorum*
Conc.	*Concilia*
Const.	*Constitutiones et acta publica imperatorum et regum*
Epp.	*Epistolae*
Form.	*Formulae Merowingici et Karolini Aevi*
L.L.	*Libelli de lite imperatorum et pontificum saeculis XI et XII*
Ss.	*Scriptores*
Ss. Rr. Mer.	*Scriptores Rerum Merovingicarum*
Migne, P.L.	J. P. Migne, *Patrologia Latina*

B. ABBREVIATIONS USED IN BIBLIOGRAPHIES

A.D.R.S.	*Archivio della R. deputazione romana di storia patria*
A.H.R.	*American Historical Review*
A.R.S.	*Archiv für Rechts- und Sozialphilosophie*
A.S.L.	*Archivio storico lombardo*
A.S.P.	*Archivio storico pugliese*
A.S.R.S.	*Archivio della società romana di storia patria*
A.U.	*Archiv für Urkundenforschung*
B.E.C.	*Bibliothèque de l'École des Chartes*
B.Z.	*Byzantinische Zeitschrift*
C.	*Cîteaux*
C.H.J.	*Cambridge Historical Journal*
C.M.H.	*Cambridge Mediaeval History*
C.O.C.R.	*Collectanea ordinis Cisterciensium reformatorum*

D.A.E.M.	*Deutsches Archiv für Erforschung des Mittelalters*
D.A.G.M.	*Deutsches Archiv für Geschichte des Mittelalters*
E.H.R.	*English Historical Review*
H.	*History*
H.J.	*Historisches Jahrbuch*
H.V.	*Historische Vierteljahrschrift*
H.Z.	*Historische Zeitschrift*
M.A.	*Moyen Âge*
M.H.P.	*Miscellanea historiae pontificiae*
M.I.Ö.G.	*Mitteilungen des Instituts für österreichische Geschichtsforschung*
M.S.	*Mediaeval Studies*
N.A.	*Neues Archiv*
P.B.A.	*Proceedings of the British Academy*
R.B.	*Revue bénédictine*
R.B.C.C.	*Revue bimensuelle des cours et conférences*
R.H.	*Revue historique*
R.H.D.	*Revue d'histoire du droit*
R.H.D.F.E.	*Revue historique de droit français et étranger*
R.H.E.	*Revue d'histoire ecclésiastique*
R.H.E.F.	*Revue d'histoire de l'Église de France*
R.I.H.P.C.	*Revue internationale d'histoire politique et constitutionnelle*
R.S.I.	*Rivista Storica Italiana*
R.S.R.	*Revue des sciences religieuses*
S.G.	*Studi Gregoriani*
S.P.A.W.	*Sitzungsberichte der preussische Akademie der Wissenschaften*
Spec.	*Speculum*
T.	*Traditio*
Z.K.	*Zeitschrift für Kirchengeschichte*
Z.S.G.	*Zeitschrift für schweizerische Geschichte*
Z.S.S.R.	*Zeitschrift der Savigny-Stiftung für Rechtsgeschichte*
g.a.	*germanische Abteilung*
k.a.	*kanonische Abteilung*

Contents

Chapter II: *Aspects of the Church and its Government in the Twelfth and Early Thirteenth Century*

PART THREE: EMPERORS AND EMPIRE
IN GERMANY AND ITALY

Chapter I: *The Ottonians and Salians*

Chapter II: *The Investiture Contest*

Chapter III: *The Reign of Frederick I*

Chapter IV: Innocent III and the Empire

Chapter V: Frederick II as Emperor and as King of Sicily

✓ PART FOUR: FRANCE AND FLANDERS

Chapter I: Feudal Problems in France and Flanders

Chapter II: The French King as Suzerain

Chapter III: Royal Administration and Justice under Philip Augustus and Louis IX

Chapter IV: Royal and Clerical Power

PART ONE

The Carolingian Empire

NOTE ON REFERENCES

Biblical references are to the Latin Vulgate. All French books cited whose place of publication is not expressly mentioned were printed in Paris.

CHAPTER I

The Origins
of the Empire in the West

THE PAPACY AND THE HOUSE OF PIPPIN,
739-754

§§ 1-3. These texts are designed to illustrate, though they can do so only very imperfectly by themselves, the special connexion formed between the Papacy and the house of Pippin in the mid-eighth century —as a result of the Lombard threat to Rome, the uneasy relationship of the Popes with the Emperor in Byzantium, and the need of the formidable mayors of the Merovingian palace to have their seizure of power legitimated.

The *Liber Pontificalis* (1A, 3A) is a collection of short semi-official biographies of Popes. The extract in 1A is an interpolation, possibly written in the time of Stephen II (752-757), into the contemporary life of Gregory III (731-741). The life of Stephen II was written under his successor Paul I (757-767).

Some of the other sources are Frankish official histories. The author of 1B was writing on the instructions of Count Childebrand, uncle of King Pippin. The *Annales Regni Francorum* (2) are not a contemporary source. Their compilation began somewhere about the last decade of the eighth century, but they were probably edited from notes of important current events taken by clerks in the royal palace. 3B is believed to have been a fragment of a chronicle drawn up at St. Denis in 805 and preserved in the Chronicle of Moissac (an abbey in Aquitaine) and the Annals of Metz.

The *Clausula de Unctione Pippini* (3C) is a note added to a manuscript copy of the *Miracula* of Gregory of Tours. Ostensibly it was written in 767, doubtless by a monk of St. Denis. Some scholars have—not very convincingly—questioned its authenticity.

On the sources, as well as the introductions to the editions from which these extracts are translated, see L. Levillain, 'L'avènement de la dynastie carolingienne et les origines de l'état pontifical (749-757)', B.E.C., 94

(1933), 237 foll.; in defence of the *Clausula*, Levillain, B.E.C., 88 (1927); M. Baudot, M.A. (1927); H. Leclercq, 'Pépin le Bref', in *Dictionnaire d'archéologie chrétienne et de liturgie*, 14 (1939), 282 foll.

For comment on the texts and for background, see L. Duchesne, *The beginnings of the temporal sovereignty of the Popes* (London, 1908); E. Caspar, *Pippin und die römische Kirche* (Berlin, 1914), discussed by L. Halphen, R.H., 121 (1916), 337 foll.; Levillain, 'L'avènement'; E. Caspar, *Geschichte des Papsttums*, II (Tübingen, 1933), 730 foll.; J. Haller, *Das Papsttum: Idee und Wirklichkeit*, I (Stuttgart-Berlin, 1934), 385 foll.; R. Aigrain, in A. Fliche and V. Martin, *Histoire de l'Église*, V (1938), 412 foll.; R. Bonnaud Delamare, *L'idée de paix à l'époque carolingienne* (1939), 103 foll., on 2; H. Pirenne, *Mohammed and Charlemagne* (London, 1939), 222 foll.; L. Halphen, *Charlemagne et l'empire carolingien* (1947), 16-17, 21 foll.; O. Bertolini, 'Il problema delle origini del potere temporale dei papi', *Miscellanea Pio Paschini*, I (Rome, 1948); W. Ullmann, *The growth of papal government in the middle ages* (London, 1962), 44 foll.

Other documents in the original Latin are collected in J. Haller, *Die Quellen zur Geschichte der Entstehung des Kirchenstaates* (Leipzig-Berlin, 1907); some are translated in S. C. Easton and H. Wieruszowski, *The era of Charlemagne* (London-New York-Toronto, 1961).

For full bibliography on sources used for Part I, see W. Levison, H. Lowe and R. Buchner, *Wattenbach-Levison, Deutschlands Geschichtsquellen im Mittelalter* (Weimar, 1952-1953).

§ 1

Pope Gregory III appeals to Charles Martel for aid against the Lombards, 739.

A. *Liber Pontificalis*, ed. L. Duchesne, I (1886), 420.

The province subject to Roman government was smitten by the wicked Lombards and their King, Liutprand. Coming to Rome, he pitched his tents in the field of Nero, ravaged Campagna, and shaved and dressed many Roman nobles in the Lombard fashion. Therefore the man of God, oppressed with grief on every side, took the holy keys from the tomb of the blessed apostle Peter and sent them by sea to the land of Francia, to the most wise Charles, who then ruled the Frankish kingdom, by his ambassadors, the most holy bishop Anastasius and the priest Sergius, to ask the most excellent Charles to free them from this great oppression by the Lombards.

B. *Chronicarum quae dicuntur Fredegarii Scholastici Continuationes*, ch. 110, ed. B. Krusch in M.G.H., Ss. Rr. Mer., II, 178–9.

Now at this time the blessed Pope Gregory twice sent to the prince from Rome, the see of St. Peter the apostle, the keys of the holy tomb and the chain of St. Peter and great and numberless gifts, an embassy without precedent, proposing an agreement whereby he would withdraw from the territories of the Emperor and decree a Roman consulship for Prince Charles. So the prince received the embassy with marvellous and sumptuous honour, gave them precious gifts, and, richly rewarding them, dispatched them to Rome, to the home of St. Peter and St. Paul, sending with them his companions Grimo, Abbot of Corvey, and Sigbert, a monk of St. Denis the Martyr.

§ 2

The deposition of the Merovingian King Childeric III and the coronation of Pippin, *circa* 750: *Annales Regni Francorum*, ed. G. H. Pertz and F. Kurze (Hanover, 1895), 8.

[749] Burghard, Bishop of Würzburg, and the chaplain Fulrad were sent to Pope Zachary, to ask him whether or not it was good that at that time there should be Kings in Francia who had no kingly power. And Pope Zachary instructed Pippin that it would be better to call King the man who had the power, rather than him who remained without regal power. That order might not be disturbed, by virtue of his apostolic authority, he commanded that Pippin should be made King.

[750] Pippin was chosen King according to Frankish custom and anointed by the hand of Archbishop Boniface of holy memory and raised to kingship by the Franks in the city of Soissons. Childeric, who was falsely called King, was tonsured and sent to a monastery.

§ 3

The meeting of Pippin and Pope Stephen II at Ponthion, 754.
A. *Liber Pontificalis*, ed. Duchesne, I, 447–8.

When King Pippin heard of the arrival of the most blessed pontiff, he made the utmost haste to meet him, together with his wife and his sons and his principal subjects. He sent his son Charles, with some of his noblemen, nearly a hundred miles to meet the angelic Pope. He himself received the most holy Pope nearly three miles from his palace at Ponthion, descending from his horse and prostrating himself with great humility upon the ground, together with his wife, sons and nobles; and he acted as groom to the Pope, running for some distance beside his horse. Then the pious Pope and all his men, giving glory and endless praise to God with a loud voice, all set out with the King for the palace, singing hymns and canticles, on the sixth day of January, on the most holy feast of the Epiphany. And there, when they were seated together within the oratory, the most blessed Pope tearfully begged the most Christian King to settle the cause of St. Peter and the commonwealth of the Romans by a peace treaty. Pippin, by taking an oath, satisfied the most blessed Pope that he would make every effort to obey all his commands and admonitions and, in accordance with the Pope's wishes, to restore the Exarchate of Ravenna and the rights or territories of the commonwealth by every means possible.

As the winter season was at hand, the King asked the Pope to go with all his men to spend it in Paris at the venerable monastery of St. Denis. When this was done and he had arrived with the most Christian Pippin at the venerable monastery, by the Lord's will, after some days, the most Christian King Pippin and his two sons were anointed Kings of the Franks by the grace of Christ by the same Pope.

B. *Annales Mettenses Priores*, ed. B. von Simson (Hanover-Leipzig, 1905), 44–5. For a very similar text, see *Chronicon Moissiacense*, ed. G. H. Pertz, in M.G.H., Ss., I, 292–3.

The same year, Pope Stephen, who had succeeded Pope Zachary of blessed memory, refusing to tolerate the menace of the Lombards and the arrogance of King Aistulf, came to seek protection from King Pippin. When King Pippin was informed of this, he was filled with great joy and ordered his eldest son Charles to meet the Pope and conduct him honourably to his presence at the manor called Ponthion. When the Pope arrived there, he was honourably received by King Pippin. He conferred many gifts on the King and his noblemen. On the following day, the Pope with his clergy, sprinkled with ash and dressed in a hair shirt, prostrating himself on the ground, entreated King Pippin by the mercy of God Almighty and the merits of the blessed apostles Peter and Paul to free him and the Roman people from the hand of the Lombards and from enslavement to the haughty King Aistulf. He refused to rise from the ground until King Pippin and his sons and the Frankish noblemen had extended a hand to him and raised him from the ground as a token of the aid and liberation to come. Then King Pippin, fulfilling every wish of the pontiff, sent him to the monastery of St. Denis the Martyr, and most earnestly and respectfully told him to pass the winter there. Then King Pippin sent an embassy to Aistulf, King of the Lombards, exhorting him out of reverence for the blessed apostles Peter and Paul to cease his ungodly oppression of the Roman cities and not to commit these insolent and impious acts against the pontiff of the city of Rome. But the ambassadors won nothing from that haughty tyrant save answers full of arrogance and insulting words concerning every point on which the most pious Prince Pippin had instructed them. . . .

c. The *Clausula de Unctione Pippini*, ed. B. Krusch in M.G.H., Ss. Rr. Mer., I (1885), 465-6.

If, reader, you wish to know when this little book was written and issued in precious praise of the holy martyrs, you will find that it was in the year of the Lord's incarnation 767, in the time of the most happy, serene and catholic Pippin, King of the Franks and Patrician of the Romans, son of the late Prince Charles of blessed memory, in the sixteenth year of his most happy reign in the name of God, indiction five, and in the thirteenth year of his sons, Kings of the same Franks, Charles and Carloman, who were consecrated Kings with the holy chrism by the hands of the most blessed lord Pope Stephen of holy memory together with their father the most glorious lord King Pippin, by the providence of God and by the intercession of the holy apostles Peter and Paul.

This most prosperous lord and pious King Pippin had, three years previously, been raised to the throne of the kingdom by the authority and commandment of the lord Pope Zachary of holy memory, and by unction with the holy chrism at the hands of the blessed priests of Gaul, and election by all the Franks. Afterwards he was anointed and blessed as King and Patrician in the name of the Holy Trinity together with his sons Charles and Carloman on the same day by the hands of Pope Stephen, in the church of the blessed martyrs Denis, Rusticus and Eleutherius, where, as is well known, the venerable Fulrad is Archpriest and Abbot. Now, in this very church of the blessed martyrs, on the same day, the venerable pontiff blessed by the grace of the sevenfold Spirit the most noble and devout and most assiduous devotee of the

B

holy martyrs Bertrade, wife of this most prosperous King, clad in her robes. At the same time he strengthened the Frankish princes in grace with the blessing of the Holy Spirit and bound all, on pain of interdict and excommunication, never to presume in future to elect a King begotten by any men other than those whom the bounty of God has seen fit to raise up and has decided to confirm and consecrate by the intercession of the holy apostles through the hands of their vicar, the most blessed pontiff.

We have inserted these things briefly, gentle reader, on the very last page of this little book so that they may become known by common report to our descendants in subsequent ages.

THE DONATION OF CONSTANTINE

§ 4. The Donation of Constantine purports to be an imperial decree issued by the Emperor in 317. It begins by describing how Constantine had been converted to the Christian faith through a dream in which the apostles Peter and Paul appeared to him, and how at his baptism by Pope Silvester he was miraculously cured of the leprosy from which he was then suffering. In recognition of the power conferred by the Saviour upon St. Peter, Constantine determined to confer on the Popes, who were the successors of St. Peter, a supreme power even greater than his own. The author of the Donation drew heavily on a popular legend, the *Vita Silvestri*, which he further expanded. For some time the Popes based their claims to universal dominion partly on the Donation of Constantine.

Since the Renaissance scholar Lorenzo Valla exposed the Donation as a forgery, there has been little attempt to maintain that it was genuinely issued by Constantine. But there is no absolute agreement among scholars about the date at which it was forged. The majority of present-day historians would probably agree that it was produced by the papal curia about the middle of the eighth century. It may even have been shown to Pippin by Pope Stephen II at Ponthion.

An enormous literature centres round the Donation of Constantine and it would be impossible to give a detailed list here. Levillain, 'L'avènement', 231 foll., lists older works on the subject; Ullmann, *Growth of papal government*, 58 foll., 456–7, refers to several more recent articles. Cf. also Halphen, *Charlemagne*, 30 foll., and R. Folz, *L'idée d'empire en occident du Vᵉ au XIVᵉ siècle* (1953), 19–21, 192–4. For

Valla's dissection of the Donation, see C. B. Coleman, trans. *The treatise of Lorenzo Valla on the Donation of Constantine* (New Haven, 1922); C. B. Coleman, *Constantine the Great and Christianity* (New York, 1914), gives a Latin version of the *Vita Sylvestri* as well as the text of the Donation.

See also below, Part III, nos. 4B, 34, 35.

§ 4

Extract from the forged Donation of Constantine: text printed by K. Zeumer in *Festgabe für Rudolf von Gneist* (Berlin, 1888), 47–59; reprinted in J. Haller, *Quellen*, 241–50, and in C. Mirbt, *Quellen zur Geschichte des Papsttum* (Tübingen, 1924), 107–12.

(13) ... We have also built the churches of the blessed Peter and Paul, the chief of the apostles, and adorned them with gold and silver. Laying their most sacred bodies there with great honour, we have made them coffins of amber, against which the elements are powerless, and on each of their coffins we have placed a cross of the purest gold and of precious stones, and fixed it there with golden nails. We have conferred estates upon them in order to provide lights, and we have bestowed divers riches upon these churches; and by our sacred imperial commandments have conferred gifts upon them in the east and west, and also in the northern and southern regions, in Judea, Greece, Asia, Thrace, Africa and Italy and divers islands, on condition that all shall be administered by the hands of our most blessed father Pope Silvester and his successors.

(14) And let all people and all nations in all the world rejoice with us; we exhort you all to join us in giving thanks without measure to our God and Saviour Jesus Christ, since he, being God in heaven above and on earth below, visiting us through his holy apostles, made us worthy to receive both the holy sacrament of baptism and health of body. In return for this, to the same holy apostles, my lords the most blessed Peter and Paul, and through them also to the blessed Silvester our father, Supreme Pontiff and Universal Pope in the city of Rome, and to all who succeed him as pontiff and sit upon St. Peter's seat, unto the end of the world, from henceforth we grant and surrender our imperial palace of the Lateran, which outshines and ranks above all other palaces in the whole world: and also the diadem, that is, the crown upon our head, and likewise the white bonnet [*frygium*] and the

'superhumeral' (i.e. the scarf which hangs about the Emperor's neck) and also the purple mantle, the purple tunic and all the imperial garments, and the honour of a guard of imperial knights; and we grant also the imperial sceptres, and likewise the spears, the orb and eagle [*signa*], the standards and various imperial ornaments, and all the pomp of the supreme position of Emperor and the glory of our power.

(15) We ordain that those most reverent men, the clergy of various orders who serve the holy Roman church, shall have that supremacy, that unique position, that power and pre-eminence with which our illustrious Senate is glorified (that is, they shall be made Patricians and Consuls); and we proclaim that they may also hold the other imperial offices. We decree that the clergy of the holy Roman church shall enjoy the same distinctions as the imperial soldiery; and we wish the holy Roman church to be dignified with various offices,—with chamberlains and doorkeepers and all the guards,—like the imperial power. And, that the glory of the pontiffs may shine forth most brilliantly, we further decree that the clerks of this same holy church of Rome shall adorn their horses with small cloths made of linen, of the purest colour, and ride with them thus, and, like our Senate, they shall wear shoes with goats' hair, shining white: so that earthly things may be decorated in praise of God like things heavenly. But above all we grant to our most holy father Silvester, Bishop of the city of Rome and Pope, and to all the most blessed pontiffs who shall ever after come to succeed him, permission that to the honour and glory of Christ our God he may make anyone he chooses out of our Senate a clerk in the great catholic and apostolic Church of God and even enrol him among the monastic clergy; and no man whatsoever may presume at this to behave arrogantly.

(16) We also decreed that our venerable father Silvester, Supreme Pontiff, and all who succeeded him as pontiff, should wear the diadem, the crown of the purest gold and precious stones, which we took from our head and gave to him, and bear it on their heads to the praise of God for the honour of St. Peter. But the most holy Pope did not on any account permit himself to wear this golden crown above the crown of his clerical office which he wears to the glory of St. Peter. However, we have with our own hands placed on his most holy head the shining white bonnet [*frygium*] which symbolizes the glorious resurrection of our Lord; and by holding the bridle of his horse we have, by way of reverence for St. Peter, acted as his groom; and we

have enacted that each and every succeeding pontiff shall wear this bonnet in processions.

(17) For the imitation of our Empire, and so as not to cheapen the supreme dignity of the pontiff, but that his honour, power and glory may even surpass that of the earthly Empire, behold! we have yielded up and abandoned our palace (as aforesaid), and likewise the provinces, territories and cities of the city of Rome and of all Italy and the western regions to the most blessed pontiff, our father Silvester, Universal Pope. And by an irrevocable decision of our imperial authority we decree by means of this our divine, sacred and pragmatic statute that they are to be administered by the dominion and government of Silvester and of the pontiffs who succeed him, and we grant that they shall remain the lawful property of the holy Roman church.

(18) Hence we have judged it fitting that our Empire and power to rule should be transferred and transplanted to the eastern regions; and that in the province of Byzantium, on the best site, a city should be built which shall bear our name; and our Empire be established there. For it is not right that an earthly Emperor should have power in a place where the government of priests and the head of the Christian religion has been established by the heavenly Emperor.

(19) We decree that all these things which we have enacted and confirmed by this our sacred imperial commandment and by other divine decrees shall remain unimpaired and inviolate unto the end of the world. . . .

THE CORONATION OF CHARLEMAGNE

§ 5. The coronation of Charlemagne by Pope Leo III on Christmas Day, 800, which inaugurated a new Empire in the west, has long been the subject of speculation among historians, who have arrived at very various interpretations of its meaning and of Charlemagne's attitude to it. Translated here are the four principal contemporary or near-contemporary accounts of the coronation—from the Frankish and papal official histories; from the life of Charlemagne compiled some time after his death by Einhard (otherwise Eginhard), a clerk in the palace, who later obtained preferment under Louis the Pious; and from the annals of the monastery of Lorsch.

For summaries of the principal theses, and for valuable bibliographies, see F. L. Ganshof, *The imperial coronation of Charlemagne: theories and facts* (Glasgow, 1949); P. E. Schramm, 'Die Anerkennung Karls des Grossen als Kaiser', H.Z., 172 (1951); R. E. Sullivan, ed. *The coronation of Charlemagne: what did it signify?* (Problems in European civilization, Boston, 1959). Also, recently, R. Folz, *Le couronnement impérial de Charlemagne* (1964).

§ 5

Accounts of the coronation of Charlemagne.

A. *Annales Regni Francorum*, ed. G. H. Pertz and F. Kurze (Hanover, 1895), 112.

The King celebrated Christmas at Rome. And the year 801 began. On that most holy day of our Lord's birth, when the King at Mass was rising from prayer before the tomb of the blessed apostle Peter, Pope Leo placed a crown upon his head, and all the Roman people cried: 'Long life and victory to Charles Augustus, great and peacemaking Emperor of the Romans, crowned by God!' And after the lauds, he was adored by the Pope in the manner of the ancient princes, and, discarding the title of 'Patrician', he was henceforth known as Emperor and Augustus.

B. Einhard, *Vita Karoli*, ed. G. H. Pertz and G. Waitz (Hanover, 1911), 32–3.

Although Charles esteemed so highly the church of St. Peter at Rome, he made only four journeys thither in the forty-seven years of his reign, to fulfil vows and offer prayers.

But these were not the only reasons for his last visit there—the Romans did Pope Leo many injuries, gouging out his eyes and cutting out his tongue, and forced him to appeal to the King's loyalty. And so, coming to Rome to restore to order the condition of the church, which was exceedingly disturbed, he passed the whole winter season there. At this time he received the title of Emperor and Augustus. At first he disliked it so much that he declared that on that day, high festival though it was, he would not have entered the church if he could have known in advance what the Pope was planning. Nevertheless he bore with great patience the jealousy evoked by the title he had received, for the Roman Emperors were indignant at it. And he overcame their insolence by his magnanimity, in which without doubt he was far superior to them, by frequently sending them embassies and in his letters calling them brothers.

c. *Liber Pontificalis*, ed. L. Duchesne, II (1892), 7.

On another day, in the church of the blessed apostle Peter, in the presence of the general assembly of archbishops, bishops and abbots and of all the Franks who were in the service of the great King and of all the Romans in the church of the blessed apostle Peter, the venerable prelate and pontiff, clasping the four holy gospels of Christ, in the presence of everyone ascended to the pulpit and in a clear voice declared on oath that: 'I have no knowledge of these crimes falsely imputed to me by the Romans who have wickedly persecuted me, and I am conscious of having done no such things.' And when this was done, all the archbishops, bishops and abbots and all the clergy, after the litany, praised God and Our Lady Mary, the ever virgin Mother of God, and the blessed Peter the chief of the apostles and all the saints of God.

Afterwards, when Christmas day came, all once more assembled in this church of the blessed apostle Peter. And then the venerable and bountiful bishop with his own hands crowned Charles with a most precious crown. Then all the loyal Romans, seeing how well he loved and protected the holy Roman church and its vicar, cried with one high-sounding voice, by the will of God and the blessed Peter, the keeper of the keys of the kingdom of heaven: 'Long life and victory to Charles the most pious Augustus, the great and peacemaking Emperor, crowned by God!' Before the sacred tomb of the blessed apostle Peter they declared this three times, calling upon various saints: and he was made Emperor of the Romans by them all. And then the most holy prelate and pontiff anointed Charles, the Emperor's most excellent son, King with the holy oil, on that day of the birth of our Lord Jesus Christ.

d. Annals of Lorsch (*Annales Laureshamenses*), ed. G. H. Pertz in M.G.H., Ss., I, 38.

And because at that time the title of Emperor had ceased to exist among the Greeks, and they were under the sway of a woman, it seemed to Pope Leo and to all the holy fathers who were present at the council, and to the rest of the Christian people, that they ought to confer the title of Emperor on Charles, King of the Franks, since he held Rome, where the Caesars had always used to reside, and other capitals in Italy, Gaul and Germany also. And because Almighty God had granted him power over all these capitals, they thought it right that he should take the title, with God's help and at the request of all the Christian people. King Charles did not wish to deny their request, and, subjecting himself to God in all humility, at the request of the priests and all the Christian people, on Christmas day he received that title of Emperor with his consecration by the lord Pope Leo. There, first of all, he recalled the holy church of Rome to peace and harmony from the strife they had had among themselves; and there he celebrated Easter. And with the approach of summer, he started forth by way of Ravenna, dispensing peace and justice, and thence he made his way to Francia and his own capital.

THE EMPIRES IN EAST AND WEST

§§ 6–7. After Charlemagne had been crowned, the existence of two Emperors in east and west created a very delicate situation, since the title of Emperor and more especially that of Emperor of the Romans implied universal dominion and superiority to all other rulers on earth. These extracts mark two stages in the development of the relationship between the two Emperors. Under the terms of the peace treaty to which 6A and B refer, Charlemagne was restoring to Byzantium the recent Frankish conquests in the Adriatic. The letter 6B was sent to Byzantium with two ambassadors who were on their way to fetch a copy of the peace treaty signed by the Emperor Michael and his high officials.

The Emperor Louis II sent the letter 7 to the Emperor Basil in the flush of triumph when, after five years of concentrated warfare against the Saracens in southern Italy, he succeeded in expelling them from Bari. It is now generally supposed that the actual author of the letter was the librarian Anastasius, a protégé of Louis II who acted as secretary to Pope Nicholas I and librarian to his successor, Adrian II. The historian Kleinclausz questioned whether the letter was genuine, but few have doubts nowadays.

See A. Kleinclausz, *L'empire carolingien* (1902), 203 foll., 441 foll.; G. Ostrogorsky, *History of the Byzantine state* (Oxford, 1956), 175–7, and F. L. Ganshof, 'La fin du règne de Charlemagne', Z.S.G., 28 (1948), 433–5, on 6; Halphen, *Charlemagne*, 134–6, 409 foll., 507; W. Ohnsorge, *Das Zweikaiserproblem im früheren Mittelalter* (Hildesheim, 1947), 27 foll., 40 foll. (pp. 15–31 are translated in Sullivan, *The coronation of Charlemagne*); F. Dölger, 'Europas Gestaltung im Spiegel der frankischbyzantinischen Auseinandersetzung des 9. Jahrhunderts', in his *Byzanz und die europäische Staatenwelt* (Ettal, 1953); P. Lamma and W. Ohnsorge, 'I due imperii nell'Italia meridionale', *Atti del 3° Congresso*

Internazionale di Studi sull'alto medioevo (Spoleto, 1959); Folz, *L'idée d'empire*, 39–42, 196–9, and Ullmann, *Growth of papal government*, 216–19, on 7.

See also below, Part III, no. 3.

§ 6

The conclusion of peace between Charlemagne and the Emperor Michael Rhangabe, 812.

A. *Annales Regni Francorum, anno 812*, ed. G. H. Pertz and F. Kurze (Hanover, 1895), 136.

The Emperor Niceforus after many glorious victories in the province of Moesia died in battle with the Bulgars, and his son-in-law Michael became Emperor, and in Constantinople received and dismissed the ambassadors of the lord Emperor Charles who had been sent to Niceforus; and with them he sent his own ambassadors, Bishop Michael and the *protospatharii* Arsafius and Theognostus, and through them he confirmed the peace begun by Niceforus. For when, at Aachen, where they came to the Emperor, they received the text of the treaty from him in the church, they praised him in their own fashion in the Greek language, calling him Emperor and *Basileus*. When they came to Rome on the return journey, they received another copy of the treaty or agreement from Pope Leo in the church of St. Peter the apostle.

B. Letter of Charlemagne to Michael, spring 813, ed. E. Dümmler in M.G.H., Epp., IV (1895), 556.

IN THE NAME OF THE FATHER AND OF THE SON AND OF THE HOLY GHOST: CHARLES, BY THE GRACE OF GOD EMPEROR AND AUGUSTUS AND LIKEWISE KING OF THE FRANKS AND LOMBARDS, TO HIS BELOVED AND HONOURABLE BROTHER MICHAEL, GLORIOUS EMPEROR AND AUGUSTUS, ETERNAL GREETING IN OUR LORD JESUS CHRIST.

We bless the Lord Jesus Christ our true God, and render him thanks with all our heart and with all our strength and with all our mind, for he has decided to enrich us with his unutterable kindness, and to establish in our time the long sought-after and always desired peace between the eastern and the western Empire. Whilst he has always seen fit to rule and protect his holy, catholic and immaculate Church which has spread throughout the whole world, in accordance with her daily prayers, he has even now in our time decided to unite and pacify her. We say this at such length because we have fulfilled every obligation on our part, and we have no doubt that you are willing to do likewise. We have faith in him who enjoined on us this work of making peace which we have on hand, because he is faithful and true and collaborates with every good worker, and we trust that he will bring to perfection the things that even we begin well.

§ 7

Extracts from the letter of the Emperor Louis II to the Emperor Basil I, 871, ed. W. Henze in M.G.H., Epp., VII (1928), 386, 388 foll.

IN THE NAME OF OUR LORD JESUS CHRIST THE EVERLASTING GOD: LOUIS, BY THE DECREE OF DIVINE PROVIDENCE EMPEROR AUGUSTUS OF THE ROMANS, TO OUR MOST BELOVED SPIRITUAL BROTHER BASIL, THE MOST GLORIOUS AND DEVOUT EMPEROR OF THE NEW ROME.

. . . It is ridiculous of you to say that the imperial title is neither hereditary nor appropriate to the people. In what way is it not hereditary?—for our grandfather was already inheriting it from his father. In what way is it inappropriate to the people, since we know that Roman Emperors have been recruited from Spaniards, Isaurians and Chazars (for the sake of brevity we mention no others)? You cannot rightly maintain that these races are more devout or more virtuous than the Frankish people, and yet you do not close the door to them or scorn to proclaim Emperors from among their number.

To reply briefly, brother, to your assertion that we are not Emperor in all Francia. Of course we are Emperor in all Francia, because without a doubt we own the territories held by our kinsmen, with whom we are one flesh and blood, and, in the Lord, one spirit. Furthermore, beloved brother, you profess to be astonished that we call ourselves Emperors, not of the Franks, but of the Romans: but you ought to know that we could not be Emperors of the Franks without being Emperors of the Romans. We took over this title and dignity from the Romans, for it is certain that this supreme and lofty title first shone forth among them; and we received from heaven this people and city to guide and the mother of all the churches of God to defend and exalt. From her the founder of our line received the authority, first to be King, and then to be Emperor. For the Frankish princes were called first Kings and then Emperors,—those at least who were so anointed by the Roman Pontiff with the holy oil. And Charles the Great, our great-

great-grandfather, was the first of our race and line (devotion abounding in him) to be anointed with oil in this manner by the Supreme Pontiff, to be called Emperor and to become the anointed of the Lord: all the more so, as men have frequently risen to be Emperor on obtaining the imperial office, not by any divine operation carried out by the pontiffs, but only from the Senate and people, who care nothing for them. Some have not even risen by this means, for they have been acclaimed and set upon the imperial throne only by the soldiers, and some of them have even been promoted by women or by other dubious means to govern the Roman Empire.

. . . Again, the Frankish race has borne the Lord much very fertile fruit, not only by being quick to believe, but also by converting others to the way of salvation. Hence the Lord rightly warned you: 'The Kingdom of God shall be taken from you and given to a nation which bears him fruit.'[1] God was able, out of stones, to raise up children for Abraham,[2] and so he could also, out of the hardness of the Franks, raise up heirs to the Roman Empire. If we belong to Christ, we are, according to the apostle, the seed of Abraham;[3] and, if we belong to Christ, we can, by his grace, do everything which those who belong to Christ can do. As we, through our faith in Christ, are the seed of Abraham, and as the Jews for their treachery have ceased to be the sons of Abraham, we have received the government of the Roman Empire for our right thinking or orthodoxy. The Greeks for their 'cacodoxy', that is, wrong thinking, have ceased to be Emperors of the Romans,— not only have they deserted the city and the capital of the Empire, but they have also abandoned Roman nationality and even the Latin language. They have migrated to another capital city and taken up a completely different nationality and language.

---

1. Matthew, xxi, 43   2. Matthew, iii, 9.   3. Galatians, iii, 29.

CHAPTER II

Law and Government

COMMENDATION

§ 8. This document tells something about the formation of the personal link between the strong and the weak which was one of the foundations of any feudal society. It is taken from a collection of formulae or specimen charters used to provide models for legal documents, named after its place of origin, Tours, and is thought to date from the very late Merovingian period.

See H. Mitteis, *Lehnrecht und Staatsgewalt* (Weimar, 1933), 27 foll.; references in C. E. Odegaard, *Vassi and fideles in the Carolingian Empire* (Cambridge, Massachusetts, 1945), 110; Halphen, *Charlemagne*, 198 foll.; F. L. Ganshof, *Feudalism* (New York, 1961), 5–8; M. Bloch, *Feudal Society* (London, 1961), 147 foll.

§ 8

Formulae Turonenses, no. 43, ed. K. Zeumer in M.G.H., Form. (1886), 158.

43. *A man who commends himself into the power of another.*

I, A., to the magnificent lord B. As it is well known to everybody that I have no means of feeding and clothing myself, I have asked you, in your pity, permission to hand over and commend myself to your protection [*mundoburdus*] and your goodwill has granted me it; and I have therefore done so, on the understanding that you must aid and comfort me with food and clothing, according as I am able to serve you and deserve well of you; and that, so long as I live, I must extend to you service and obedience of the kind expected of a free man [*ingenuili ordine*]; and throughout my life I shall have no power of withdrawing from your power and protection [*mundoburdus*], but must remain all the days of my life under your power and protection [*defensio*]. Hence it is fitting that, if one of us attempts to depart from this agreement, he must pay so many *solidi* to his partner, and the agreement shall nonetheless remain in force.

Hence it is fitting that the parties should exchange and confirm two letters of the same tenor on this matter; and so they have done.

VASSALAGE, FEALTY AND THE 'MISSI DOMINICI'

§§ 9–10. Extracts 9 and 10A and B, which historians have often discussed in conjunction with one another, provide important evidence on the institution of vassalage, on the oath of fealty which accompanied it, and on the relationship which Charlemagne tried to establish with his subjects. 10A also illustrates the function of the *missi* or royal commissioners in the Carolingian Empire (though this law did not originate them) and gives a broad indication of Charlemagne's ideals of government shortly after he became Emperor.

On Tassilo and on the oath of fealty, Fustel de Coulanges, *Histoire des institutions politiques de l'ancienne France*, VI (1892), 238 foll.; Mitteis, *Lehnrecht*, 49 foll., 65 foll.; R. Schröder and E. von Künssberg, *Lehrbuch der deutschen Rechtsgeschichte* (Berlin-Leipzig, 1932), 167 foll.; C. von Schwerin, *Grundzüge der deutschen Rechtsgeschichte* (Munich-Leipzig, 1934), 79 foll.; F. L. Ganshof, 'Benefice and vassalage in the age of Charlemagne', C.H.J., 6 (1939), 155–6, 170 foll.; L. Halphen, 'L'idée d'état sous les carolingiens', R.H., 185 (1939), 61 foll.; C. E. Odegaard, 'Carolingian oaths of fidelity', *Spec.*, 16 (1941) (summarizing the controversy of A. Dumas and F. Lot), 'The concept of royal power in Carolingian oaths of fidelity', *Spec.*, 20 (1945) and *Vassi and fideles*, 24 foll.; Halphen, *Charlemagne*, 165 foll.; F. L. Ganshof, 'Charlemagne et le serment', *Mélanges Louis Halphen* (1951) and *Feudalism*, 29–30, 34–5.

On the *missi*, V. Krause, 'Geschichte des Institutes der *missi dominici*', M.I.Ö.G., II (1890); Fustel de Coulanges, *Histoire des institutions*, VI, 534 foll.; Schröder and von Künssberg, *Lehrbuch der. Rechtsgeschichte*, 142 foll.; von Schwerin, *Grundzüge der Rechtsgeschichte*, 71 foll.; A. Kleinclausz, *Charlemagne* (1934), 220 foll.; Halphen, *Charlemagne*, 150 fol.; H. Fichtenau, *The Carolingian Empire* (Oxford, 1957), 107 foll.

On other aspects of the legislation of 802: Fustel de Coulanges, *Histoire des institutions*, VI, 461; Kleinclausz, *Charlemagne*, 308 foll.; Halphen, *Charlemagne*, 210 foll.; Ganshof, 'La fin du règne de Charlemagne', 438 foll.

On the legislation of Charlemagne in general, R. Buchner, *Die Rechtsquellen* (*Beiheft* of Wattenbach-Levison, *Deutschlands Geschichts-*

quellen), 44 foll.; F. L. Ganshof, 'Recherches sur les capitulaires', R.H.D.F.E. (1957). Other translations of it appear in D. C. Munro, ed. 'Selections from the laws of Charles the Great', *Translations and reprints from the original sources of European history*, 6 (Philadelphia, Pa., 1900).

§ 9

Duke Tassilo does homage to King Pippin, 757: *Annales Regni Francorum*, ed. G. H. Pertz and F. Kurze (Hanover, 1895), 14, 16.

King Pippin held his court [*placitum*] with the Franks at Compiègne; and to that place came Tassilo, Duke of the Bavarians, and he commended himself into vassalage by his hands, and swore many, indeed numberless oaths, placing his hands on relics of saints. And he promised to be faithful to King Pippin and his aforesaid sons, the lords Charles and Carloman, as by law a vassal of right intentions and steadfast loyalty ought to do, and as a vassal ought to be towards his lords.

Tassilo declared upon the bodies of St. Denis, Rusticus and Eleutherius, and St. Germanus and St. Martin, that he would keep the promises made in his oaths all the days of his life. The more important of his men who were with him declared this also, as has been said, both in the places named above and in many others.

§ 10

A. General Capitulary of the Commissioners, 802, chs. 1–9, ed. A. Boretius in M.G.H., Cap., I (1883), 91 foll.

First chapter. Of the commission [legatio] *sent out by the lord Emperor.* The most Serene and Christian lord Emperor Charles has chosen from among his nobles men of the greatest wisdom and experience, archbishops, bishops, venerable abbots and pious laymen, and sent them to every part of his kingdom, and through them he has granted men the opportunity to live in accordance with the correct law, in all the chapters which follow. Where the law decrees anything which is not right or just, he has ordered these men to inquire most industriously into it and to inform him: he is anxious, God willing, to improve this. And let no one out of cunning or slyness dare (as many do) to obstruct the written law or disturb the rights of the Emperor or those of the churches of God, or of the poor, of widows and of orphans, or, indeed, of any Christian man. But all men without exception are to live justly under the rule of justice in accordance with God's commandment, and every man is advised to live at peace with others in the same occupation or calling. Canons must entirely follow the canonical way of life, without pursuing sordid gain; nuns must industriously watch over their way of life; laymen and secular clergy must observe their laws correctly and undeceitfully, and all should live together in perfect mutual love and peace. And the commissioners [missi] shall make thorough inquiries whenever anyone complains that an injustice has been done him, as they desire to retain the favour of Almighty God for themselves and keep the faithful promise they have made to him—they shall extend law and justice to all men without exception in every place, to the holy churches of God and to the poor, to orphans and widows and all the people, according to the will of God and in the fear of him. If there is anything they are unable to correct and adjust by themselves, together with the counts in the provinces, they must without a doubt refer it to the Emperor's judgment together with their reports; and the straight path of justice shall not be obstructed by anyone, by means of the flattery or bribery of any man, by any tie of relationship or by fear of the mighty.

2. *Of the fealty to be promised to the lord Emperor.* He has ordered that every man in all his kingdom, ecclesiastic or layman, each according to his vows and occupation, who has already promised to be loyal to him as King, shall now make the same promise to him as Emperor; and all those aged twelve and over who have not yet made this promise shall do likewise. A public announcement shall be made so that everyone may realize how many and how important are the points covered by this oath. It does not only, as many have hitherto supposed, demand loyalty to the lord Emperor as far as his life is concerned, and forbid introducing any enemy into his kingdom for a hostile purpose, and forbid being a party to or concealing the disloyalty of any man to him. Everyone ought to know that this oath contains the following meanings:

3. Firstly, that every man should personally strive, within the limits of his own ability and intelligence, to devote himself fully to the holy service of God according to God's commandment and his own promise, because the lord Emperor cannot himself give the necessary care and discipline to every individual man.

4. Secondly, let no man, by perjury or by any other deceit or trickery, or by flattery or bribery of any man, dare in any way to dispute about,

to take away or to conceal any serf of the lord Emperor or any district or land or anything which he has a right to possess; and let no man presume to conceal or take away by means of perjury or other deceit fugitive serfs of the Crown who wrongfully and fraudulently call themselves free men.

5. That no one shall presume to defraud, rob or otherwise injure the holy churches of God, or widows, or orphans, or pilgrims—for the lord Emperor himself, after the Lord and his saints, has been appointed their protector and defender.

6. That no man shall dare to lay waste a benefice of the lord Emperor, or make one of his own out of it.

7. That no man shall presume to ignore a summons to arms from the lord Emperor; and no count be so bold as to exempt anyone from military service because he is his kinsman or out of flattery and bribery.

8. That no man whatsoever may presume to obstruct the edicts or commands of the lord Emperor in any way, or delay, hinder or detract from his work, or otherwise oppose his wishes and commands. And that no man shall dare to withhold from him his dues or taxes.

9. That no man may make a practice of wrongfully defending another in court, pleading a weak case out of desire for gain, impeding a just judgment by the cunning of his argument, or wishing to oppress, even though his case is weak. But every man shall give an account of his own case, or tax, or debt, unless he is infirm or ignorant of pleading. If so, the commissioners or the chief men in court or a judge who knows the case shall plead before the court on his behalf; or, if necessary, let a pleader who is acceptable to everybody and who knows the case well be provided. This, however, shall be done entirely at the convenience of the chief men or commissioners who are present. But it shall be done entirely in accordance with justice and the law; and let no one succeed in interfering with justice by means of a bribe or fee, by dint of evil flattery or by considerations of relationship. And let no man wrongfully conspire with another, but let all be prepared most earnestly and willingly to do justice.

All the points in the imperial oath mentioned above ought to be observed.

B. One version of the oath of fealty which Charlemagne's commissioners were charged to impose on all his subjects: extract from the Special Capitularies of the Commissioners, early 802: M.G.H., Cap., I, 101.

I once more swear an oath that from this day forward I will be loyal to the lord Charles, the most devout Emperor, son of King Pippin and Queen Berthana, as a man must rightfully be to his lord, with a pure intention on my part towards him, without deceit and to the honour of his kingdom. So help me God, and the saints whose relics are here defend me, that all the days of my life, of my own wishes and within the limits of the understanding which God has given me, I may strive to observe this oath.

c. The four annual visits of the commissioners: extract from the Capitulary on the administration of justice, 811/813: M.G.H., Cap., I, 176–7.

8. It is our will that, to deal with the cases which have been referred to them by the counts, our commissioners shall make their visits during four months of the year only: in winter in January, in spring in April, in summer in July, in autumn in October. In the other months each of the counts is to hold his own court [*placitum*] and administer justice. But our commissioners are to hold their sessions together with these counts four times in the month and in four different places in which it shall be convenient for them to assemble.

FRANKISH LAW COURTS

§ 11. These paragraphs from the laws or capitularies of Pippin, Charlemagne and Louis the Pious help to define the competence and composition of the various law courts in the Kingdom and Empire.

See, on this subject and on the counts, L. Beauchet, *Histoire de l'organisation judiciaire en France: époque franque* (1886), 123 foll., 293 foll., 327 foll.; Fustel de Coulanges, *Histoire des institutions*, VI, 418 foll., 494 foll.; Schröder and von Künssberg, *Lehrbuch der d. Rechtsgeschichte*, 175 foll.; Kleinclausz, *Charlemagne*, 206 foll.; H. M. Cam, 'Suitors and scabini', *Spec.*, 10 (1935); F. N. Estey, 'The meaning of *Placitum* and *Mallum* in the Capitularies', *Spec.*, 22 (1947), and 'The scabini and the local courts', *Spec.*, 26 (1951); Halphen, *Charlemagne*, 185 foll.

§ 11

A. ch. 7 of a Capitulary of Pippin, 754–5: M.G.H., Cap., I, 32.
Of the administration of justice. Let all officials, both royal and ecclesias-

C

tical, administer justice. If any man brings his case to the palace without first informing the count in the assembly [*mallum*] before the judges [*racemburgii*], or if his case has been before the count in the assembly [*mallum*] before the judges [*racemburgii*] and he has refused to allow them to judge him lawfully, he shall be flogged; or, if he is an important person, the King shall decide his fate. But if he claims that the court has not judged him lawfully, then he shall have permission to bring his case to the palace. And if he can prove that it has not judged him lawfully, the palace shall see that amends are made to him. And if the count and judges [*racemburgii*] can prove that they judged him lawfully and he would not accept the sentence, amends shall be made to them. Similarly with ecclesiastics: if they come to appeal to the palace over their superior's head, let them be flogged.

B. ch. 13 of the First Aachen Capitulary of the Commissioners, 810: M.G.H., Cap., I, 153.

Those who are guilty of desertion shall be sent under sureties to the King.

C. ch. 12 of a Capitulary of Aachen, 801/813: M.G.H., Cap., I, 171.

That men of good family who behave wickedly or wrongfully in a county shall be brought before the King; and the King shall impose on them the penalty of imprisonment or exile until they reform.

D. ch. 2 of a Capitulary on the Administration of Justice, 811/813: M.G.H., Cap., I, 176.

That bishops, abbots, counts and all the more powerful men, if they have a dispute among themselves and refuse to make peace, shall be ordered to come before us. Their dispute may not be determined in any other place, and the causes of the poor and the less powerful may not be deferred because of it. The count of our palace shall not presume to judge the cases of the more powerful without orders from us, but shall understand that it is open to him to dispense justice only to the poor and the less powerful.

E. ch. 3 of the First Aachen Capitulary of the Commissioners, 810: M.G.H., Cap., I, 153.

No judgment concerning property or liberty shall be pronounced or obtained in the court of a vicar or hundredor: this shall always be done in the presence of the imperial commissioners or in the presence of the counts.

F. ch. 2 of a Capitulary of Louis the Pious, 815: M.G.H., Cap., I, 262.

Those who have been prosecuted or sued by their neighbours and ordered to come to the court in the more important cases, such as homicide, rape, arson, plunder, mayhem, theft, brigandage, offences against other men's property or anything else, may on no account refuse to come to their count's assembly [*mallus*]. But men shall not be forbidden to decide other cases of less importance among themselves in their own fashion, as they are known to have done hitherto.

G. ch. 14 of an Italian Capitulary of Pippin (son of Charlemagne), 801 (806?)/810: M.G.H., Cap., I, 210.

No criminal action may be determined before the vicars except for petty cases which can easily be decided; and no one may claim a man as his serf in the vicars' courts, but the parties shall be sent upon security before the count. And the vicars shall not make free men attend any further sessions [*placita*] after they have attended the statutory three, unless one of them happens to be accusing another, except for those *scabini* who must sit repeatedly with the judges.

H. ch. 20 of a Capitulary of the Commissioners, 803: M.G.H., Cap., I, 116.

No one may be summoned to court [*placitum*] unless he is bringing an action or another party is bringing one against him, except for the seven *scabini* who must be present at all sessions [*placita*].

THE GENERAL ASSEMBLY

§ 12. The agenda for the general assembly of 811 provide some hints on the nature of the relationship between Charlemagne and his magnates and of the process by which his laws were made, as well as indicating the kind of problems which his government set itself to solve.

See Fustel de Coulanges on general assemblies, *Histoire des institutions*, VI, 356 foll.; Schröder and von Künssberg, *Lehrbuch der d. Rechtsgeschichte*, 158 foll.; Halphen, *Charlemagne*, 161 foll.

§ 12

Points to be discussed with the counts, bishops and abbots, 811: M.G.H., Cap., I, 161-2.

First, we wish to divide our bishops and abbots, on one hand, from

the counts on the other, and to question each group separately on the
following points:

1. What causes one man to refuse aid to another on the frontier or in
the army, where he ought to do something to help the defence of his
country?

2. Why the persistent litigation in which men demand of one another
everything they see in the possession of their fellows?

3. Concerning those who receive the fugitive vassals of others.

4. They shall be asked in what places and concerning what matters
ecclesiastics obstruct laymen or laymen ecclesiastics in the execution of
their duties. At this point they ought to debate and to find out how far
a bishop or abbot should intervene in worldly matters and how far a
count or other layman in ecclesiastical affairs. Here there must be a very
penetrating inquiry into the meaning of the apostle's saying: 'No
soldier of God may involve himself in the affairs of this life.'[1] To whom
does this remark apply?

5. What is the meaning of the words that every Christian says at
baptism, and of the things that he then renounces?

6. What must he do or fail to do in order to invalidate this declaration and renunciation?

7. That he who thinks he can with impunity ignore God's commandments, and who disdains his threats as if they will never be carried out,
does not truly believe in God.

8. That we must examine ourselves to see whether we are true
Christians. This can be discovered very easily by considering our life
and habits: should we be willing to discuss our conduct thoroughly in
public?

9. Of the life and habits of our pastors, the bishops, who must set a
good example to the people of God, not only in their teaching, but in
their lives also—for we think the apostle was talking to them when he
said: 'Be followers of me and watch those who walk in my way, so that
you have us for an example.'[2]

10. How ought those who are called canons to live?

11. Of the monastic way of life: can anyone be a monk other than
those who observe the Rule of St. Benedict? It must also be asked
whether there were any monks in Gaul before the Rule of St. Benedict
was transmitted to these parts.

12. You shall observe these things in a fitting manner. I trust you,

1. 2 Timothy, ii, 4.   2. Philippians, iii, 17.

most pious bishops, and have no hesitation in sending and writing to you everything I can discover.

Farewell in the Lord.

CHARLEMAGNE'S LETTER ON EDUCATION

§ 13. For comment on Charlemagne's famous letter (associated with Alcuin) on the duty of cathedral and monastic clergy to provide education, and accounts of his other legislation to similar ends, see J. B. Mullinger, *The schools of Charles the Great* (London, 1877), 97 foll.; L. Maître, *Les écoles épiscopales et monastiques en Occident avant les universités* (Ligugé-Paris, 1924), 6 foll.; M. Deanesly in C.M.H., V (1926), 774 foll.; E. S. Duckett, *Alcuin, friend of Charlemagne* (New York, 1951), 121 foll.; L. Wallach, 'Charlemagne's *De litteris colendis* and Alcuin', *Spec.*, 26 (1951) and in his *Alcuin and Charlemagne* (New York, 1959); J. Fleckenstein, *Die Bildungsreform Karls des Grossen* (1953); M. L. W. Laistner, *Thought and letters in western Europe, A.D. 500 to 900* (London, 1957), 189 foll.

§ 13

Charlemagne's *Epistola de Litteris Colendis*, late eighth century: M.G.H., Cap., I, 79.

We, Charles, by the grace of God King of the Franks and Lombards and Patrician of the Romans, send loving greeting to you, Abbot Baugulf, and to all the congregation and to our loyal teachers who are entrusted to you, in the name of Almighty God.

Be it known to you, whose devotion is pleasing to God, that we and our loyal servants have considered it profitable that the bishoprics and monasteries committed by Christ's favour to our guidance should, in addition to following the monastic way of life and living together under a holy Rule, offer earnest instruction in the study of literature to those who, by the gift of God, are capable of learning, according to the capacity of each of them. Observing a Rule imparts order and grace to honourable conduct, and perseverance in teaching and learning does the same for connected speech: so that those who are eager to please God by rightly living may not neglect to please him by speaking correctly. For it is written: 'Either by your words shall you be justified, or by your

words shall you be condemned.'[1] It may be better to do well than to
know: but knowledge comes before action. So every man must learn
about the thing he wants to accomplish: that the mind may know more
fully what it ought to do and the tongue run on in praise of Almighty
God without stumbling in errors. All men must avoid errors: how
much more then, must they be shunned, as far as possible, by those
who were chosen for the sole purpose of specially serving the truth. In
recent years we have frequently received letters from certain monasteries informing us how the brethren who lived there were fighting for
us with their holy and pious prayers; and we have noticed that in most
of these writings there were proper sentiments but uncouth expres-
sions—because of failure to learn, the uninstructed tongue could only
faultily express what devout piety was faithfully dictating to the mind.
Hence we began to fear that, there being too little skill in writing, there
might also be far too little wisdom in understanding the holy Scriptures.
And we all know that, though verbal errors are dangerous, errors of
thought are much more so. Therefore we exhort you, not only not to
neglect the study of letters, but also to strive to learn, with efforts that
are humble but pleasing to God, to penetrate more easily and correctly
the mysteries of the holy Scriptures. Since metaphors, figures of speech
and other similar things are found in the sacred pages, there is no doubt
that everyone who reads them will understand the spiritual meaning
more rapidly if he is first more fully instructed in the craft of letters.
Let men be chosen for this work who have the will and ability to learn
and the desire to instruct others. And let this be done with a zeal as
great as the earnestness with which we command it. We wish you, as
befits soldiers of the Church, to be devout in thought and erudite in
speech, chaste in your strict conduct and learned in your eloquence, so
that if anyone seeks to see you out of reverence for the Lord or because
of your noble and holy life, he may both be edified by your appearance
and enlightened by the wisdom he perceives in your reading and
singing, and may go home joyfully rendering thanks to Almighty God.

If you wish to enjoy our favour, do not fail to send copies of this
letter to all your suffragans and fellow bishops and to all the monasteries.

MILITARY ORGANIZATION

§ 14. Charlemagne's Capitulary of Boulogne, in addition to providing

1. Matthew, xii, 37.

useful information on the way in which military service was organized in the Carolingian Empire, also tells something about the law on the termination of the feudal contract (see 15 below), the extent to which lords were becoming responsible for the conduct of their vassals, and so on. See, on this and on military organization, Fustel de Coulanges, *Histoire des institutions*, VI, 509 foll.; H. Delbrück, *Geschichte der Kriegs-kunst im Rahmen der politischen Geschichte*, III (Berlin, 1907), 35 foll.; Kleinclausz, *Charlemagne*, 89 foll., 317–18; Mitteis, *Lehnrecht*, 149 foll., 178 foll.; Ganshof, 'Benefice and vassalage', 168–9, 175; Halphen, *Charlemagne*, 167 foll.

§ 14

Charlemagne's Capitulary of Boulogne, October 811: M.G.H., Cap., I, 166–7.

The articles which the lord Emperor decreed at Boulogne, which is on the coast, in the month of October in the forty-fourth year of his reign, indiction five.

1. If a free man has been summoned to the host and has refused to come, he shall pay the full *heriban* of sixty *solidi*; and if he has not the means of paying that sum, he shall deliver himself as a pledge into servi-tude to the prince, until such time as he has paid the fine; and then he may return to a state of freedom. But if the man who has delivered himself into servitude on account of the *heriban* dies in servitude, his heirs shall not lose the inheritance which belongs to them nor their own freedom, nor shall they be liable to any harm as a result of that *heriban*.

2. That no count shall presume upon any occasion—whether for guard or garrison duty or any other [*nec de wacta nec de warda nec pro heribergare neque pro alio banno*]—to exact the *heriban*; our com-missioner [*missus*] must first receive the *heriban* on our behalf, and he shall then give the count his share, one third of it, upon our orders. The *heriban* shall not be exacted in the form of lands or chattels, but in gold and silver, in cloaks, weapons, beasts and cattle or things of that kind which are of immediate use.

3. If any vassal who holds honours [*honores*] of ours is sum-moned to the host and does not come to the assembly [*placitum*] which has been arranged, he shall abstain from meat and wine for as many days as he is proved to have been late for this assembly.

4. If anyone returns from the host without permission from the

prince—an act which the Franks call *herisliz*—we wish to retain the ancient law whereby he is punished by sentence of death.

5. If any of those who have a benefice from the prince leaves a colleague when advancing with the army against the common enemy and refuses to go on or stay with him, he shall lose his honour and his benefice.

6. That in the host nobody must ask a comrade or any other man to drink. And if anyone in the army is found drunk, he shall be set apart so that he can drink only water until he realizes that he has done wrong.

7. Concerning the King's vassals who serve in the household and yet are known to have benefices, it is ordained that if any of them remain at home with the lord Emperor they are not to keep their own vassals who have benefices [*vassallos suos casatos*] with them, but shall allow them to go with the count to whose district they belong.

8. It is ordained that preparations for the host shall continue to be required according to the ancient custom: that is, food for a period of three months after crossing the border, and weapons and clothing for half a year. It shall be observed, however, that those who march from the Rhine to the Loire shall provide this amount of food from the Loire onwards; and those who are journeying from the Loire to the Rhine must have three months' victuals from the Rhine onwards; and those who live beyond the Rhine and march through Saxony shall know that their border is the Elbe; and those who live beyond the Loire and have to start for Spain shall know that the Pyrenees form their border.

9. If any free man is found not to have been with his lord in the host this present year, he shall be forced to pay the full *heriban*. But if his lord or count has left him at home, the lord shall pay the fine for him; and a fine shall be exacted from the lord for every man he has left at home. And because this present year we have allowed all lords to leave two men at home, we wish them to show them to our commissioners, because we have remitted the fine on account of them alone.

10. It is ordained that no bishop, abbot, abbess, rector or guardian of a church shall presume to give or sell a breastplate or sword to any outsider without our permission: he may do so only to his own vassals. If it happens that any church or holy place has more breastplates than are needed by the guardians of the church, the rector of the church shall ask the prince what should be done about them.

11. That whenever we wish to send out a fleet, the lords shall sail on the ships and shall be prepared to do so.

THE FEUDAL CONTRACT

§§ 15–18. These texts are evidence of some of the main developments in feudal law. The extracts from the Capitularies in 15 state some of the legal grounds for terminating the contract between lord and vassal when both were still alive which were recognized at the beginning of the ninth century. 16A is cited by Professor Ganshof to show how—in the mid-ninth century—a benefice might be withdrawn on the death of a lord and the vassal have to renew the contract with his successor. 16B and 17 throw further light on the question of how far benefices and counties were becoming inheritable property, and how far a lord was free to dispose of them to whom he would when a vassal died. 16B is taken from a tract addressed to Charles the Bald by his formidable partisan, Hincmar, Archbishop of Reims, in 868. The Capitulary of Quierzy (17) was issued by the assembly summoned by Charles the Bald on the eve of his departure for Italy in 877. 18, taken from a legal instrument signed in Tours, is the earliest known certain case of a vassal holding benefices of more than one lord.

On 15: Mitteis, *Lehnrecht*, 87 foll., 149 foll.; Halphen, *Charlemagne*, 201; Ganshof, *Feudalism*, 30–1, 43; Bloch, *Feudal Society*, 227 foll.

On 16 and 17: Mitteis, *Lehnrecht*, 165 foll.; Ganshof, *Feudalism*, 40–3, 46–9; Bloch, *Feudal Society*, 190 foll.; and on 17, E. Bourgeois, *Le capitulaire de Kiersy-sur-Oise* (1885), esp. 127 foll., and Halphen, *Charlemagne*, 432 foll., 506.

On 18: F. L. Ganshof, 'Depuis quand a-t-on pu en France être vassal de plusieurs seigneurs?' in *Mélanges Paul Fournier* (1929); Mitteis, *Lehnrecht*, 102 foll.; Ganshof, *Feudalism*, 49–50; Bloch, *Feudal Society*, 211 foll.

§ 15

The termination of the contract of vassalage.

A. From the Capitulary of Aachen, 801/13: M.G.H., Cap., I, 172.

ch. 16. That no man may leave his lord after he has received from him one valid *solidus*, unless his lord tries to kill him or to strike him with a rod or to defile his wife or daughter or to deprive him of his inheritance.

ch. 20. If any of our loyal servants [*fideles nostri*] wishes to engage in battle or in any contest with an adversary, and summons to him one of his comrades to lend him aid, and his comrade refuses and continues to fail him in this, the benefice which he has shall be taken away from him and given to someone who has remained steadfast and loyal.

B. From a Capitulary of indeterminate date, issued either by Charlemagne or Louis the Pious: M.G.H., Cap., I, 215.

ch. 8. Supposing anyone wishes to leave his lord and can prove him guilty of one of the following offences: firstly, that his lord has attempted to reduce him wrongfully to servitude; secondly, that he has given him advice dangerous to his life; thirdly, that the lord has committed adultery with the vassal's wife; fourthly, that he has wilfully attempted to kill him with a drawn sword; fifthly, it shall be lawful for the vassal to leave his lord if the lord has failed to defend him, when capable of doing so, after the vassal has commended himself by placing his hands within the lord's. If the lord has committed any of these five offences against his vassal, it shall be lawful for the vassal to leave him.

§ 16

A. *Cartulaire de l'Abbaye de Redon en Bretagne*, ed. A. de Courson (1863), 72–3.

[867] A record of those into whose presence came Ritcant shortly after he had been installed as Abbot of St. Saviour's, and other brothers with him, before Count Rivel in Bronjudwoc. He cited certain men, whose names were Milun and Haelwoc, the son of Risoc, and Bidwor, and Haelwoc, the son of Standulf, concerning the manor [*villa*] which Abbot Conwoy, with the consent of his monks, had conferred upon them as a benefice in fealty to St. Saviour's and to the Abbot of Redon and to all the monks of Redon, and called upon them to return the benefices into his hands, because he had been elected Abbot to succeed Conwoy. Then the above-named men returned into the hands of Ritcant, the new Abbot, their benefices, which they had hitherto held by the gift of Conwoy.

Then Ritcant, at their humble prayers, returned the benefices to them with the consent of his brothers, in fealty and service to St. Saviour's and to him and to all the monks of Redon; and so that they might defend the whole abbey of St. Saviour's, unless, which God forbid, the count in Poillac were opposing the monks of Redon. In that case they should return their benefices into the hands of Abbot Ritcant or of whoever was then Abbot of Redon. These men gave securities to Ritcant that they would be loyal after this manner to St. Saviour's and the Abbot of Redon and the monks of Redon. The securities Milun gave for this fealty and service were Haelwoc, son of Standulf, and Haelwoc, son of Risoc; and Haelwoc, son of Risoc, gave Milun and Haelwoc, son of Standulf, and Maban; and Bidwor gave Maban, Christian and Arthur; and Haelwoc, son of Standulf, gave Arthur again, as he had given him to Abbot Conwoy.

This was done in the community of Poillac, in Bronjudwoc, on February 24th, before Count Rivel, in the presence of many noblemen whose names are there. . . .

B. Extract from Hincmar, *Pro Ecclesiae libertatum defensione*, a tract addressed to Charles the Bald, 868: Migne, P.L., 125, 1050.

When the bishop has disposed of the aids due to him and his church, to the clergy, to the poor and to his guests, and is giving out of the property of the church a benefice for military service, he ought to give it either to the sons of fathers who have done good to the church, if they can usefully succeed their fathers (since, as somebody has written, unless the calf is fed, the ox cannot be yoked to the plough); or else he ought to give it to men who are fit to render to Caesar the things that are Caesar's and to God the things that are God's—excepting the benefices which must be granted to servants of the church and men vital to it, whom we must not and cannot do without, for the Lord commands us, 'You shall not muzzle the mouth of the ox that treads the corn'.[1] These military vassals must strive to serve the bishop, and hence the church, loyally and profitably according to the extent of the benefice, and, in obedience to the King, to work in general for the defence of the holy church of God.

Suppose a bishop takes away a benefice on any pretext from them, or from one who has long been of service to the Church and especially to that particular church and its needs, and has been useful to the common-wealth and the army, but now, being worn out with age and sickness, cannot serve any longer in person; and suppose especially that he has a son serving him who can do these things for him: if the vassal cannot obtain justice through the prayers and admonitions of a neighbouring bishop or any other person, it will be reasonable for him not to pro-ceed against the bishop before the public judges (which is not lawful), but to have recourse to you (the King). The military benefice is like the payments which used formerly to be made to soldiers out of public

1. 1 Corinthians, ix, 9.

funds, and which still are today in other places. The devotion of the faithful having increased among our people, the Church for the sake of her own defence furnishes benefices out of ecclesiastical property, which consists of the offerings of the faithful, of fines for sin, of the patrimony of the poor, of alms for the servants and handmaids of the Lord and of other gifts to be dispensed by the prince's servants. She also pays to the King and commonwealth the taxes which are called our annual gifts, keeping the commandment of the apostle: 'Tribute to whom tribute is due; honour to whom honour.'[1] This means, supply the King and your defenders. Those who, whatever their estate, position or rank, accept maintenance from the Church and do not work diligently to the best of their ability for its safety, peace, honour and defence, are as good as usurping this maintenance for themselves. For just as the property and resources of the Church are entrusted to the bishop to administer and dispense, even so are they entrusted to the power of the King to defend and protect.

§ 17

The Capitulary of Quierzy, 877.

A. chs. 3–4 of the portion of the Capitulary promulgated on June 16th, 877 (a more explicit version of ch. 9 of the Capitulary of June 14th, 877): ed. A. Boretius and V. Krause in M.G.H., Cap., II (1897), 362.

3. If a count of this realm dies and his son is accompanying us, our son and our other loyal servants [*fideles*] shall appoint, from among those who have been closest and most familiar to the count, men to look after the county together with the officials of the county and the bishop in whose diocese it is situated, until the death is reported to us, so that we may confer upon his son who is accompanying us the honours which were his [*de honoribus illius honoremus*]. But if the count has left a young son, his son, together with the officials of the county and the bishop in whose diocese it is situated, shall look after the county until we are informed of the death of the count and until the honours which were his are conferred upon his son by our grant. But if the count has left no son, our son and our other loyal servants shall appoint a man to look after the county together with the officials of the county and with its bishop, until we give orders about it. And he who looks after the county must not be angry

<hr>

1. Romans, xiii, 7.

if we give the county to some other person chosen by us, rather than to him who has hitherto looked after it. The same must be done concerning our vassals [*vassalli*]. And we wish and command bishops, abbots, counts and our other loyal subjects to strive to observe this rule concerning their own vassals [*homines*].

4. We also wish and expressly command that if any bishop, abbot, abbess, count or vassal of ours dies, no one shall plunder the property or resources of the church, or presume to invade or usurp the property or resources of any count or vassal of ours or of any dead person, or to commit any violence against the wives and children of dead laymen, and no one shall prevent their almoners from giving alms. But if anyone does presume to do so, he shall both compound this offence according to secular law by paying our fine [*bannus*], and make satisfaction for it according to ecclesiastical law to the church which he has damaged; and furthermore he must pay our penalty [*harmiscara*], according to the nature of the offence and as it pleases us.

B. ch. 10 of the Capitulary of June 14th, 877: M.G.H., Cap., II, 358.

If any of our loyal servants after our death, prompted by love for God and for us, wishes to renounce the world, and has a son or some such close relative who can be of service to the commonwealth, he may dispose of his honours to him as he chooses [*suos honores, prout melius voluerit, ei valeat placitare*]. And if the man wishes to live peaceably upon his own property [*alodis*], no one shall presume to interfere with him in any way, and no duty shall be required of him save only that of going to the defence of his country.

§ 18

The case of a vassal who held more than one benefice, 895: *Gallia Christiana*, ed. B. Hauréau, XIV (1856), *Instrumenta*, col. 53.

A record of how Ecfred, the provost, with Adalmar, the advocate of St. Martin, on the twenty-fourth of April, in the city of Le Mans, came before Count Beringar and complained that a vassal of the monastery named Patericus was keeping in an unseemly manner the property of the brothers, which Guitto had formerly held on account of his advocacy. Then Count Beringar answered that Patericus was not his vassal only, although he had something in benefice from him: he was, rather, the vassal of his friend Robert, because he held a larger benefice of Robert. But, for love of St. Martin, the Count immediately restored what belonged to the monastery, saying 'If he wishes to enjoy my benefice, he shall no longer keep any of the land of St. Martin'. And so they departed. . . .

IMMUNITIES

§ 19. This specimen grant of immunity, made by Louis the Pious to one Abbot Arnulf between about 814 and 825, shows primarily how the authority of the ruler was limited by the creation of privileged areas in which his officials had no power, either judicial or fiscal.

See Beauchet, *Histoire de l'organisation judiciaire*, 418 foll.; M. Kroell, *L'immunité franque* (1910); von Schwerin, *Grundzüge der Rechtsgeschichte*, 83 foll.; Schröder and von Künssberg, *Lehrbuch der d. Rechtsgeschichte*, 213 foll.; Halphen, *Charlemagne*, 193 foll., 510; cf. K. F. Drew, 'The immunity in Carolingian Italy', *Spec.*, 37 (1962).

§ 19

From the *Formulae Imperiales e Curia Ludovici Pii*, ed. K. Zeumer in M.G.H., Form. (1886), 290–1.

When, for love of divine worship, we accede to the just and reasonable requests of the servants of God and with God's assistance carry them into effect, we are not merely acting in accordance with royal custom: we feel confident that the Lord will grant to us for this act the gift of prosperity in this present life and of happy enjoyment of his sublime favour in the future one. Hence all our loyal servants [*fideles*], both present and future, shall know that the venerable A., Abbot of the monastery called B., erected in honour of St. C., in the district of D., on the river E., coming before Our Serene Highness, asked us to take this monastery, which he governs by gift from us, under our protection and the protection of immunity, so that the attacks of evil men may be repelled and he and the brothers who live there may rejoice in more freely serving God and praying for us and for the stability of the Empire committed to us by God. Therefore you shall know that we have deemed the petition of the aforesaid venerable Abbot Arnulf worthy to be heard by us, and have assented and inclined the ear of our mildness to it, and have taken the aforesaid monastery under our protection and that of immunity, and have decided to make this decree of our mildness concerning the monastery.

We therefore command and ordain that no public judge, and no one by virtue of his judicial powers, shall dare at any time to enter the churches, places, fields or other possessions which the said monastery justly and reasonably holds at the present time in any districts and territories, or to enter any property that has been conferred on the monastery for the love of God, and which the kindness of God has chosen to add to the possessions of the monastery, for the purpose of hearing and discussing cases in the manner of a judge, or of exacting fines [*freda*], or of making a halt or claiming hospitality there [*mansiones vel paratas faciendas*], or of taking post-horses [*paravereda*], or of exacting securities [*fideiussores tollendos*], or of wrongfully coercing the men of the monastery who live upon its land, whether they are free-men or serfs; or in order to demand payment of taxes or public imposts or any unlawful exaction; nor may they presume to exact any of the things listed above. And for the sake of an eternal reward we entirely remit to the said monastery any dues the public treasury could expect to be paid out of the monastery's property, so that this may perpetually increase to provide alms for the poor and to support the monks who serve God in that place. And whenever, at the summons of God, the said Abbot or his successors depart this life, so long as the monks can find among themselves men capable of governing the congregation according to the Rule of St. Benedict, they shall by our authority and consent have permission to elect Abbots, so that it may please these servants of God, who serve God in that monastery, to pray continually to the Lord to have mercy upon us and our wife and children, and to pray for the stability of the whole Empire committed to us to preserve. Hence we absolutely ordain and command that the property of the aforesaid monastery, which the aforenamed man has up to the present time obtained, either through the generosity of the Kings of the Franks who preceded us or by the offerings of other faithful persons, and any property which the monastery shall hereafter succeed in justly obtaining by the grace of God, shall be held and possessed by him and his successors under the protection of our immunity, all judicial power being wholly excluded from it.

THE 'ORDINATIO IMPERII' OF LOUIS THE PIOUS

§ 20. The *Ordinatio Imperii* of Louis the Pious, though ultimately ineffectual, was an intelligent attempt to reconcile the unity of the Empire with the multiplicity of the kingdoms which had to be granted to the Frankish princes, and to check the process of disintegration which would result from subdividing these kingdoms into smaller and smaller portions.

See Fustel de Coulanges, *Histoire des institutions*, VI, 277 foll., 624–5; J. Doizé, 'Le gouvernement confraternel des fils de Louis le Pieux et l'unité de l'empire', M.A. (1898), 258 foll.; Kleinclausz, *L'empire carolingien*, 277 foll.; J. Calmette, *L'effondrement d'un empire et la naissance d'une Europe (IXe-Xe siècles)* (1941), 27 foll.; Halphen, *Charlemagne*, 236 foll.; F. L. Ganshof, 'Observations sur l'*Ordinatio Imperii* de 817', *Festschrift Guido Kisch* (Stuttgart, 1955); F. L. Ganshof, 'Louis the Pious reconsidered', H., 42 (1957); W. Mohr, 'Die kirchliche Einheitspartei und die Durchführung der Reichsordnung von 817', Z.K. (1961).

§ 20

The *Ordinatio Imperii* of Louis the Pious, July 817: M.G.H., Cap., I, 270–3.

In the name of the Lord God and our Saviour Jesus Christ, Louis, by the decree of divine providence Emperor Augustus.

Whën, in God's name, in the month of July of the year of the Lord's incarnation 817, indiction ten, in the fourth year of our reign, we had at our palace of Aachen in the customary manner gathered together the sacred assembly and common council of our people in order to study the welfare of the Church and our whole Empire and were engaged upon these things, it happened all at once that by divine inspiration our loyal subjects advised us to deal with the state of the whole realm and with the question of our sons in the same way as our parents, maintaining the peace and security which God had everywhere granted us. But although this advice was given with devoted loyalty, it did not seem to us nor to men of sound judgment that, out of love or favour to our sons, the unity of the Empire preserved for us by God ought to be destroyed by men, lest this should allow any scandal to arise in the Holy Church and lest we should offend him who holds all kingdoms in his possession. Therefore we thought it necessary that, with fasting and prayer and almsgiving, we should obtain from him the answer which we in our weakness did not presume to give. After three days of such solemn celebration, and, we believe, at the command of Almighty God, it was accomplished that we and all our people together voted to elect our beloved eldest son Lothar. So, as the divine decree had pointed to him, it pleased us and all our people to crown him solemnly with the imperial diadem, and to appoint him our consort and, God willing, successor to the Empire by common vote. It was generally agreed to confer upon his brothers, Pippin and our namesake Louis, the title of King, and to determine the places (those named below) in which upon our decease they shall wield royal power under their elder brother according to the articles drawn up below, which contain the arrangement we have established between them. It has pleased us to debate with all our loyal subjects these articles for the welfare of the Empire, for the preservation of everlasting peace between our sons and for the protection of the whole Church; and, having discussed them, to write them down and afterwards sign them with our own hands, so that with God's help they may be preserved inviolate by the common devotion of all men even as they have been enacted by their unanimous vote, to maintain everlasting peace between our sons and all the Christian people: saving in all things our imperial power over our sons and our people, and all the obedience which is shown to a father by his sons and to an Emperor and King by his people.

1. We wish Pippin to have Aquitaine and Gascony and the entire mark of Toulouse, and four counties in addition to that: Carcassonne in Septimania, and Autun, Avallon and Nevers in Burgundy.

2. Again, we wish Louis to have Bavaria and the Carinthians, Bohemians, Avars and Slavs to the east of Bavaria, and, in addition, to have two royal manors, Lauterhofen and Ingolstadt, at his service in the district of Nordgau.

3. We wish the two brothers who bear the title of King to have power of their own to distribute all honours within their dominion, provided only that in bishoprics and abbeys the proper ecclesiastical procedure is observed and that other offices are given in an honourable and useful manner.

4. Again we wish them, once a year at a suitable time, to go to their elder brother with gifts, either together or separately as circumstances permit, in order to visit and see him and in mutual brotherly love discuss vital matters and those connected with the common welfare and everlasting peace. And if it happens that one of them is unavoidably prevented from coming at the usual suitable time, he must inform the eldest brother of this by sending him ambassadors and gifts. He must

not, on a flimsy pretext, slide out of coming as soon as a suitable opportunity presents itself.

5. We wish and advise the eldest brother, when either one or both
his brothers, as aforesaid, come to him with gifts, to reward them in
kind and brotherly love with a still more generous gift, as greater
power is by God's consent vested in him.

6. When his younger brothers make a reasonable request for aid
against foreign nations, we wish and command the elder brother, as
reason dictates and the situation allows, to bring them suitable help
either in person or through his loyal lieutenants and armies.

7. Again, we wish them henceforth not to presume to declare war
upon or make peace with foreign nations hostile to this Empire preserved by God without the advice and consent of their eldest brother.
But they must try to repress sudden hostile risings or unexpected in-
vasions by themselves, as far as they are able.

8. Supposing ambassadors have been sent by foreign nations to
make peace or declare war, or hand over cities or castles, or on any
other important business, they shall on no account answer them or
send them back without their eldest brother's knowledge. But if ambassadors are sent to him from any country and reach one of them first,
he shall send them honourably with his own loyal ambassadors to his
brother's presence. But they may give an answer by themselves concerning matters of less consequence, depending on the nature of the
embassy. But we advise them never to fail to inform their eldest
brother how matters stand within their own territories, so that he may
be found always alert and prepared to do anything that the need and
profit of the kingdom shall demand.

9. We also see fit to ordain that, to avoid discord, after our decease
the vassal of each brother shall hold a benefice only in the dominion of
his own lord and not in that of another. But every man may honourably
and securely keep his own property and inheritance, wherever it is,
having regard for justice, according to his law and without being wrongfully disturbed. And every free man who has no lord shall be allowed
to commend himself to any of these three brothers he shall choose.

10. But if, which God forbid, a thing we do not desire, it happens
that any of the brothers, out of that greed for earthly possessions which
is the root of all evil, dismembers or oppresses churches and poor men,
or uses that tyranny which is the height of cruelty, let him first (as the
Lord commands)[1] be secretly warned to amend once, twice and thrice,

1. Matthew, xviii, 15.

through loyal ambassadors. If he will not yield to them, let him be summoned by one brother and in the presence of the other admonished and reprimanded in fatherly and brotherly love. And if he utterly despises this salutary admonition, let the common decision of all determine what is to be done about him; that the imperial power and the common decision of all may coerce the man who cannot be restrained from his wicked deeds by a salutary admonition.

11. The rectors of churches in Francia shall have the same power over their possessions in Aquitaine or in Italy or in other regions and provinces subject to this Empire as they had in the time of our father and are recognized as having in our own.

12. The brothers may have any tribute, taxes or moneys they can demand and obtain within their dominion, so that they may use them to provide for their own needs and can the better prepare gifts to be sent to their eldest brother.

13. If, after our decease, the time comes for any of the brothers to marry, we wish him to take a wife with the advice and consent of his eldest brother; and we decree that care must be taken, in order to avoid discord and take away opportunities for harm, that none of them presumes to take a wife of foreign nationality. But the vassals of all the brothers, for the purpose of strengthening the ties of peace, may take wives from any country they choose.

14. If any of them dies and leaves legitimate children, his dominion shall not be divided between them, but the people shall assemble and elect the one of them whom God desires. The eldest brother shall receive him as a brother and son, and, being honoured as a father, shall in every respect observe this decree in his relations with him. They shall discuss with dutiful love how to take care of the other children and treat them wisely as our parents did.

15. But if any of the brothers dies without legitimate children, his dominion shall revert to the eldest brother. And if it happens that he has children by mistresses, we advise the eldest brother to show mercy to them.

16. If it happens that any of the brothers on our death is not yet lawfully of age according to Ripuarian law, it is our will that, until he reaches the prescribed age, the eldest brother shall take charge of and govern him and his kingdom in the same way as we have done. And when he comes of age he shall wield his power over all things in the approved manner.

17. May the Kingdom of Italy be subject to our son Lothar in every-

thing, if God wishes him to succeed us, just as it was to our father and as it is subject to us, God willing, at the present time.

18. Also, we advise all our people in their devotion, and in their steadfast and most sincere loyalty, which is celebrated among all peoples, that, if our son who succeeds us at God's command departs this life leaving no legitimate children, they may for the safety of all, for the peace of the Church and for the unity of the Empire, in electing one of our children, if any survive their brother, follow the procedure we laid down for his election, so that in the appointment they may seek to fulfil, not the will of man, but the will of God.

PART TWO

The Church and the Papacy

CHAPTER I

The Papacy

GELASIUS ON THE TWO POWERS

§ 1. These pronouncements of Gelasius, Pope from 492 to 496, fall outside the normal chronological boundaries of this collection of texts. They are included because of their outstanding importance for later Popes, canonists and ecclesiastical political theorists. They were originally issued during the late fifth century as a protest against the extended powers claimed by the Emperor in pronouncing on matters of Christian dogma. The Emperor Zeno had attempted to conciliate the Monophysites of Egypt by issuing, in 482, the dogmatic statement known as the Henoticon, a compromise between Catholicism and Monophysitism. He did this on the advice of the Patriarch Acacius, but without summoning a council or sounding the general opinion of the bishops. Acacius was in any case anxious to exalt his own see of Constantinople at the expense of the see of Rome. He was vigorously opposed by Popes Simplicius and Felix; Gelasius, dealing with Zeno's successor, the Emperor Anastasius, was continuing their opposition, whilst retaining considerable respect for the Emperor.

See R. W. and A. J. Carlyle, *A history of mediaeval political theory in the west*, I (Edinburgh-London, 1927), 184 foll., 253 foll.; C. H. McIlwain, *The growth of political thought in the west* (New York, 1932), 164 foll.; E. Caspar, *Geschichte des Papsttums* (Tübingen, 1933), II, 64 foll.; J. Haller, *Das Papsttum: Idee und Wirklichkeit*, I (Stuttgart-Berlin, 1934), 213 foll.; L. Knabe, *Die gelasianische Zweigewaltentheorie bis zum Ende des Investiturstreits* (Berlin, 1936); T. G. Jalland, *The Church and the Papacy* (London-New York, 1944), 325 foll.; F. Dvornik, 'Pope Gelasius and Emperor Anastasius', B.Z., 44 (1951); E. J. Jonkers, 'Pope Gelasius and civil law', R.H.D., 20 (1952); M. Pacaut, *La théocratie: l'Église et le pouvoir au moyen âge* (1957), 22 foll.; W. Ullmann, *The growth of papal government in the middle ages* (London, 1962), 14 foll., *passim*.

§ 1

A. Extract from the letter of Pope Gelasius I to the Emperor Anastasius I, 494, expounding the theory of the two powers ruling over the world and of the relationship between them: *Epistolae romanorum pontificum genuinae*, ed. A. Thiel (Brunswick, 1868), 350–2.

There are two powers, august Emperor, by which this world is ruled from the beginning: the consecrated authority of the bishops, and the royal power [*auctoritas sacrata pontificum et regalis potestas*]. In these matters the priests bear the heavier burden because they will render account, even for rulers of men, at the divine judgment. Besides, most gracious son, you are aware that, although you in your office are the ruler of the human race, nevertheless you devoutly bow your head before those who are leaders in things divine and look to them for the means of your salvation; and in the reception and proper administration of the heavenly sacraments you know that you ought to submit to Christian order rather than take the lead, and in those matters follow their judgment without wanting to subject them to your will. For if, in matters relating to public law and order, Christian priests themselves obey your laws in the knowledge that your Empire is conferred upon you by heavenly disposition, and lest they appear to be resisting your judgment, which is unchallengeable in worldly affairs, then how eagerly one ought to obey those who are assigned to the administration of the hallowed mysteries! There is no slight danger to the bishops in not having spoken up for the worship of God as they should; and, which God forbid, there is no inconsiderable peril in store for those who behave contemptuously when they ought to be obedient. And if it be right that the hearts of the faithful should submit to all bishops everywhere who rightly administer the things that are divine, how much more then must they give their support to the bishop of this see, who, even by the supreme divine will, was to be superior to all other priests, and whom the Church has obediently honoured with universal loyalty!

B. Extract from the Tractatus IV or Tome of Gelasius: Thiel, *Epistolae pontificum*, 567–8.

But if Emperors are afraid to attempt these things, and know that they do not fall within their own scant measure of power, which is permitted to judge only human affairs and not to take the lead in things divine: how then can they presume to judge those through whom

things divine are administered? Before the coming of Christ it happened that certain men, although at that time they were only appointed
to carry out worldly functions, were in a sense both kings and priests,
because Scripture tells us that the holy Melchisedech was such a person.[1] And the devil imitated this among his own people, since he always
strives to claim for himself, like a usurper, things pertaining to the worship of God, with the result that heathen Emperors were also called
Supreme Pontiffs [*maximi pontifices*]. But after the coming of the
true King and Pontiff, the Emperor no longer assumed the title of
Pontiff, nor did the Pontiff lay claim to the royal supremacy. For even
though the body of the true King and Pontiff is said to have embraced
both these attributes in holy nobility, according to their participation
in his majestic nature, so that a nation may be at once royal and priestly,[2]
yet Christ, thinking of human frailty, by a majestic disposition took the
appropriate measure for the salvation of his people, and distinguished
the sphere of each power by appropriate functions and distinct titles,
wishing his people to be saved by the physic of humility and not be
struck down again by human arrogance. Hence at the same time
Christian Emperors needed bishops for the sake of eternal life, and
bishops availed themselves of imperial decrees for the good order of
temporal affairs. Hence the spiritual function might be immune from
worldly interference, and 'No soldier of God might involve himself in
the affairs of this life',[3] and conversely no man who was involved in the
affairs of this life might take charge of things divine. Hence both orders
might be restrained and neither be boosted and exalted above the
other, and each calling might become specially competent in certain
kinds of function.

PAPAL ELECTIONS, 769–962

§§ 2–5. The four documents which follow—translated in whole or in
part—are designed to show the means by which the Papacy attempted
to free papal elections from all forms of lay influence, and the process by
which the influence of the Emperor none the less reasserted itself
through the imperial duty of protecting the papal territories.

The election decree of Stephen III (2) followed the conspiracy of a
group of laymen, led by Duke Toto, against the government of the
clergy in the papal states. On the death of Pope Paul I, they had in-

1. Genesis, xiv, 17–20.   2. Cf. 1 Peter, ii, 9; 2 Peter, i, 4.
3. 2 Timothy, ii, 4.

stalled their candidate, Toto's brother, as Pope Constantine II, and had forced the Bishop of Prenesto to consecrate him.

The agreement concluded in 817 by Louis the Pious and Pope Pascal I (3) contains the earliest known text of a Carolingian 'donation' to the church of Rome—it confirms the gifts conferred upon St. Peter by Pippin and Charlemagne.

The *Lotharianum* (4)—ostensibly an agreement reached in 824 by the Emperor Lothar and Pope Eugenius II—was designed to give the Emperor legal means of continually intervening in the government of the papal states and supervising their administration. It resulted from the need to curb the antagonism which kept breaking loose between nobles and clergy and their rivalry for control of the papal states. The authenticity of this document is open to dispute.

The *Ottonianum* (5) is, on the face of it at least, a privilege granted by the Emperor Otto to St. Peter and to his vicar Pope John XII on February 13th, 962, after Otto had intervened in Rome to protect the papal states from the advancing armies of Berengar II, King of Italy. Dr. Ullmann, however, has argued that the later chapters of the *Ottonianum* (from ch. 15, translated here, onwards) were inserted at the end of 963, when Otto had deposed John for treason to him, had ceased to be merely the protector of the papal states, and was becoming their master.

See P. Hinschius, *System des katholischen Kirchenrechts*, I (Berlin, 1869), 227 foll.; T. Sickel, *Das Privilegium Ottos I für die römische Kirche vom Jahre 962* (Innsbruck, 1883); L. Duchesne, *The beginnings of the temporal sovereignty of the Popes* (London, 1908), 71 foll., 125 foll., 222 foll.; E. Amann, in A. Fliche and V. Martin, *Histoire de l'Église*, VI (1937), 32 foll., 205 foll.; VII (1940), 44 foll.; L. Halphen, *Charlemagne et l'empire carolingien* (1947), 233 foll., 253 foll. (on 3 and 4); W. Ullmann, 'The origins of the *Ottonianum*', C.H.J., 11 (1953); L. Santifaller, *Zur Geschichte des ottonisch-salischen Reichskirchensystems* (*Sitzungsberichte der Österreichische Akademie der Wissenschaften*, 229, Vienna, 1954); W. Ullmann, *Growth of papal government*, 87–8, 322 (on 2), 229 foll. (on 5).

§ 2

The election decree of Pope Stephen III issued at the Council of Rome, April 769: ed. A. Werminghoff in M.G.H., Conc., II, 86.

It was necessary that this our holy lady church of Rome should be set in order according to what St. Peter and his successors ordained, and that one of the cardinal priests or deacons should be consecrated to the Apostolic Supremacy.

We decree upon pain of anathema that no layman, whether he is a soldier or whether he belongs to any other order, may presume to be present at the election of a Pope: but the election of the Pope shall derive from all the priests and leaders of the church and from all the clergy. But after the Pope has been elected and taken to the patriarchal palace, then the military chiefs and all the army and the citizens of rank and the whole assembly of the people of this city of Rome must hasten there to greet him as lord of all. In the customary manner they must make a decree and, all being in agreement, subscribe to it.

We decree that the same procedure shall be observed in other churches in the name of God's judgment and on pain of anathema.

§ 3

The agreement of Louis the Pious with Pope Paschal I, 817 (the *Ludovicianum*): ed. A. Boretius in M.G.H., Cap., I, 353–5.

In the name of the Lord God Almighty, Father, Son and Holy Spirit.

I, Louis, Emperor Augustus, decree and grant by this treaty of confirmation to you, St. Peter, Chief of the Apostles, and through you to your vicar, the lord Paschal, Supreme Pontiff and Universal Pope, and to his successors in perpetuity, the city of Rome and its duchy and all its subject cities, castles, towns and villages and its mountainous and maritime territories, coasts and ports, and all the cities, castles, towns and villages in Tuscany [*a detailed list of these follows*—ED.] as you and your predecessors have hitherto held dominion over them.

[*The document goes on to list the territories in the possession of which the Emperor confirms the Pope—in Campagna, the Exarchate of Ravenna, the Pentapolis and the Sabine territory—and those in which he upholds his claims: the islands of Corsica, Sardinia and Sicily, and the patrimonies of Benevento, Salerno, Calabria and Naples. It confirms all the gifts conferred by Pippin and Charlemagne of their own free will upon St. Peter, including the tribute formerly paid to the Lombard Kings by the remainder of Lombard Tuscany and the Duchy of Spoleto.—ED.*]

As we have said, we confirm to you by this decree of confirmation all the things named above, so that they may remain in the possession of you and your successors and under their rule and government, and so that your dominions shall not be reduced by us or by our sons and successors on any kind of pretext or by any intrigue, and so that you and your successors shall not be deprived of any of these provinces, cities, towns, castles, villages, islands, territories and estates, or taxes and tributes. We will not deprive you of them, nor will we consent to any-one else attempting to do so. Rather do we promise to defend as far as we are able all the things mentioned above, provinces, cities, towns, castles, territories, estates, islands, taxes and tributes, for the church of St. Peter the apostle and for the pontiffs who shall ever after reside in his most holy see, so that they can without disturbance use, enjoy and set in order everything under St. Peter's government. We do not claim for ourselves any part in these things or any power to order, to judge, to withdraw or to diminish them, save when we are asked to do so by the man who for the time being governs this holy church. And should any man come to us from these cities which belong to your church, wishing to withdraw himself from subjection to you, contemplating some other wicked design or escaping after committing some crime, we will not receive him save for the purpose of justly interceding for him, provided that the crime he has committed is found to be pardonable. If it is not, we will arrest him and hand him over to you. We except those who have suffered violence or oppression from the powerful and who come to us that they may obtain justice through our intervention. This is an entirely different matter from those mentioned before it.

And when, at the summons of God, the bishop of this most holy see departs this life, no man from our kingdom subject to us, be he Frank or Lombard, no matter what his race, shall be allowed to oppose the Romans either publicly or privately or to make any choice of a suc-cessor. Nobody shall presume to commit any evil act on account of this in the cities or territories in the possession of the church of St. Peter the apostle. But the Romans shall be allowed to give their bishop honourable burial in all reverence and without any disturbance, and to consecrate in the canonical fashion without any uncertainty or oppo-sition the man whom, on the inspiration of God and intercession of St. Peter, all the Romans have unanimously, and without having promised their votes, elected to the pontificate. And when he has been consecrated, legates shall be sent to us or to succeeding Kings of the Franks to seal the friendship, love and peace between them and us, as it was customary to do in the time of the lord Charles our great grandfather of holy memory, of the lord Pippin our grandfather, and of the lord Emperor Charles our father. . . .

§ 4

Extracts from the *Constitutio Romana* of the Emperor Lothar (the *Lotharianum*), November 824: M.G.H., Cap., I, 322–4.

We have decreed that all who have been taken under the special protection of the Pope or of ourselves may inviolably make use of the just protection they have obtained; and if anyone does presume to disdain and to violate it, he shall know that he will thereby jeopardize his life.

We wish no one (be he freeman or serf) to presume to come to the election of a Pope for the purpose of obstructing the Romans in any way, for they alone were granted in ancient times by decree of the holy fathers the customary right to elect a Pope. If anyone presumes to disobey this our order, he shall be sent into exile.

We wish representatives [*missi*] to be appointed on behalf of the Pope and ourselves to report to us annually on how every duke and judge is doing justice to the people and how well they are observing our decree. We decree that these representatives must, as soon as possible, bring to the attention of the Pope all complaints which have arisen through the negligence of dukes or judges, and he shall choose one of two alternatives: either the situation shall be corrected immediately by these representatives themselves, or our representative shall inform us so that it can be corrected by other representatives whom we shall send.

We wish all the people of Rome to be asked by what law they wish to live, that they may live by the law they declare they wish to live by; and an announcement shall be made to them, that everybody—dukes, judges and the rest of the people—shall know that they will be subject, at the decree of the Pope or ourselves, to the law which they choose if they contravene it.

It is our pleasure that all the judges, and those who must govern all the people, those through whom the judicial power must be exercised in this city of Rome, shall come before us: for we wish to know their names and their number and to give them instructions concerning the function which has been entrusted to them.

Finally every man shall be instructed to offer obedience and reverence to the Pope in this manner, as he wishes to enjoy the favour of God and ourselves:

I, A., promise by Almighty God and by these four holy Gospels, and by this cross of our Lord Jesus Christ, and by the body of the most blessed Peter the Chief of the Apostles, that from this day forward I will be loyal to our lords the Emperors Louis and Lothar all the days of my life, to the best of my ability and understanding, without deceit and ill-will, reserving only the loyalty which I have promised to the Apostolic Lord; and that, to the best of my ability and understanding, I will not acquiesce in any papal election taking place other than canonically and justly; and he who is elected with my consent shall not be consecrated Pope until, in the presence of the lord Emperor's representative and the people, he has made upon oath a promise similar to the one which the lord Pope Eugenius has willingly made in writing for the preservation of all.

§ 5

Extract from the *Ottonianum*, ostensibly a Privilege of the Emperor Otto, granted to St. Peter and to his vicar, Pope John XII, February 13th, 962: ed. L. Weiland in M.G.H., Const., I, 26.

In all things our power and that of our son and our descendants must be respected, according to the contents of the pact, constitution and certain promise of Pope Eugenius and his successors: which declares that all the clergy and all the noble Roman people shall bind themselves, for various urgent reasons and for the purpose of restraining the unreasonable harshness of the Popes towards the people subject to them, to ensure that every future papal election takes place justly and canonically; and that no one shall consent to the man who is elected to this holy and apostolic rulership being consecrated Pope before he has made in the presence of our representatives [*missi*], or of our son, or of the whole assembly of people, a promise for the satisfaction and future preservation of all, such as our lord and venerable spiritual father Leo is known to have made of his own free will.

We perceive that some minor additions ought to be made to this: i.e. that no man, be he freeman or serf, shall presume to come to the election of a Pope for the purpose of obstructing the Romans, who are admitted to this election by ancient custom established by the holy fathers: and if anyone presumes to contravene this decree of ours, he shall be exiled. Moreover, we forbid any of our representatives to presume to concoct evidence of any impediment to a papal election.

ELECTION DECREE OF NICHOLAS II, 1059

§ 6. The election decree of Pope Nicholas II in 1059 was an important step in the developing campaign to free the clergy in general from lay control—the campaign which culminated in the pontificate of Gregory VII and the deposition of the Emperor Henry IV. Parallel to this decree, which attempted to free papal elections from the strong influence which the Ottonian and Salian Emperors had come to exert over them, Nicholas II issued other legislation which applied to all bishoprics and not merely to the papacy (see Part III, no 8). There are two known versions of the papal election decree: one of them assigns to the Emperor a part in the election of the Pope, and is thought to have been a forgery circulated by the anti-Gregorian party during the Investiture Contest. This translation is made from the pontifical version, generally believed to be authentic.

See Hinschius, *System des Kirchenrechts*, I, 248 foll.; C. J. Hefele and H. Leclercq, *Histoire des conciles* (1907–1931), IV, ii, 1139 foll.; A. Fliche, *La réforme grégorienne* (Louvain-Paris, 1924–1937), I, 314 foll., III, 327 foll.; E. Voosen, *Papauté et pouvoir civil à l'époque de Grégoire VII* (Gembloux, 1927), 47 foll.; A. Michel, *Papstwahl und Königsrecht oder das Papstwahl-Konkordat von 1059* (Munich, 1936), discussed by R. Holtzmann, Z.S.S.R., k.a., 27 (1938), and by B. Schmeidler, H.V., 31 (1938); A. Fliche in Fliche-Martin, *Histoire de l'Église*, VIII (1946), 16 foll.; A. Michel, 'Humbert und Hildebrand bei Nikolaus II', H.J., 72 (1953); H. G. Krause, *Das Papstwahldekret von 1059 und seine Rolle in Investiturstreit*, S.G., 7 (Rome, 1960); Ullmann, *Growth of papal government*, 323–4.

§ 6

The election decree of Pope Nicholas II, April 1059, ed. L. Weiland in M.G.H., Const., I (1893), 539–41.

In the name of our Lord God and Saviour Jesus Christ, in the month of April in the year of his incarnation 1059, indiction 12, having set out the holy Gospels, with the most reverend and blessed Apostolic Pope

Nicholas presiding in the basilica of Constantine of the patriarchal
palace of the Lateran and with the most reverend archbishops, bishops
and abbots and venerable priests and deacons seated round about, the
venerable pontiff, speaking with apostolic authority, decreed concerning the election of a Supreme Pontiff:

Most beloved brothers and fellow bishops, you in your blessedness
know, and so do the lesser members of the Church, how many adversi-
ties this Apostolic See of which God has made me servant suffered at the
death of the lord Stephen, our predecessor of affectionate memory, and
how many hammer-strokes and repeated blows it sustained at the hands
of dealers in the heresy of simony, so that the pillar of the living God
seemed almost to be toppling at the shock and the chief fisherman's net
was plunged by the swelling hurricanes into the depths of a shipwreck.
Hence, if it please you, brethren, we must with God's assistance prudently provide against future mishaps and provide for the constitution
of the Church in future lest–which God forbid–the evil revive and
triumph once more. Hence, equipped with the authority of our predecessors and of other holy fathers, we decree and ordain:

That, on the death of a Bishop of this universal Roman church, the
cardinal bishops, having first very thoroughly discussed the matter together, shall then summon the cardinal clerks to them, and then the
rest of the clergy and people shall in the same way come to consent to
the new election.

That—lest the disease of corruption have any opportunity to creep in
—the churchmen shall take the lead in electing the Pope and the others
shall merely follow. This electoral procedure will be found to be correct and lawful if we examine the laws and deeds of various fathers and
recollect especially the opinion of our blessed predecessor Leo: 'Reason
does not permit', he says, 'that men be recognized as bishops unless they
have been chosen by the clergy, demanded by the people or consecrated
by the bishops of the same province with the approval of the metropolitan.'[1] Since the Apostolic See is set above all the other churches in
the world and so cannot have a metropolitan over it, the cardinal
bishops undoubtedly perform the office of a metropolitan: that is, they
promote the chosen bishop to the summit, the apostolic throne.

Let them choose someone from the bosom of the Roman church,
if a suitable man can be found; if none can be found there, let them
take one from another church.

1. From a letter of Leo the Great to Rusticus, Bishop of Narbonne, in the year 458/9
(Migne, P.L., 54, 1203).

Due honour and reverence shall be preserved for our beloved son Henry, who is at present recognized as King, and who, it is hoped, will become Emperor if God permit it, as we have already permitted it; and so shall the honour and reverence due to his successors who personally obtain this right from the Apostolic See.

But if the corruption of depraved and wicked men has brought it about that a pure, genuine and spontaneous election cannot be held in Rome, the cardinal bishops, with clerks of the church and catholic laymen (even a few), may be lawfully empowered to elect the Bishop of the Apostolic See in any place which they deem more suitable.

Once the election has been made, if the storm of war or the malignant endeavours of men prevent the man elected to the Apostolic See from being enthroned according to custom, nevertheless he shall be authorized to rule the holy Roman church as Pope and to administer all its property, as we know that St. Gregory did before his consecration.

But if anybody is elected and even ordained and enthroned in violation of this our decree promulgated by decision of the Council, everyone shall hold and recognize him not as a Pope but a devil, not an apostle but an apostate; and by the authority of God and of the holy apostles Peter and Paul he shall be cast out from the doors of the holy Church of God and subjected to perpetual anathema, together with those who have made, supported and followed him, as an Antichrist, an invader and destroyer of all Christendom. He shall not be granted any hearing on this matter, but shall be irrevocably deprived of any ecclesiastical rank which he previously held. If anyone adheres to him or shows him reverence as if he were Pope or in any way presumes to defend him, he shall be subject to a similar sentence. If anyone defies our decretal and attempts to confuse and disturb the Roman church with his presumption in violation of this statute, he shall be condemned to perpetual anathema and excommunication and counted among the wicked who shall not rise again in judgment.[1] He shall feel the wrath of God Almighty, Father, Son and Holy Spirit against him and shall sustain the fury of the holy apostles, Peter and Paul, whose church he presumes to confound, in this life and the next. Let his habitation be made desolate and let there be no one to dwell in his tabernacles.[2] Let his children become orphans and his wife a widow. Let him be cast out with violence and let his children be expelled from his dwellings and go a-begging. Let the usurer pick over all his property and strangers

1. Psalms i, 5.   2. Psalms lxix, 25.

plunder his work.[1] Let the whole world fight against him and all the elements oppose him,[2] and the merits of all the saints at rest confound and openly wreak vengeance upon him in this life.

But let the grace of Almighty God protect all who keep this our decree and loose them from the fetters of all their sins by the authority of the blessed apostles Peter and Paul.

I, Nicholas, Bishop of the holy, catholic and apostolic Roman church subscribe to this decree promulgated by us as it is read above. I, Boniface, by the grace of God Bishop of Alba, have subscribed. I, Humbert, Bishop of the holy church of Silva Candida, have subscribed. I, Peter, Bishop of the church of Ostia, have subscribed. And 76 other bishops have subscribed together with the priests and deacons.

URBAN II AND THE CRUSADE

§ 7. The account of Pope Urban II's speech at Clermont in 1095 (7A) provides valuable information about the connexion of the Popes with the Crusade; about the developing concept of holy warfare; and (if read in conjunction with one of the canons issued by the Council of Clermont, 7B) about the spiritual rewards offered to those who went on the Crusades. The Council summoned by the Pope at Clermont was generally concerned with the enforcement of decrees for the reform of the Church. A few months earlier, at a Council held by the Pope at Piacenza, the Byzantine Emperor Alexius had appealed for military aid to defend the eastern Church.

To some extent this version of Urban's speech may be a 'rhetorical exercise' composed by the chronicler Fulcher of Chartres. On the other hand, it may genuinely embody—in essence if not in detail—the exhortations of the Pope.

Fulcher, the author of the chronicle from which this speech is taken, took part in the First Crusade and settled in the east, where he lived for about thirty years. He may have begun the chronicle about the year 1101.

See D. C. Munro, 'The speech of Urban II at Clermont, 1095', A.H.R., 11 (1906); A. Fliche, 'Urbain II et la Croisade', R.H.E.F., 13 (1927); U. Schwerin, *Die Aufrufe der Päpste zur Befreiung des Heiligen Landes* (Berlin, 1937); A. Fliche, 'La papauté et les origines de la Croisade', R.H.E., 34 (1938); P. Rousset, *Les origines et les caractères de la*

1. Psalms cix, 8–10.   2. Wisdom of Solomon, v, 21.

première Croisade (Neuchâtel, 1945); S. Runciman, *A history of the Crusades*, I (Cambridge, 1951), 106 foll.; F. Duncalf, 'The Councils of Piacenza and Clermont' in K. M. Setton, ed. *A history of the Crusades*, I (Philadelphia, Pa., 1955); A. Waas, *Geschichte der Kreuzzüge*, I (Freiburg, 1956), 53 foll.

On Fulcher of Chartres, see D. C. Munro, 'A Crusader', *Spec.*, 7 (1932).

§ 7

A. The Papacy and the Crusades: Pope Urban II's exhortation to the Crusade at Clermont, 1095: Fulcher of Chartres, *Historia Hierosolymitana*, ed. H. Hagenmeyer (Heidelberg, 1913), 130–8.

When these and many other matters had been properly dealt with, everybody present, both clergy and laity, giving thanks to God, willingly approved what the lord Pope Urban had said and ratified his decrees with a faithful promise to keep them truly. But he added that another disaster, which was no less grave than the afflictions already mentioned, but was indeed greater and most terrible, was now confronting Christendom from the other half of the world.

'O children of God', he said, 'since you have promised God, more earnestly than usual, to keep the peace among yourselves and faithfully preserve and maintain the rights of the Church, it is fitting that you, being invigorated by the discipline of God, should devote the full force of your righteousness to another matter which concerns God and yourselves. For it is vital that you should make a rapid expedition to help your brothers who live in the east, who need your assistance and have now many times appealed for it. For, as most of you have already been told, they have been invaded as far as the Mediterranean sea, up to the point called the Arm of St. George, by the Turks, a Persian people, who have overrun an increasing amount of Christian territory on the frontiers of Romania, and have conquered and overcome your brothers seven times over in war, killing or capturing many of them, ruining churches and ravaging the Kingdom of God. If you leave them any longer thus unmolested, they will go much further afield to trample upon the faithful of God. It is not I but the Lord himself who begs and exhorts you, as the heralds of Christ, to persuade all men, be they knights or common soldiers, be they rich or be they poor, by repeated proclamations, to devote themselves to helping their fellow Christians, like a hurricane, to sweep away this evil race out of our people's country. I say this to you who are present, and I send to those who are absent: but Christ himself commands it. And all who end this mortal life upon that journey, on the march or on the crossing, or in the fight against the heathen, shall obtain an immediate remission of their sins. I promise this to all who go, for I have received it as a gift from God. How inglorious that this degenerate outcast race, the demons' minion, should thus overthrow a people fortified with faith in Almighty God and resplendent with the name of Christ! How gravely will the Lord himself reproach you if you do not help those who are recognized, even as you are, to be of the Christian persuasion!

'Let them go forth', said the Pope, 'to the fight against the infidels which is now ready to begin and to end in victory, all those who have been privately feuding with their fellow Christians! Let those who are brigands become soldiers of Christ; let those who have been fighting against their own brothers and kinsfolk now fight lawfully against the barbarian; let those who are hired for a few sous now find eternal rewards! Let those who have toiled to the destruction of body and soul now work for the honour of body and soul! The poor and sad shall be rich and gay and the Lord's enemies shall become his friends. Those who are going must not delay their journey, but lease their property and gather the money they need, and when winter ends and the spring follows, let them set forth eagerly upon the way, with the Lord going before them'.

B. The Papacy and the Crusades: Canon II of the Council of Clermont, 1095: Mansi, *Concilia*, XX, 815.

If any man sets forth to liberate the church of God at Jerusalem out of devotion alone, and not for love of glory or of gain, the journey shall be accounted a complete penance on his part.

PAPAL SUPREMACY AND THE POSSIBILITY OF JUDGING THE POPE

§ 8. Humbert of Moyenmoutier, Cardinal of Silva Candida (*circa* 1000–1063), was an eminent member of the papal curia from the time of Leo IX onwards, and a vigorous champion of the rights of the Roman church. A portion of the Fragment translated here—the sentences which mention the possibility of judging the Pope—became incorporated in the *Decretum* or *Concordia Discordantium Canonum* of Gratian,[1] where it is attributed to St. Boniface the Martyr. It was later to provide valuable material for conciliarists in the fourteenth and fifteenth centuries who were seeking legal justification for putting the Pope on trial. The commentary of Huguccio (or Hugh of Pisa, an influential canonist teaching at Bologna, who completed his commentary on the *Decretum* towards the end of the twelfth century) is an important example of the way in which Humbert's teaching was interpreted.

See P. E. Schramm, *Kaiser, Rom und Renovatio* (Leipzig-Berlin, 1929), I, 240 foll.; A. Michel, 'Die folgenschweren Ideen des Kardinals Humbert und ihr Einfluss auf Gregor VII', S.G., 1 (1947); W. Ullmann, 'Cardinal Humbert and the *Ecclesia Romana*', S.G., 4 (1952); B. Tierney, *Foundations of the conciliar theory* (Cambridge, 1955), 57 foll.

Cf. also the *Dictatus Papae*, below, Part III, no. 9.

§ 8

A. Humbert of Silva Candida, *De sancta Romana ecclesia*, Fragmentum A: Schramm, *Kaiser, Rom und Renovatio*, II, 128–9.

The holy Roman and apostolic church, being made (after Christ Jesus) head of all churches by a privilege of special authority, both divine and human, influences the members of all Christendom according to the character and ability of its bishop or rector—so that their soundness corresponds to the soundness of the Roman church, and they rejoice or languish in unison with it.[2] As they are exalted by its glory, as the apostle says, so also are they brought low by its downfall, and thus we find here particular fulfilment of the prophecy: 'The whole head is listless and the whole heart is mourning; from the sole of the foot to the crown of the head there is no health therein.'[3] Indeed, all men look up to the pinnacle of the Apostolic See with so much reverence that they seek to discover rulings of the sacred canons or the ancient law of the Christian religion in the sayings of the master of the Apostolic See rather than in the Holy Scriptures and the writings handed down from the Fathers. Men merely find out what the Pope wishes or does not wish, so that they too may submit or adjust their lives to his will.

1. *Decretum Magistri Gratiani*, I, dist. XL, ch. vi, ed. E. Friedberg (Leipzig, 1879), 146. 2. Cf. 1 Corinthians, xii, 26. 3. Isaiah, i, 5–6.

If, as is supremely expedient to him and to all men, being continually consumed by zeal for the house of God[1] and being a faithful and wise steward,[2] the Pope strives to keep himself blameless in deed and word before God and man, I say truly that he makes the whole world run after God, being stirred and inspired together with him; that he leads to his Lord a multitude of peoples of both sexes and different callings, ranks and ages; and that he shall be set above all his Lord's goods. But if, being careless of his own and his brothers' salvation, he is found to be useless and remiss in his works[3] and failing to point out the good, which is still more harmful to him and to all men, he is likewise leading numberless people to the threshold of hell, and will afflict them, together with himself, with many plagues unto eternity. No mortal dares to reprove his offences, because he who shall judge all men must not be judged by anyone,[4] unless perchance he is found to be straying from the faith. The whole body of the faithful pray for his perpetual preservation all the more urgently as they reflect that their salvation depends (after God) most of all upon his soundness.

With due respect to the mystery of the omnipotence of God, the remarks of the blessed Job may not inappropriately be applied (after God) to the Roman church: 'Where it destroys, there is no one who can build again. And if it imprisons a man, there is no one who can release him. If it withholds the waters, all things shall be dried up. And if it sends them forth, they shall overwhelm the land.'[5] Together with Almighty God, the Roman church shall deservedly hold the reins of heaven and earth, especially through Peter; and since it is the special mother of all the faithful in Christ, no one must refuse to be disciplined by it or to be corrected by its sentence, according to the proverbs of Solomon: 'Lest you forsake the law of your mother, bind it to you upon your heart. Unhappy is he who rejects instruction, and foolish is the man who despises his mother.'[6] And again: 'Accursed of God is he who angers his mother, and a mother's curse uproots the foundations.'[7] Those things which are separated from the see of him to whom it was divinely said: 'You are Peter, and upon this rock I will build my church',[8] are proved to be founded upon the sand[9] of carnal concupiscence or human presumption. For a stream cannot flow if it is cut off from its source.

B. The gloss on the words 'Nisi deprehendatur a fide devius' in the

1. Psalms, lxix, 9; John, ii, 17.   2. Luke, xii, 42.   3. Ecclesiasticus, iv, 34.
4. 1 Corinthians, ii, 15.   5. Job, xii, 14–15.   6. Proverbs, vi, 20–21; xv, 20, 32.
7. Ecclesiasticus, iii, 11, 18.   8. Matthew, xvi, 18. 9. Cf. Matthew, vii, 26.

Decretum of Gratian by the canonist Huguccio: Tierney, *Foundations of the conciliar theory*, 248–50.

'*Unless he is found to be straying from the faith*'. Here the Pope can be condemned for heresy by his subjects, whereas *Distinctio* xxi 'nunc autem' is against this. There it is said that Marcellinus committed heresy, but his subjects did not condemn him.[1] Some say that they did not want to, but I say that they could not and had not to condemn him because he confessed his error humbly and of his own free will. Therefore the Pope can be condemned for heresy when he resists defiantly and obstinately and tries to defend and substantiate his error (*arg.* xxiii, q. iii, 'dixit apostolus' and 'qui in ecclesia').[2] But if on admonition he is willing to come to his senses, he cannot be accused or condemned for his error, whether it is heresy or any other notorious crime ... But he must be summoned and condemned when he publicly preaches things of this sort and on being admonished refuses to come to his senses, and not before. ...

But supposing the Pope devises a new heresy, and somebody wishes to prove that it is heresy, and the Pope says it is no heresy but is the catholic faith: should the other be allowed to prove it heresy? I think not. It follows that the heresy is secretly condemned. Some people know this and wish to prove that the Pope is following such a heresy. But he denies it. Ought they to be listened to? I think not. Therefore the Pope can be accused of heresy when it is agreed that the deed committed is heresy, and the Pope does not deny that he is committing it, and on being admonished refuses to come to his senses and defiantly defends his error. But if it is not agreed that the deed is heresy; or if it is agreed to be heresy but the Pope denies that he is committing it; or if it is agreed that the deed is heresy and the Pope is committing it and does not deny it, but is willing to stop and come to his senses: then nobody can accuse or condemn him for it.

Cannot the Pope be accused of simony or of some other crime? Some say he cannot, be it notorious or no, because we must not make exceptions which the canon does not make. These people also say that the reason for the distinction whereby the Pope can be accused of heresy and not of any other crime is that if the Pope were a heretic he would harm not only himself but the whole world also, especially as simple and foolish people might easily follow that heresy, not believing it to be heresy. But if the Pope commits simony, fornication, theft and the like he appears to be harming only himself, since everybody knows

1. *Decretum*, ed. Friedberg, 71–2.   2. Ibid., 998 (II, c. XXIV, q. iii, chs. xxix, xxxi).

it is not lawful for any man to fornicate or steal or commit simony and the like. But I think the same applies to any notorious crime—that the Pope can be accused and condemned if on admonition he is not willing to desist. Suppose he publicly thieves, publicly fornicates, publicly commits simony, publicly keeps a mistress, and publicly has intercourse with her in the church by or even upon the altar, and on admonition refuses to desist, shall he not be accused? . . . Shall he not be condemned? Is it not as good as committing heresy, so to scandalize the Church? Moreover, defiance is the crime of idolatry and as good as heresy—*Distinctio* lxxxi 'si quis presbyter'[1]—and hence a defiant man is called an infidel—*Distinctio* xxxviii 'nullus'.[2] So in other notorious crimes there is the same rule as in heresy.

Then why does Boniface mention heresy rather than any other notorious crime? I say that he has put it here by way of example, or perhaps there is a difference between heresy and other notorious crimes in that the Pope can be accused of the crime of heresy if he publicly preaches heresy and will not desist, even though such a crime be not notorious. But he cannot be accused of any other crime unless it be notorious. Therefore he cannot be accused of a secret crime. But supposing two, three or four persons know of the Pope's secret crime, can they not accuse him of it? Can they, after admonition, denounce this crime according to the rule of the Church 'si peccaverit'?[3] Why shall this rule of the Gospel not apply where the Pope is concerned? By the word 'brother' do we not understand 'any of the faithful' and therefore even the Pope?—*Distinctio* xi q. iii 'ad mensam'.[4] I answer: it appears that this rule does not apply to the Pope because there is no judge before whom he could be summoned, since he is himself the supreme judge; and to what Church would the report be made, since he is himself the Church?

Again I ask whether the Pope can rule out all possibility of being accused of heresy or notorious crime. I answer that he could in practice, but would have no right to do so, because he would thereby be teaching heresy; and besides, if the Pope were openly a heretic and could not be accused of heresy, the whole Church would be endangered and the general constitution of the Church thrown into confusion. I do not think he can ordain anything to the prejudice of the general constitution of the Church,—*Distinctio* xv 'sicut'. . . .[5]

---

1. *Decretum*, ed. Friedberg, 284–5: 'Si qui sunt presbiteri.'   2. Ibid., 144.
3. Matthew, xviii, 15–17.   4. *Decretum*, ed. Friedberg, 650 (II c. XI, q. iii. ch. xxiv).
5. *Decretum*, ed. Friedberg, 35–6.

Again, some people are in the habit of asking how a Pope could impose this law on his successors, so that they could be accused of heresy. But I say that there was no question of it. For the Pope did not ordain that a Pope could be accused of heresy: he established a privilege that he could not be accused of crimes. However, he did not wish to extend the privilege to all crimes, so that he could not be accused of anything. There was a general rule that everyone, including the Pope, should be punished for crimes, but he modified this general rule as far as the Pope was concerned by establishing a privilege that he could not be accused of crimes. But, since danger to the Church and general confusion within it must be avoided, he did not wish by that privilege to exclude heresy or notorious crime.

Cannot the Pope renounce this privilege? Yes—*arg.* ii q. v. 'mandastis' and 'auditum'[1] and q. vii 'nos si'.[2] But this would in no way prevent his successor from decreeing the same thing again if he so wished —*arg.* ii. q. v. 'mandastis' and 'auditum'.

BERNARD OF CLAIRVAUX
ON THE POWERS OF THE POPE

§ 9. Bernard, the Cistercian Abbot of Clairvaux, addressed the treatise *De Consideratione* (which he wrote between 1149 and 1153) to his disciple Bernardo Paganelli of Pisa, formerly Abbot of Tre Fontane and a fellow Cistercian, who had been elected Pope in 1145 as Eugenius III. The first of the extracts translated here is a declaration of the unlimited power of the Pope over the whole Church, which consists of all Christians. The second is a statement of the theory of the two swords.

See E. Vacandard, *Vie de Saint Bernard* (1897), II, 453 foll.; J. Rivière, *Le probléme de l'église et l'état au temps de Philippe le Bel* (Paris-Louvain, 1926), 26 foll. and *passim*; R. P. Lecler, 'L'argument des deux glaives', R.S.R., 21–2 (1931–2); McIlwain, *Growth of political thought*, 228 foll.; H. X. Arquillière, 'Origines de la théorie des deux glaives', S.G., 1 (1947); M. Maccarrone, 'Il papa "Vicarius Christi" ', *Miscellanea Pio Paschini*, I (Rome, 1949), 435 foll.; Watkin Williams, *Saint Bernard of Clairvaux* (Manchester, 1953), 242 foll.; B. Jacqueline, 'Bernard et l'expression "Plenitudo Potestatis" ' and A. Fliche, 'Bernard et la société civile de son temps', both in *Bernard de Clairvaux*, pub. by Commission d'histoire de l'ordre de Cîteaux (1953); G. B. Ladner,

---

1. *Decretum*, ed. Friedberg, 458, 461.   2. Ibid., 496.

'The concepts of "Ecclesia" and "Christianitas" and their relation to the idea of papal "Plenitudo Potestatis" from Gregory VII to Boniface VIII', M.H.P., 18 (1954); W. Levison, 'Die mittelalterliche Lehre von den beiden Schwerten', D.A.E.M., 9 (1953), 32 foll; M. Pacaut, *Alexandre* III (1956), 380 foll.; Pacaut, *La théocratie*, 109 foll.; Ullmann, *Growth of papal government*, 426 foll.

For theories of the two swords, cf. also below, Part III, nos. 10, 20A, 35.

§ 9

Bernard of Clairvaux: extracts from *De Consideratione*. A. II, viii: Migne, P.L., 182, 751–2.
He discusses the excellence of the pontifical office and power.

Let us, then, investigate more thoroughly the question of who you are and what part you play for the time being within the Church of God. Who are you? A great priest, a Supreme Pontiff. You are the chief of bishops, the heir of the apostles, a primate like Abel, a pilot like Noah, a patriarch like Abraham, of the order of Melchisedech, in the office of Aaron, with the authority of Moses and the judgment of Samuel, a Peter in power and a Christ by anointing. To you were the keys delivered, to you the sheep entrusted. Others are doorkeepers of heaven and shepherds of flocks: but you have inherited both these titles in a more glorious and a more distinctive fashion than have they. They have flocks assigned to them, particular people particular ones: but all are entrusted to you, one flock to one man. You are the one pastor, not only of all sheep, but also of all shepherds.

Do you ask me how I would prove this? From the word of the Lord. For to which apostle (let alone which bishop) are all sheep committed so absolutely and without distinction? 'If you love me, Peter, feed my sheep'.[1] Which sheep? The people of this or that city or province or such and such a kingdom? "My sheep", he said. Is it not obvious to everyone that the Lord did not merely point out certain particular ones, but assigned Peter all? Nothing is excepted where no distinction is made. And perhaps the other disciples were also present, since, when committing it to one man, he commended to all men unity in one flock under one shepherd, according to the dictum: 'One is my dove, my beautiful, my perfect one.'[2] Where there is unity, there is perfection.

1. John, xxi, 15.   2. Song of Solomon, vi, 8.

Other numbers have not perfection but division, as they are receding from unity. Hence it is that the other individual apostles who knew the mystery received particular peoples. Hence James, who appeared as the pillar of the Church, was content with one place, Jerusalem, and gave up the whole company to Peter. He was excellently placed there to raise up the seed of his dead brother, after he was killed: for James was called the brother of the Lord.[1] If even the Lord's brother gives way, who else shall obtrude upon the prerogative of Peter?

Therefore, according to your canons, others are summoned to part of the care [*in partem sollicitudinis*], but you to the wholeness of power [*in plenitudinem potestatis*]. The power of others is confined within definite limits: but yours is extended even to those who have received power over others. Can you not, if there is reason, close heaven to a bishop, can you not even depose him from his bishopric and deliver him to Satan? Your privilege, then, is inviolate, consisting both in the keys which were given and in the sheep which were commended to you.

Receive another privilege which the Lord none the less confirms to you. The disciples were in their boat and the Lord appeared on the shore—and, which was even better, he was once more in living flesh. Peter, knowing that it was the Lord, sprang upon the sea and so came to him whilst the other disciples came in the boat.[2] What was this? Assuredly it was the sign of the pontificate peculiar to Peter, by which he did not receive only one ship to pilot, like the others did, each one his own: he received the very world itself. For the sea is the world; the ships, churches. Hence it is that, walking upon the waters like the Lord, alternately with him, he marked himself out as the one vicar of Christ, who was to govern not one people only, but all: for indeed 'the many waters are many peoples'.[3] Therefore, whilst each of the others has his own ship, the one which is greatest is entrusted to you: the universal Church made out of all, spread throughout the entire world.

B. From IV, iii: Migne, P.L., 182, 776.

You say, 'You are advising me to feed serpents and scorpions, not sheep'. Because they are scorpions, I say, attack them all the harder— but with the word, and not the steel. Why try again to usurp the sword which you were once ordered to put back in the sheath? If anybody denies that it is yours, it seems to me he has not sufficiently pondered the word of the Lord when he says: 'Put *your* sword into its sheath'.[4] It

1. Galatians, i, 19.   2. John, xxi, 1–8.   3. Revelations, xvii, 15.   4. John, xviii, 11.

is yours, therefore, and must be drawn, perhaps at your behest, but not by your own hand. Had this sword not in any respect belonged to you, our Lord would not have answered 'That is enough', when the apostles said 'Here are two swords', but 'That is too much'.[1] Both swords, therefore, the spiritual and the material, belong to the Church—but the material sword is to be exercised on behalf of the Church, the spiritual even by the Church itself: the spiritual by the hand of the priest, the material by that of the soldier, but, to be sure, at the behest of the priest and the command of the Emperor.

DECREE ON PAPAL ELECTIONS, 1179

§ 10. On the first canon of the Third Lateran Council of 1179, which introduced more precise rules for the election of a Pope, see Hefele-Leclercq, *Histoire des conciles*, V, ii, 1086 foll.; H. J. Schroeder, *Disciplinary decrees of the general councils* (St. Louis-London, 1937), 214–15; J. Rousset de Pina in Fliche-Martin, *Histoire de l'Église*, IX, ii (1953), 162–3; L. Moulin, 'Les origines religieuses des techniques électorales et délibératives modernes', R.I.H.P.C., 3 (1953), 123 foll.; L. Moulin, '*Sanior et maior pars*. Note sur l'évolution des techniques électorales dans les Ordres religieux du VIe au XIIIe siècle', R.H.D.F.E. (1958), 385 foll.

§ 10

Canon I, 'Licet de evitanda', of the Third Lateran Council, 1179, on the election of the Pope: Mansi, *Concilia*, XXII, 217–18.

On the election of a Supreme Pontiff.

Although sufficiently clear laws for avoiding discord in the election of a Supreme Pontiff have been issued by our predecessors, nevertheless, as the Church has since frequently suffered serious division because of the effrontery of evil ambition, we have decreed, on the advice of our brothers and with the approval of the holy Council, that some addition be made to these decrees for the purpose of avoiding this evil. We decree therefore that if an enemy sows tares and there cannot be full agreement among the cardinals about replacing the Pope, and two-thirds of them agree but the other third refuses to agree or presumes to

1. Luke, xxii, 38.

ordain another Pope for itself, the man who has been chosen and accepted by the two-thirds shall be recognized as the Roman Pontiff. If anyone, relying on his nomination by the remaining third, usurps for himself the title of bishop (because he cannot usurp the bishopric itself), both he and those who accept him shall be subject to excommunication and punished by deprivation of all holy orders, so that the communion of the viaticum shall be denied them save in the last extremity, and unless they recover their senses they shall share the fate of Dathan and Abiram, whom the earth swallowed up alive.[1] Moreover, if anybody is elected to the office of the Apostolate by less than two-thirds, he shall not be installed unless greater agreement is reached, and he shall be subject to the same penalty if he refuses humbly to withdraw. But out of this no prejudice shall arise to the canonical decrees and to other churches, in which the opinion of the greater and sounder part ought to prevail— because if any doubt arises in them, it can be resolved by the judgment of a superior. But in the Roman church a special arrangement is made, because there can be no recourse to a superior.

POPE INNOCENT III ON THE RELATIONSHIP
OF PAPAL AND TEMPORAL POWER

§§ 11–12. The decretals 'Per venerabilem' and 'Novit ille' of Pope Innocent III contained pronouncements of supreme importance for canon law on the relationship between lay and ecclesiastical, spiritual and secular jurisdictions, and on the extent to which the Apostolic See was prepared to acknowledge and respect the rights of princes. 'Per venerabilem', addressed by Innocent III in 1202 to the Count of Montpellier, shows how a Pope could, on a comparatively trivial occasion, make significant pronouncements on matters of general principle. Some of the phrases used by the Pope in this letter were subjected to thorough discussion by medieval canonists and have been diversely interpreted by modern scholars. Debates have centred mainly round the nature of the 'occasional' jurisdictional powers which Innocent III claimed for the Apostolic See, and round the implications of his remark that 'the [French] King himself recognizes no superior in temporal matters' [*rex ipse superiorem in temporalibus minime recognoscit*]. 'Novit ille' was designed to justify Innocent's intervention in the current war between Philip of France and John of England. It reinforced an

1. Numbers, xvi, 31–3.

earlier letter replying to Philip's claim that he was not bound to submit to the papal jurisdiction in feudal matters: in dealing with John he was simply punishing a rebellious vassal. Innocent III claimed jurisdiction, not in feudal matters, but *ratione peccati*—'by reason of the sin committed' (see also below, Part IV, nos. 9–10).

See W. Molitor, *Die decretale 'Per venerabilem' von Innocenz III und ihre Stellung im öffentlichen Recht der Kirche* (Munich, 1876); R. W. and A. J. Carlyle, *History of mediaeval political theory in the west* (Edinburgh-London, 1903–1936), II, 231 foll., V, 143 (on 11), II, 219 foll., V, 165 foll. (on 12); E. W. Meyer, *Staatstheorien Papst Innocenz III* (Bonn, 1919), 24 foll.; E. F. Jacob, 'Innocent III', C.M.H., 6 (1929), 4–6; McIlwain, *Growth of political thought*, 231–2, 267; M. Maccarrone, *Chiesa e stato nella dottrina di papa Innocenzo III* (Rome, 1940), 108 foll., 118 foll.; W. Ullmann, *Medieval papalism* (London, 1949), 70–1, 102 foll., and 'The development of the medieval idea of sovereignty', E.H.R., 64 (1949); S. Mochi Onory, *Fonti canonistiche dell'idea moderna dello stato* (Milan, 1951), 8, 66, 209 foll., 271 foll. (on 11), 8, 34, 205–6 (on 12); H. Tillmann, 'Zur Frage der Verhältnisse von Kirche und Staat in Lehre und Praxis Papst Innocenz' III', D.A.E.M., 9 (1951); A. M. Stickler, 'Sacerdozio e regno nei decretisti e decretalisti', M.H.P., 18 (1954); G. B. Ladner, 'Ecclesia, Christianitas, Plenitudo Potestatis', ibid.; F. Kempf, *Papsttum und Kaisertum bei Innocenz III* (Rome, 1954—M.H.P., 19), 258 foll.; H. Tillmann, *Papst Innocenz III* (Bonn, 1954), 20 foll.; B. Tierney, 'Some recent works on the political theories of the medieval canonists', T., 10 (1954), 612 foll.; Pacaut, *La théocratie*, 143–4; B. Tierney, ' "Tria quippe distinguit iudicia . . . " A note on Innocent III's decretal "Per venerabilem" ', *Spec.*, 37 (1962).

§ 11

Innocent III's decretal 'Per venerabilem', 1202: *Decretalium collectio*, ed. Friedberg (Leipzig, 1881), 714–16.

To the noble William of Montpellier.

Through our venerable brother, the Archbishop of Arles, who approached the Apostolic See, you humbly begged us to legitimate your children, so that their illegitimate birth should be no impediment to their succeeding you. That the Apostolic See has full power in this matter appears from the fact that it has examined various cases, and in dealing with illegitimate children it has legitimated for the purpose of spiritual functions not only natural ones but even children born in adultery, so that they can be promoted to bishoprics. Hence it seems more likely and probable that it can legitimate them for secular functions also—especially if they recognize no earthly superior who has the power of legitimating other than the Roman Pontiff.

Greater foresight, authority and aptitude is required in spiritual matters, and what is permitted in the greater is lawful also in the less. This can be proved by analogy, since when a man is raised to the heights of a bishopric, he becomes exempt from the power of his father. Moreover, should even an ordinary bishop knowingly ordain priest the serf of another man, although the ordainer would be bound to compensate the lord as the canons prescribe, nevertheless the man ordained would still escape from the yoke of his serfdom. It would seem monstrous that a man who was legitimate for the purpose of spiritual functions should remain illegitimate for secular. Hence, if a dispensation is made in spiritual matters, it is understood that in consequence one has also been made in temporal matters. The Apostolic See may freely do this within the patrimony of St. Peter, where it both exercises the authority of a Supreme Pontiff and wields the power of a supreme prince. Since it appears from this that authority to legitimate, not only in spiritual but also in temporal matters, resides in the Roman church, the Archbishop humbly on your behalf requested us to do a favour to your sons in this matter on account of your merits and those of your ancestors, who have always been devoted to the Apostolic See.

Apparently he was further emboldened to make this request because a precedent was not far to seek, and in favour of this request he was able to adduce the decision which he said we ourselves had taken in a similar case. For our dearest son in Christ, Philip, the illustrious King of the French, put from him our dearest daughter in Christ, Ingeborg, illustrious Queen of the French, and had a boy and a girl by another woman with whom he later formed a liaison; and you likewise put away your lawful wife and took up with another, by whom you had children. It was thought that the Apostolic See would kindly make a dispensation for your children as it had for his, especially as the need for this was greater and you are more specially subject to us. For the King of the French had already had a legitimate heir by the Queen of the French of famous memory—one who is desirable to him and who, it is thought, will succeed him on the royal throne—whilst you have no male heir by your lawful wife to succeed you in devotion to us and in his own inheritance. Again, whilst the King himself is subject to us in things spiritual, you are subject to us in things both spiritual and temporal, since you hold a part of your land from the church of Maguelonne; and as this church acknowledges that this land comes temporally from the Apostolic See, the Archbishop asserted that you were temporally subject to us by means of the church of Maguelonne.

But, if we inquire diligently into the truth, this case does not appear to resemble yours: it is really very different. For the King himself was separated from the Queen by the judgment of the Archbishop of Reims, of happy memory, legate of the Apostolic See; but you, it is said, separated your wife from you by your own presumption. The King formed a liaison with another woman, who, as is well known, bore him twins, before the veto on contracting with another reached him; but you sought to form a liaison with another woman in contempt of the Church, and because of it the Church wielded the sword of ecclesiastical punishment against you. Again, the King objected that his kinship with the Queen was an impediment to his marriage with her and produced witnesses to this in the presence of the Archbishop. The Archbishop's decision was invalidated only because the correct judicial procedure was not observed, and we ordered that other judges should be appointed to deal with this matter after the reinstatement of the Queen. But you, it is said, did not raise against your wife any objection which would lead to a divorce, since, although faithfulness to the marriage bed is one of the three good things of marriage, nevertheless breaking faith to it would not cut the marriage tie. There can be justifiable doubts as to whether the King's children were legitimate or illegitimate, so long as the dispute over the impediment of kinship is pending. For if the kinship is proved, it will appear that the Queen is not the King's wife, and consequently the other woman will seem to be lawfully joined to him and to have born him legitimate children. But you do not suggest that your children were born legitimate, and no reason at all for such a contention is advanced.

Moreover, since the King himself recognizes no superior in temporal matters, he could subject himself in this matter to our jurisdiction, and indeed did so, without infringing the rights of his superior. It might seem to some people that he could deal with this matter himself, not as a father with his children, but as a prince with his subjects. But you are known to be subject to others. Hence you could not subject yourself to us in this matter without the risk of doing them wrong (unless they had agreed to the case going to us). And you are not of such authority that you have the right to deal with these matters yourself.

We were induced by these arguments to grant the King the favour which he asked, deriving both from the Old and the New Testament the reason why we exercise temporal jurisdiction occasionally [*casualiter*] not only within the patrimony of the church, over which we wield full power in temporal matters, but also in other regions, where we have examined certain determinate cases [*certis causis inspectis*]. It is not that we wish to prejudice the rights of another or usurp power that does not belong to us, for we know that Christ in the Gospel answered: 'Render to Caesar the things that are Caesar's, and to God the things that are God's'.[1] Hence, being asked to divide an inheritance between two people, 'Who' he asked, 'appointed me a judge over you?'[2]

But it is said in Deuteronomy: 'If you see that there is a difficult and doubtful matter to be determined among you, between blood and blood, cause and cause, or leprosy and leprosy, and you see that the words of the judges within your gates are at variance: then rise and go up to the place which the Lord your God chooses, and come to the priests of the tribe of Levi and to the judge for the time being, and ask them; and they shall show you the truth of the judgment; and you shall do what they say who preside over the place which the Lord has chosen, and follow their decision without straying to the left or to the right. And if anyone is arrogant and refuses to obey the commandment of the priest who at that time is serving the Lord your God, he shall die by the judge's decree, and you shall put away the evil from Israel'.[3] Now as 'Deuteronomy' is understood to mean 'the second law', the very word itself proves that what is decreed in Deuteronomy must be observed in the New Testament also. For the 'place which the Lord has chosen' is known to be the Apostolic See, because the Lord founded it with himself as the corner stone. For when Peter fled from the city, and the Lord wanted to recall him to the place he had chosen, when Peter asked him: 'Lord, where are you going?' he answered 'I am going to Rome to be crucified again'.[4] Realizing that this was meant for him, Peter returned forthwith to that place. The 'priests of the tribe of Levi' are our brothers, who by the law of Levi assist us in performing priestly duties. The priest or 'judge' over them is the one to whom the Lord said in Peter: 'Whatsoever you shall bind on earth shall be bound in heaven also, and whatsoever you shall loose on earth shall be loosed

---

1. Matthew, xxii, 21; Mark, xii, 17. 2. Luke, xii, 13–14. 3. Deuteronomy, xvii, 8–12. 4. *Apocryphal Acts of Peter*: Greek text, ed. R. A. Lipsius (Leipzig, 1891), 88; trans. B. Pick (Chicago, 1909), 115.

F

in heaven also.'[1] He is vicar of him who is a priest forever after the order of Melchisedech, and was appointed by God judge of the living and of the dead.[2]

Deuteronomy distinguishes three forms of judgment: the first, 'between blood and blood', by which we understand crimes to be dealt with by a lay judge [*per quod criminale intelligitur et civile*]; the third, 'between leprosy and leprosy', which denotes crimes within the jurisdiction of an ecclesiastical judge [*per quod ecclesiasticum et criminale notatur*]; the second, 'between cause and cause', which refers to cases which are either ecclesiastical or secular [*quod ad utrumque refertur, tam ecclesiasticum quam civile*]. If anything in these is difficult or uncertain, one must have recourse to the judgment of the Apostolic See, and if anyone is arrogant and scorns to abide by its sentence, he must die and 'the evil be put away from Israel': that is, be separated from the communion of the faithful like a dead man by the sentence of excommunication. Paul, in order to explain the fullness of power, said when writing to the Corinthians: 'Do you not know that we shall judge angels? How much more, then, things of this life!'[3] Moreover, he was accustomed to discharge the function of a secular power in some matters personally and in some matters through other people.

Admittedly we thought that a dispensation should be made for the sons of the King of the French, for there was some possibility that they were legitimate in the first place. But both the Mosaic and the canon law detest the offspring of adultery, and the Lord bears witness that bastards and children of harlots shall not enter the Church even unto the tenth generation,[4] and the canon forbids them to be promoted to holy orders, and the secular laws not only exclude them from succeeding their fathers but even deny them the right to be supported by them. Therefore we do not see fit to assent to your petition, until you can show both that your fault is less serious and that we are freer to judge the case—although we embrace you with special love and would like to show you special favour, in so far as we can do so in a godly and honourable fashion.

§ 12

The decretal 'Novit ille' of Innocent III, April 1204: *Decretalium collectio*, ed. Friedberg, 242–3.

1. Matthew, xvi, 19.   2. Acts, x, 42.   3. 1 Corinthians, vi, 3.   4. Deuteronomy, xxiii, 2.

Innocent III to the prelates in France.

He knows, who is ignorant of nothing, who examines men's hearts and knows their secrets, that we love our dearest son in Christ, Philip, illustrious King of the French, with a pure heart, a good conscience and unfeigned loyalty, and that we are striving effectively for his honour, advancement and prosperity: for we believe that the exaltation of the French Kingdom is the sublimation of the Apostolic See, since this Kingdom, which is blessed of God, has always been devoted to him and will never, we think, abandon that devotion. Although, from time to time, from here or there, wicked angels loose their shafts, we who know the cunning of Satan will strive to frustrate his manœuvres, believing that the King will not allow himself to be seduced by his trickery.

Therefore let no one think that we want to diminish or upset the jurisdiction or power of the illustrious King of the French. For he does not wish to, and indeed must not, obstruct our jurisdiction and power; and, since we cannot adequately exercise to the full even our own jurisdiction, why should we wish to usurp that of another man? But, as the Lord says in the Gospel: 'If your brother has sinned against you, go and tell him his fault between you and him alone. If he listens to you, you have won your brother over. If he will not listen to you, take with you one or two others, so that every word may be established by the mouths of two or three witnesses. But if he will not listen to them, tell the Church; and if he will not listen to the Church, regard him as a pagan and a tax collector.'[1] The King of England, or so he says, is prepared to give sufficient proof that the King of the French is sinning against him, and that he has himself proceeded according to the rule in the Gospel in order to correct him, and has at last, since he has made no progress, told the Church. How then, being summoned by divine decree to rule over the universal Church, can we not hear the commandment of God and not proceed according to it, unless the King of the French shows su............

church of Milan: 'You shall arrange that in the episcopal see there be
one to whom even we who govern the Empire may sincerely bow our
heads, and whose advice we shall be bound to accept like the medicines
of a physician when, being but men, we commit offences'. And let us
not omit that very humble rule which the Emperor Theodosius
originated and Charles, of whose line King Philip is well known to
descend, renewed: 'Suppose anyone is involved in a law suit, whether
as plaintiff or defendant: at the beginning of the suit or after some
time has elapsed, or when the proceedings are being concluded, or even
when the sentence is already beginning to be issued, if he chooses to be
judged by the bishop of a holy see, he may without a doubt be sent to
him, even if the other party is opposed to this, for the litigants to speak
and the bishops to judge the matter.'[1]

Now, since we do not take our stand on any decree of man, but
rather upon the law of God, because our power is not derived from
man, but from God: every man of sound mind is aware that it belongs
to our office to snatch any Christian away from any mortal sin, and, if
he scorns to be corrected, to coerce him by means of ecclesiastical sanctions. That we can and must pronounce censure appears from each page
of the Scripture where the Lord cries through the Prophet: 'Cry, and
cease not, lift up your voice like a trumpet, and proclaim their crimes
to my people',[2] and he adds in the same place: 'Unless you proclaim
his impiety to the impious one, he will die in the wickedness which he
has committed: but I will hold you responsible for his death.' The
apostle, too, advises us to censure troublemakers, and in another place
he says: 'Accuse, appeal, rebuke, with all patience and teaching.'[3] That
we can and indeed must coerce appears from what the Lord said to the
prophet who came of the priests of Anathot: 'Behold, I have set you
above peoples and kingdoms, to pluck up and destroy, to scatter, to
build and to plant.'[4] It is generally agreed that the thing to be plucked

he must bind on earth those who, it is generally agreed, are bound in heaven.

But perhaps it will be said that we must deal with kings in one way and with other men in another. However, we know that it is written in the divine law: 'You shall judge the great as the small, and you shall not respect persons'—St. James testifies that this respect of persons arises 'if you say to the well-dressed man "you sit in this good seat" but to the pauper you say "you stand over there, or sit under my footstool" '.[1]

But although we can in this way proceed against any criminal sin in order to recall the sinner from vice to virtue and from error to truth, we must do so especially when a sin is committed against peace, which is the bond of love, concerning which Christ specially commanded the apostles: 'Whenever you enter a house, first say: "Peace to this house", and if there is a son of peace there, your peace shall rest upon him.'[2] 'But if any will not receive you or listen to your arguments, go out of their doors and shake the dust off your feet as evidence against them.'[3] The apostles' 'going out of the doors of such people' can only mean their denying them apostolic communion. 'Shaking the dust off their feet' can only mean their applying ecclesiastical sanctions. For this is the dust which, when Moses scattered the ash from the furnace, was as a plague of sores throughout all the land of Egypt.[4] How terrible is the sentence which those who do not receive the messengers of peace and do not listen to their arguments will suffer at the last judgment the true Scripture itself then shows, for it says, not just plainly, but with some emphasis: 'I say to you, "Amen": it will be more bearable for the land of Sodom and Gomorrah on the day of judgment than for that town.'[5] In the town Christ included the citizens, and did not except the kings themselves.

Moreover, if anyone establishes according to the proper laws a right against anyone else, another person may use it against him; and Solomon protests 'There is a law, which shall be applied to you yourself'. The King of the French himself made use of our offices and favour in the war against Richard, the late King of the English, who was not of a rank inferior to his own (may we say this without offending the King, for we say it not to embarrass him but to justify ourselves?). How then can he not allow what was used on his behalf against King Richard to be used against him on behalf of another man? Should we not weigh up and measure which of them is detestable in the sight of God?

1. James, ii, 3.   2. Luke, x, 5–6.   3. Mark, vi, 11.   4. Exodus, ix, 10.
5. Matthew, x, 15.

Finally, since peace treaties were again drawn up between the Kings and signed with each taking his own oath, and yet were not observed up to the appointed time: then why can we not judge the religious element in the oath (for there is no doubt that it pertains to the jurisdiction of the Church) so that the broken treaties may be restored? Lest, therefore, we appear to be fostering this grave discord under cover of pretence, concealing the destruction of Christian places and paying no attention to the ruin of the Christian people, we have given orders to our beloved son, the Abbot of Casamari, the aforesaid legate, to proceed against the King of France according to the instructions we have given him unless the King of France either re-establishes a firm peace with the King of England, or initiates an adequate truce, or at least humbly suffers the Abbot and our venerable brother the Archbishop of Bourges to investigate informally [de plano] whether the complaint which the King of the English is lodging against him before the Church is just, or whether the defence against the King of England which he chose to expound in his letters to us is lawful.

And so by the apostolic letters we command all your corporations and strictly order you, by virtue of your obedience, when the Abbot has carried out the apostolic commandment on this matter, humbly to accept his sentence, or rather ours, to observe it yourselves and to make others observe it, in the sure knowledge that if you do otherwise we will punish your disobedience.

Given at the Lateran, . . . in the seventh year of our pontificate, 1204.

CHAPTER II

Aspects of the Church and its Government in the Twelfth and Early Thirteenth Century

HUGH OF ST. VICTOR ON THE NATURE OF THE CHURCH

§ 13. Hugh of St. Victor joined the monastery and theological school of St. Victor in Paris about the year 1115 and served as its head from 1133 until his death in 1141. He was the author of one of the first major pieces of theological synthesis, *De sacramentis*, which dates from the 1130s. The extract from this work which is translated here is an important expression of the concept of the whole of Christian society as a Church, and a description of the relationship which clergy and laity could in consequence be expected to assume within it.

See Ewart Lewis, *Medieval political ideas* (London, 1954), I, 208, II, 521, 576 foll.; F. W. Witte, 'Die Staats und Rechtsphilosophie des Hugo von St. Viktor', A.R.S., 43 (1957); F. Merzbacher, 'Recht und Gewaltenlehre bei Hugo von St. Viktor', Z.S.S.R., k.a., 44 (1958); Ullmann, *Growth of papal government*, 437 foll.; M. Wilks, *The problem of sovereignty in the later middle ages* (Cambridge, 1963), 50 foll.

§ 13

Hugh of St. Victor, *De sacramentis*, II, ii–iv: Migne, P.L., 176, 416–18.
    Of the Church, and what the Church is.
    The holy Church is the body of Christ, made alive by one spirit and united and sanctified by one faith. Individual faithful are the members of this body; all are one body, on account of the one spirit and the one faith. But just as in the human body all the individual members have their own distinct functions, and yet each of them does not do for itself alone what it alone does, even so are the gifts of grace distributed in the

77

body of the holy Church, and yet each man does not have for himself alone the gift which he alone has. For only the eyes can see: and yet they do not see for themselves alone, but for the whole body. Only the ears can hear, and yet they do not hear for themselves alone, but for the whole body. Only the feet can walk, and yet they do not walk for themselves alone, but for the whole body. And in this way a man does not have for himself alone any gift which he has: it merely rests with him, since, according to the order established by the most excellent giver and wise dispenser of gifts, everything belongs to all men, and all things to everybody.

Whoever, therefore, has deserved to receive the gift of God's grace, shall know that what he has does not belong to him alone, even if he alone has it. Therefore, by this simile, the holy Church, that is, the whole company of the faithful [*universitas fidelium*], is called the body of Christ on account of the Spirit of Christ which it has received and whose participation in a man is pointed out when he is called by Christ a Christian.

This name therefore means the members of Christ partaking of the Spirit of Christ, as each is anointed by the anointed, because he is called a Christian by Christ. For 'Christ' is interpreted as meaning 'anointed' —anointed by that oil of gladness which he received according to his wholeness before all who form part of him, and which he transmitted to all who form part of him according to their participation, like a head to the members: 'Like the ointment on the head, which runs down' from the head 'to the beard' and thence 'to the skirt'[1]—that is, which flowed down to the edge of the garment so that it might flow to all and make all alive. When, therefore, you become a Christian you are made a member of Christ, a member of the body of Christ partaking of the Spirit of Christ. What, then, is the Church but the mass of the faithful, the whole company of Christians [*multitudo fidelium, universitas Christianorum*]?

Of the two walls of the Church, clerks and laymen.

Now this whole company embraces two orders, laymen and clerks, like the two sides of one body. The laymen who serve the needs of the present life are, as it were, on the left hand side.

I do not mean they are on the left hand in the same way as they are placed upon the left to whom it shall be said: 'Go, cursed ones, into everlasting fire'.[2] God forbid that I should presume to put good laymen there! For good men will not go there, be they laymen or be they

1. Psalms, cxxxiii, 2.   2. Matthew, xxv, 41.

clerks; and evil men will go there, be they laymen or be they clerks.

I do not therefore place Christian laymen who are true Christians upon that left hand: but upon the left hand of which it is said 'Length of life is in her right hand; but in her left hand are riches and glory'.[1] For what lies to the left within the body is part of the body and is good, although it is not the best.

Therefore, Christian laymen who deal with earthly things and those necessary to the earthly life are the left hand side of the body of Christ. But the clerks, since they dispense the things which belong to the spiritual life, are like the right hand side of the body of Christ.

But the whole body of Christ, which is the Universal Church, is composed of these two parts. 'Lay' is understood to mean 'of the people', for the Greek *laos* is called 'people [*populus*]' in Latin. Hence also *basileus* is considered to mean 'king'—*basis laou*, 'the support of the people'. A clerk is called in Greek *kleros*, which, translated into Latin, becomes 'lot' or 'portion' [*sors*], whether because he was chosen by lot by God to serve God or because God himself is his lot; and because a clerk must not have any other portion on earth save God and the things which belong to God, for it is decreed that he shall be supported by the tithes and oblations which are offered to God. Faithful Christian laymen, then, are permitted to own earthly things; but only spiritual things are entrusted to clerks—as, in that earlier people, the tribes which symbolized laymen received portions of hereditary property, whilst only the tribe of Levi, which stood for churchmen, was fed on tithes and oblations and victims of sacrifices.

There are two lives, and, corresponding to the two lives, two peoples; and among the two peoples are two powers, and in each of them are various grades and orders of office; and one is inferior, the other superior.

There are two lives: one earthly, the other heavenly; one corporal, the other spiritual. One by which the body takes life from the soul, the other by which the soul takes life from God. Each has its own goods by which it is given life and fed so that it can subsist. The earthly life is fed by earthly goods, the spiritual life by spiritual goods. To the earthly life belong all things which are earthly; to the spiritual life belong all spiritual goods. So that in each life justice may be preserved and progress may be made, men have been assigned to one or the other to acquire good of either sort by effort and labour, according to need and to reason.

Then there are some who are empowered by the office which is

1. Proverbs, iii, 16.

entrusted to them to provide in an equitable manner that no one oppresses his brother in their dealings together, but that justice is preserved
inviolate. Hence powers have been established within the people that is
assigned to each life. Among the laymen there is an earthly power,
since they are concerned to provide for things which are necessary to
life on earth. Among the clergy, whose office is concerned with the
goods of the spiritual life, there is a divine power. The first is therefore
called the secular power, the second is known as the spiritual. Within
each power there are various grades and orders of powers, but they are
placed under one head for each of them, and, as it were, drawn from
and traced to one origin. The earthly power has the King as its head.
The spiritual has the Supreme Pontiff. To the power of the King belong
the things that are earthly and all actions to do with the earthly life. To
the power of the Supreme Pontiff belong the things which are spiritual
and all attributes of the spiritual life. But as the spiritual life has greater
worth than the earthly and the spirit than the body, so does the spiritual
power surpass the earthly or secular in honour and dignity.

For the spiritual power must both bring the earthly into existence,
and judge it if it is not good. The spiritual is the power first established
by God, and when it errs it can only be judged by God, as it is written:
'The spiritual man judges all things and is himself judged by no one.'[1]
But the spiritual power (in as much as it was established by God) is both
the first in time and the greater in rank. This plainly appears from the
ancient people of the Old Testament, where the priesthood was established by God first; and later the royal power was ordained by the
priesthood upon God's commandment.

Hence in the Church to this day the priestly dignity consecrates the
royal power, both sanctifying it by benediction and forming it by
institution. If, therefore, as the apostle says, he who blesses is greater
and he who is blessed is lesser,[2] it is agreed without any doubt that the
earthly power, which receives benediction from the spiritual, is rightly
regarded as inferior to it.

THE CISTERCIAN ORDER AND THE CHAPTER-GENERAL

§§ 14–16. Any medieval source-book which deals with the history of
the Church is bound to include some illustration of the way in which
monks and other ascetics lived their lives. Unfortunately, the two most

1. 1 Corinthians, ii, 15.   2. Hebrews, vii, 7.

important documents in the history of medieval Christian asceticism, the Rule of St. Benedict and the Rule of St. Francis, are far too long to be included here. It would be impossible to select from them in a manner which was other than highly subjective. There is a further justification for excluding them in the fact that it is quite easy to obtain modern English translations of both of them. In this century the Rule of St. Benedict has been translated at least by D. O. Hunter-Blair (1907), by F. A. Gasquet (1909) and by J. McCann—with a commentary by P. Delatte (1921) and with a parallel Latin text (1952). An English translation of the Rule of St. Francis has recently appeared in L. Sherley-Price, *St. Francis of Assisi* (London, 1959), 205 foll.

The constitutions of the Cistercian Order, however, have not received comparable attention from translators—in spite of the fact that the Cistercians were as influential a reforming movement in the twelfth century as the Mendicant Orders in the thirteenth. The essential purpose of the twelfth-century Cistercians was to return to the strict observance of the Rule of St. Benedict, which they sought to interpret in a literal sense. Document 14 consists of some of the early legislation issued for this purpose by the Chapter-General meeting at the mother house of Cîteaux (founded in 1098), from which all Cistercian monasteries were ultimately descended. There is some evidence for the existence of such a Chapter-General in the second decade of the twelfth century.

Document 15, the *Carta Caritatis*, or Charter of Love, is the constitution governing the relationship between all Cistercian abbeys. The text here translated was dated by its nineteenth-century editor, Philip Guignard, between 1191 and 1194; earlier texts have since been discovered. Some form of a *Carta Caritatis* seems to have been in existence in 1114, when Pontigny, the second daughter abbey of Cîteaux, was founded. The *Carta Caritatis*, as M. Lefèvre has recently shown, was a body of law constantly undergoing accretions—different parts of it mark successive stages in the development of the Cistercian Order throughout the twelfth century.

Document 16 shows how the Cistercian institution of the Chapter-General was imposed by the Fourth Lateran Council summoned by Innocent III in 1215 upon all monastic orders which had not yet adopted it. Many already had.

See J. B. Mahn, *L'ordre cistercien et son gouvernement des origines au milieu du XIIIᵉ siècle (1098–1265)* (1945), 60 foll., 239 foll.; P. Schmitz, *Histoire de l'ordre de Saint-Benoît*, III (Maredsous, 1948), 27 foll., 46 foll.; D. Knowles, *The religious orders in England*, I (Cambridge, 1948), 9 foll., on 16, and his *The monastic order in England, 943–1216* (Cambridge, 1963), 208 foll., with references; J. A. Lefèvre on the *Carta Caritatis* and *Instituta generalis capituli* in C.O.C.R., 16 (1954) and R.B., 65 (1955); J. B. Van Damme, 'Genèse des *Instituta generalis capituli*', C., 12 (1961). For references to the recent controversy concerning the origins of the monastery of Cîteaux, see C. Dereine, 'La fondation de Cîteaux d'après l'*Exordium Cistercii* et l'*Exordium parvum*', C., 10 (1959); D. Knowles, *Great historical enterprises and problems in monastic history* (London, 1963), 198 foll.

§ 14

Customs of the Cistercian Order: early legislation of the Chapter General: P. Guignard, *Monuments primitifs de la règle cistercienne* (Dijon, 1878), 250–2.

I. *Where monasteries must be constructed.*

No monasteries of ours must be constructed in cities or fortresses or on manors, but in places far from where men associate.

II. *Of uniformity of conduct in divine and human affairs.*

That an indissoluble unity may be forever maintained between the abbeys, it is first laid down that all shall interpret the Rule of St. Benedict in one way and observe it in one way, so that the same divine service books, the same food, the same clothing, and, in short, the same customs in all things shall be found everywhere.

III. *That it is not lawful to have different books.*

Everywhere they shall use the same missal, epistle-book, book of collects, gradual, antiphonary, Rule, hymnal, psalter, lectionary and calendar.

IV. *Of clothing.*

The dress shall be plain and cheap, without furs, linen or linsey-woolsey—such, in a word, as the Rule describes.

V. *Where food for the monks shall come from.*

Food must come to the monks of our Order by the work of their hands, by the cultivation of land and by the rearing of sheep, and hence it is lawful for us to possess for our own use waters, woods, vineyards, meadows and lands distant from the dwellings of men in the world; and also animals (other than those which usually arouse curiosity and show off their own vanity rather than serve any useful purpose—such as deer, cranes and the like). We can have granges, which must be looked after by lay brothers [*conversi*], for the purpose of using, rearing and keeping these things, either near to or far from the monasteries, but not more than a day's journey from them.

VI. *That no monk must live outside the cloister.*

A monk, who ought by the Rule to live in his cloister, may go to the granges whenever he is sent, but he may not dwell there too long.

VII. *That in our Order it is forbidden to live with women and even entry through the gate of the monastery is denied to them.*

On no pretext—whether of increasing or preserving food supplies, or of laundering property of the monastery as is sometimes necessary, or, in short, of any need whatever—may women be permitted to live with us and our lay brothers [*conversi*]. Therefore they may not be housed within the yards of the granges and may not pass through the gate of the monastery.

VIII. *Of the lay brothers.*

Work at the granges must be done by lay brothers and by hirelings. By permission of the bishops we receive these lay brothers as indispensable to us and to assist us, and we take them under our care like monks and regard them, no less than the monks, as brothers and as participants in our goods, both spiritual and temporal.

IX. *That we are not to have revenues.*

The law of our name and Order forbids us to own churches, altars, tombs, tithes of other men's labour or sustenance, manors, villeins, rents from land, revenues from furnaces or mills, and other like things which are repugnant to monastic purity.

X. *What it is lawful and what not lawful for us to have in the way of gold, silver, jewels or silk.*

Altar cloths and the vestments of ministers shall have no silk in them —apart from the stole and maniple. The chasuble shall be of one colour only. All ornaments of the monastery, vessels and utensils shall be free the lord Stephen and his brothers ordained that in no way might abbeys be founded within the diocese of any bishop before he had had a constitution drawn up, ratified and confirmed by the monastery of Cîteaux and the others that had sprung from it—for the purpose of avoiding unseemliness between the bishop and the monks. In this constitution, the said brothers, seeking to prevent the peace between them from foundering in the future, declared and ordained and laid down for their successors by what arrangement, by what means and especially with what love their monks in abbeys in various parts of the world, though divided in their bodies, might be inseparably welded together in their souls. They decided to call this decree the Charter of Love, because it refuses to impose any taxes and pursues only love and the interests of souls in divine and human affairs. As we know that we are all servants, however unprofitable, of the one true King, Lord and Master, we do not exact any earthly benefits or temporal contributions from the abbots and from our fellow monks whom the kindness of God has placed under the discipline of the Rule by means of us, the most wretched of men. Wishing to do good to them and to all sons of Holy Church, we have decided not to burden them or diminish their substance in any way, lest, in our desire to become rich by impoverishing them, we run into the evil of avarice, which is condemned as idolatry by the apostle.

But we do wish to retain the care of their souls out of love for them: so that, supposing (which God forbid) they attempt to depart from their holy resolution and from the observance of the holy Rule, our concern for them may recall them to a righteous way of life. We wish and command them to observe the Rule of St. Benedict in all things as it is observed in the New Monastery.[1] Let them not introduce any different interpretation in reading the holy Rule: they shall interpret and keep it as our forebears the holy fathers the monks of the New Monastery, interpret and keep it and the common constitutions of the Order or dare by any means to keep one which has already been obtained.

When the Abbot of the New Monastery comes to visit any of these other monasteries, the abbot of the other monastery shall give way to him in all parts of the monastery by way of acknowledging that the church of the New Monastery is the mother of his own church, and the abbot who has come thither shall take the place of the abbot of the monastery he is visiting, save that he shall not eat in the guesthouse, but in the refectory with the brothers, for the preservation of discipline, unless the abbot of the monastery is away. All visiting abbots of our Order shall do likewise. If several arrive at the same time and the abbot of the place is absent, the first of them shall eat in the guesthouse. Even in the presence of the senior abbot, the abbot of the monastery which is being visited shall bless his novices after their period of probation according to the Rule. The Abbot of the New Monastery shall take care that he does not presume against the wishes of the abbot or the brothers to deal with, regulate or interfere in the affairs of the monastery to which he comes. But if he realizes that the precepts of the Rule or of our Order are being transgressed in that place, he shall do his best to correct the brothers in a spirit of love with the advice of the abbot, if he is there: but if the abbot is away, the Abbot of the New Monastery shall correct anything he finds to be wrong.

The abbot of a greater church shall, either in person or through one of his fellow abbots, visit once a year all the monasteries which he has founded. And if he visits the brothers more frequently than that, all the more shall they rejoice. The house of Cîteaux shall be visited simultaneously by the four senior abbots, i.e. those of La Ferté, Pontigny, Clairvaux and Morimond, in person, on a day which they agree upon among themselves which shall not be that of the annual chapter, unless any of them happens to be prevented by serious illness. When any abbot of our Order comes to the New Monastery, due reverence shall be shown to him. He shall take the Abbot's stall and eat in the guesthouse if the Abbot of the New Monastery is absent. But if he is there the visiting abbot shall do none of these things, but shall eat in the refectory. The Prior of the New Monastery shall deal with its business.

Between abbeys of which one did not give birth to the other, the following rule shall be observed. Every abbot shall give way to a visiting fellow-abbot in every part of his monastery and they shall vie with one another in showing mutual respect. If two or more abbots come to the same place, the first to arrive shall take precedence. But all, apart from the abbot of that place, shall eat in the refectory as we have said above. Otherwise, wherever they assemble, they shall keep their places, according to the date of their abbeys, so that he whose church is older shall come first. Wherever they sit down together they shall defer to one another.

When, by the grace of God, one of our churches has so grown that it is able to build another monastery, they shall observe the same regulations as we do between us and our fellow brothers, save that they shall not hold an annual chapter between them. But all the abbots of our Order shall, putting aside every excuse, assemble every year for a general chapter at Cîteaux—save only those who are prevented by bodily infirmity. These must appoint a suitable messenger to announce to the chapter why they needed to remain behind. Also excepted are those who live in the more distant regions, and these shall come at a time appointed for them in the chapter. But if anybody at any time presumes not to attend our general chapter on any other pretext, he shall ask pardon for his fault at the chapter held the following year and shall not escape without a severe punishment.

In this chapter the abbots shall provide for the salvation of souls; if there are any additions or adjustments to be made in the observation of the holy Rule or the statutes of the Order they shall make them; and they shall re-establish the benefits of peace and love among themselves. If any abbot is not diligent enough in observing the Rule or too intent on worldly matters or is found to be at fault in anything, let him be proclaimed there in a spirit of love; and on being proclaimed let him ask pardon and carry out the penance imposed on him for his fault. Only abbots shall make this proclamation. If it happens that controversy arises between abbots, or that any of them is charged with such a serious fault that he deserves suspension or even deposition, the chapter's decision on the matter shall be observed and may not be revoked. If there are different views on the case and disagreement about it arises, the decision of the Abbot of Cîteaux and of those who seem better qualified and whose judgment appears to be sounder shall be inviolably observed, with a proviso that no one who has a special interest in the case may take part in determining it. If any church becomes unbearably impoverished, the abbot of that monastery shall take pains to inform the whole chapter of this matter. Then all the abbots, fired with the warmest love, shall make haste to relieve the penury of that church out of the property which they have conferred on them by God.

If any house of our Order is bereaved of its own abbot, the senior abbot out of whose house it originated shall have all the responsibility for governing it until another abbot is elected. A day shall be fixed for the election, and abbots of daughter houses of the abbey concerned (if any) shall be summoned, and these abbots and the monks of the abbey concerned shall elect the new abbot. But when the house of Cîteaux, which is the mother of all our monks, loses its own abbot, the four senior abbots, i.e. those of La Ferté, Pontigny, Clairvaux and Morimond, shall look after and take care of Cîteaux until a new abbot is chosen and installed in it. When a day has been named and fixed for the election of an Abbot of Cîteaux, abbots whose houses originated from Cîteaux shall be summoned with at least fifteen days' notice, and so shall some others whom the said abbots and the brothers of Cîteaux know to be suitable, and, having assembled in the name of the Lord, the abbots and the monks of Cîteaux shall elect an abbot. It shall be lawful for any mother church of our Order to choose an abbot freely not only from the monks of her daughter churches but, if need be, from their abbots also. None of our churches may elect as their abbot a member of another Order, and no member of our Order may be given to other monasteries which are not of our Order.

If any abbot, because of his inadequacy or timidity, asks his father the abbot of the house from which his own originated if he may be relieved of the burden of being abbot, the father abbot must take care not to assent to this lightly and without reasonable cause and urgent need. If there is such need, he must not take any action by himself, but shall summon certain other abbots of our Order and shall do on their advice what they all agree is necessary.

But if any abbot is known to be offending against the holy Rule, or transgressing the regulations of the Order, or abetting the faults of the brothers entrusted to him, then the abbot of the mother church shall up to four times admonish him to amend, either by himself or through his prior or by whatever means are most fitting. But if he is not corrected thereby and will not give way voluntarily, then a certain number of abbots of our congregation shall assemble and shall remove this transgressor of the holy Rule from his office, and then another who is worthy of it shall (as is said above) be elected by the monks of the church in question and by the abbots of any daughter houses with the advice and approval of the senior abbot. But if the deposed abbot or his monks (which God forbid) wish to be defiant and rebellious and refuse to submit to their sentences, they shall be subjected to excommunication

G

by the abbot of the mother church and by his other fellow abbots, and then he shall coerce them in whatever way he can and as he knows to be politic. But if any of them, coming to himself, wishes to rise again from the death of his soul and return to his mother, he shall be received like a penitent son. Save for this reason (which we must take the utmost trouble to avoid), no abbot may detain a monk who is subject to any other abbot of our Order without that abbot's consent; and no one may introduce monks to live in the house of any other abbot without that abbot's approval.

In the same way, if, which God forbid, the abbots of our Order realize that our mother the church of Cîteaux is flagging in her holy resolution and departing from the observation of the Rule or of the precepts of our Order, then, through the four senior Abbots of La Ferté, Pontigny, Clairvaux and Morimond, acting in the name of the other abbots, they shall admonish him up to four times to correct himself and to correct the others. The other rules which are laid down to deal with other abbots who appear to be incorrigible shall be diligently enforced against him, save that if he refuses to give way spontaneously they shall not be able to depose or anathematize the defiant abbot. They must wait to depose this unprofitable man from his office either in a general chapter, or, if it seems that the matter cannot wait, in another assembly attended by the abbots of the daughter houses of Cîteaux and some abbots of other houses. Then both they and the monks of Cîteaux shall strive to elect a suitable abbot. But if the former abbot and the monks of Cîteaux defiantly attempt to resist, the other abbots shall not be afraid to smite them with the sword of excommunication. But if any of the transgressors then comes at last to his senses and, wishing to save his soul, takes refuge at one of our four churches of La Ferté, Pontigny, Clairvaux or Morimond, he shall be received with satisfaction, according to the Rule, as a servant and a co-heir of the Church, in such a way that he may, as is right, be restored to his own church at any time when it is reconciled. Meanwhile, the annual chapter of abbots shall not be held at Cîteaux, but in a place which the four abbots named above shall determine.

§ 16

Canon XII of the Fourth Lateran Council, 1215: Mansi, *Concilia*, XXII, 999–1002.

Of the common chapters of monks.

In each realm or province, saving the rights of diocesan bishops, there shall be held every three years a common chapter of abbots and of priors who have no abbots above them, who have not been accustomed to hold such a chapter. It shall be held in one of the monasteries that is suited to this purpose, and let all attend it if there is no canonical reason to the contrary; and all shall be limited to bringing no more than six horses and eight men. When this new arrangement is beginning they shall lovingly summon two neighbouring abbots of the Cistercian Order to offer them suitable advice and aid, since as a result of long practice they are more fully experienced in holding chapters of this kind. These two shall without opposition choose two others, who they see will be useful, to join them. And the four of them shall preside over the whole chapter, and no one shall assume the authority of a leader. When it is advisable, they may upon prudent deliberation be changed. This chapter shall continue for a certain number of days according to the usage of the Cistercian Order, and there shall be a thorough discussion concerning the reformation of the Order and the observation of the Rule: and anything that is decreed with the approval of these four shall be inviolably observed by all, without the possibility of any exemption, opposition or appeal. They shall determine where the next chapter must be held. Those who attend shall live communally and meet all common expenses together, each according to his share. If they cannot all live under the same roof, they shall at least dwell together in groups under their different roofs.

In the same chapter there shall be appointed godly and prudent persons who shall take pains to visit in our place each abbey in the same realm or province, not only of monks but of nuns as well, according to the procedure determined for them, correcting and reforming where they see that correction and reform is needed. If they find that the rector of a place ought to be removed altogether from administering it, they shall report him to his own bishop, that he may arrange for his removal: and if the bishop does not do this, the visitors shall send the matter to be examined by the Apostolic See. We wish and command regular canons to observe this procedure according to their Order. If any difficulty arises in this new arrangement which cannot be dealt with by the aforesaid persons, it shall without unseemliness be referred to the Apostolic See for judgment, whilst the other decrees which were laid down by friendly deliberation shall be inviolably observed.

Moreover, diocesan bishops shall strive to reform the monasteries subject to them, so that when the said visitors come to them they will find in them more that deserves commendation than that deserves correction. They shall take very special care not to lay undue burdens upon these monasteries. For we wish the rights of superiors to be preserved, but without inferiors sustaining injuries.

To this end we strictly order diocesan bishops and all persons who preside over the chapters that must be held to restrain by ecclesiastical censure, without the possibility of appeal, advocates, patrons, *vidames*, governors and consuls, great lords and soldiers and all other persons from presuming to commit offences against the people or property of monasteries: and if these persons do happen to offend, they shall not fail to compel them to make amends, that the monasteries may more freely and peacefully serve Almighty God.

HERESY AND NEW RELIGIOUS ORDERS

§§ 17–19. These and the following documents are pieces of legislation issued by the Third and Fourth Lateran Councils summoned by Alexander III and Innocent III in 1179 and 1215 to make laws for the reform of the whole Church. Document 17 renewed and confirmed for the whole Church various particular laws which had previously been enacted against heretics. It was directed especially against the Albigensians or Cathars of southern France, against whom a Crusade was already in progress. Documents 18 and 19 throw some light on the process by which the Mendicant preaching Orders were founded and on Innocent III's attitude to them.

On the Lateran Councils in general, see J. Rousset de Pina in Fliche-Martin, *Histoire de l'Église*, IX, ii (1953) and A. Fliche, ibid., X (1950); also Hefele-Leclercq, *Histoire des conciles*, V, ii, 1316 foll., and A. Luchaire, *Innocent III: le Concile de Latran et la réforme de l'Église* (1908)..

On 17: see also J. Guiraud, *Histoire de l'Inquisition au moyen âge* (1935–1938), I, 411 foll.; H. Maisonneuve, *Études sur les origines de l'Inquisition* (1960), 229 foll. On the heresies at whose suppression this canon was chiefly aimed, see, for example, A. Luchaire, *Innocent III: la croisade des albigeois* (1905); chapters by A. Fliche and C. Thouzellier in Fliche-Martin, *Histoire de l'Église*, X, with bibliographies; A. Borst, *Die Katharer* (Stuttgart, 1953). On heresy and the Inquisition in general, see H. C. Lea, *A history of the Inquisition of the middle ages* (London,

1888; reprinted in part, London, 1963, with introduction by W. Ull-mann); A. S. Turberville, *Mediaeval heresy and the Inquisition* (London, 1920); W. Ullmann, 'The significance of Innocent III's decretal "Vergentis" ', *Études G. Le Bras* (1964).

On 18 and 19: see also P. Mandonnet, *Saint Dominique: l'idée, l'homme et l'œuvre* (1937), I, 46 foll.; M. H. Vicaire, 'S. Dominique et le pape en 1215', ibid.; H. Grundmann, *Religiöse Bewegungen im Mittel-alter* (Hildesheim, 1961), 140 foll.

§ 17

The suppression of heresy: Canon III of the Fourth Lateran Council, 1215: Mansi, *Concilia*, XXII, 986–90.

III. *Of heretics.*

We excommunicate and anathematize every heresy which rears itself against this holy, orthodox and catholic faith which we have ex-pounded above, and we condemn all heretics, no matter by what names they are known: they may have different faces, but they are tied to-gether by their tails, since they are united by their emptiness.

After being condemned, they shall be left to be visited with the proper punishment by the secular powers in person or by their bailiffs; clerics shall first be deprived of their orders. The property of such con-demned persons shall, if they are laymen, be confiscated; if they are clergy, it shall be applied to the churches from which they received their stipends.

Those who are merely under suspicion of heresy shall be smitten with the sword of anathema and shunned by everyone until they make suitable amends, unless they prove their own innocence by clearing themselves properly (the nature of the suspicion and also their personal character being taken into account). If they have persisted in their ex-communication for one year, they shall then be condemned as heretics.

The secular powers, no matter what offices they hold, shall be ad-vised and persuaded and, if necessary, compelled by ecclesiastical censure, as they desire to be held and accounted faithful, to take an oath publicly for the defence of the faith that they will, as far as they are able, strive in good faith to exterminate all heretics indicated by the Church from the lands subject to their jurisdiction—so that whenever anyone is appointed to a spiritual or temporal office he shall be bound to confirm this decree by an oath.

If any temporal lord fails to purge his land of this heretical foulness after being required and warned to do so by the Church, he shall be bound with the fetters of excommunication by the metropolitan and other bishops of the province. And if he refuses to make amends within one year, the Supreme Pontiff shall be informed of this, that he may declare the lord's vassals freed from fealty to him, and lay his land open to occupation by catholics, who, after exterminating the heretics, shall possess it without any opposition and preserve it in the purity of faith—saving the rights of the lord-in-chief so long as he does not obstruct or hinder this in any way. This law shall none the less be applied to those who do not have lords-in-chief.

Catholics who have taken the sign of the Cross and girded themselves for the extermination of the heretics shall enjoy the same indulgence and be endowed with the same holy privilege as is granted to those who go to assist the Holy Land.

We decree that those who believe the heretics and those who receive, defend or support them are subject to excommunication: and we firmly ordain that when any of these has been marked out by excommunication, if he refuses to make amends within one year he shall then by the law itself become infamous and shall not be admitted to public offices or councils or be allowed to elect anyone to them or to give evidence in a court of law. He shall also become 'intestable'—deprived of the power of freely making a will or of succeeding to an inheritance. Again, nobody shall be forced to answer to him concerning any matter, but he shall be made to answer to others. If he happens to be a judge, his decisions shall have no validity and no cases shall be brought to be heard by him. If he is an advocate, he shall not be allowed to defend anyone. If he is a notary, the deeds which he has drawn up shall have no force, but shall be condemned with their condemned author. And we order the same rule to be observed in all similar cases. If the man is a cleric, he shall be deprived of every office and benefice—so that, where the guilt is greater, a more severe penalty may be inflicted.

If anybody refuses to shun such men after they have been pointed out by the Church, they shall be smitten with sentence of excommunication until they make suitable amends. The clergy shall not offer the sacraments of the Church to pests of this kind and shall not presume to give them Christian burial or accept their alms or offerings: otherwise they shall be deprived of their office, to which they shall never be restored without a special dispensation [*indulto*] from the Apostolic

See. Likewise with all regular clergy—they may suffer a further penalty, in that their privileges shall be annulled in any diocese in which they presume to commit such excesses.

As some persons, 'having an appearance of godliness', but, as the apostle says, 'denying the power thereof',[1] claim for themselves the authority to preach; and since the same apostle says 'How can men preach, unless they are sent?';[2] all those who have been forbidden to preach, or have not been sent, and presume to usurp the duty of publicly or privately preaching without receiving authority from the Apostolic See or the catholic bishop of the place, shall be bound with the fetters of excommunication: and, unless they come to their senses with the utmost rapidity, they shall undergo another sufficient penalty.

We further decree that every archbishop or bishop, either in person or through his archdeacon or through suitable respectable persons shall twice or at least once a year go round his own diocese if it is rumoured that heretics are living there: and there they shall compel three or four reliable men, or even the whole neighbourhood if it seems expedient, to swear that if anyone knows there are heretics in that place or that anybody is holding secret meetings or in his life and habits departing from the common way of the faithful, he shall be at pains to point them out to the bishop. The bishop shall summon the accused to his presence: and unless they can clear themselves of the charge against them, or if after clearing themselves they relapse into their former treachery, they shall be canonically punished. But if perchance any of them with damnable obstinacy reject the religious element in the oath and refuse to swear they shall by this very fact be accounted heretics.

We therefore wish and ordain and by virtue of their obedience strictly command bishops to keep a thorough watch in their dioceses that these orders may be effectively carried out, if they wish to escape canonical penalties. For if any bishop is negligent or remiss in clearing out of his diocese the ferment of depraved heresy: when this is definitely proved, he shall be deprived of episcopal office, and another suitable person, who can and is willing to rout depraved heresy, shall be put in his place.

§ 18

Canon X of the Fourth Lateran Council: Mansi, *Concilia*, XXII, 998–9.

1. 2 Timothy, iii, 5.   2. Romans, x, 15.

X. On the appointment of preachers.

Among other things which pertain to the salvation of the Christian people, the nourishment of the word of God is especially necessary, because the soul is fed upon spiritual food just as the body is upon material food—for 'man does not live by bread alone, but by every word which proceeds from the mouth of God'.[1] It often happens that bishops are not capable of serving the word of God to the people, especially in large and extensive dioceses, because of their manifold occupations or their bodily infirmities or because of the assaults of enemies or for other reasons (to say nothing of lack of knowledge, which in them is altogether reprehensible and must not be tolerated in future).

Therefore we decree by a general edict that bishops shall appoint suitable men, who are vigorous in deed and word, to discharge the salutary function of holy preaching, to visit assiduously the congregations entrusted to the bishops in their place when they are unable to do so themselves, and to instruct these congregations with word and example. The bishops shall supply these men in a suitable fashion with what they need, lest for lack of necessities they be forced to desist from the work they have begun. Hence we decree that suitable men shall be appointed in cathedral and in other conventual churches whom the bishops may have to assist and work with them, not only in the function of preaching, but also in hearing confessions and ordering penances and other things which have a bearing on the salvation of souls.

If anyone fails to execute this decree, he shall be liable to a severe penalty.

§ 19

Canon XIII of the Fourth Lateran Council: Mansi, *Concilia*, XXII, 1002–3.

XIII. *Of the prohibition of new religious Orders.*

Lest an excessive number of different religious Orders introduce grave confusion into the Church of God, we firmly forbid anyone henceforth to found a new religious Order. If anyone wishes to enter an Order, let him choose one of the approved ones. Likewise if anyone wishes to found a new religious house, let him take a rule and constitution from an approved Order.

We also forbid anyone to presume to be a monk in more than one monastery; and no abbot shall preside over more than one monastery.

1. Matthew, iv, 4.

DISCIPLINARY DECREES OF THE LATERAN COUNCILS

§§ 20–22. On this legislation of the Lateran Councils, see the general accounts cited above; and, on the problem of elections (20 and 21), Moulin, 'Les origines religieux des techniques électorales' and '*Sanior et maior pars*'.

§ 20

Canon XVI of the Third Lateran Council: Mansi, *Concilia*, XXII, 227.

XVI. *Of the ordering of churches.*

Since in all churches the decisions of the majority of brothers and the more prudent ones [*saniores*] ought to be observed without delay, it is a serious matter, deserving of censure, that a few people in certain churches should many times hinder the ordering of the church and not allow it to proceed, not on reasonable grounds, but out of their own wilfulness. Hence we ordain by the present decree that, unless the minority and the less important of the brothers advance some reasonable objection, the decision of the greater and more prudent part of the chapter shall always prevail and be carried into effect, there being no appeal against it. Supposing anyone says that he is bound by oath to preserve the custom of his church, this shall not stand in the way of our decree. For oaths that go against the interests of the church and the decrees of the holy fathers are not to be called oaths, but rather perjuries. If any man presumes to swear to customs of this kind, which have no reason on their side and are at odds with the holy canons, then he shall be prevented from receiving communion until he has done a suitable penance.

§ 21

Canons XXIII, XXIV and XXV of the Fourth Lateran Council: Mansi, *Concilia*, XXII, 1011–14.

XXIII. *That no cathedral or regular church shall be vacant for more than three months.*

That no ravening wolf may attack the Lord's flock because it is without a pastor and that no bereaved church may incur severe loss of property, wishing to fend off the danger to souls and to provide for the safety of churches, we decree that no cathedral or regular church may be without a prelate for more than three months. If the election has not been held within three months, there being no just impediment, those who should have elected shall lose the power to elect to that office, and the power of electing shall devolve upon the immediate superior. The man upon whom this power devolves, keeping the Lord before his eyes, shall not, if he wishes to escape canonical punishment, delay more than three months before canonically appointing to the bereaved church (on the advice of his chapter and of other prudent men) a suitable member of that church or, if no worthy candidate can be found there, one of another church.

XXIV. *Of making an election by scrutiny or compromise.*

Since, because of the different forms of election which certain people try to devise, many difficulties arise and great dangers threaten the bereaved churches, we decree that when an election is to be held, in the presence of those who wish to, ought to and can fittingly take part, three reliable members of the assembly shall be chosen and they shall secretly and carefully find out, one by one, the votes of all of them and, having set them down in writing, they shall then reveal them to all, without being obstructed by any appeal whatsoever. When the votes have been added together, the man on whom all the chapter or the greater or more prudent part of it agree shall be the one elected. Or at least the power of electing shall be entrusted to certain suitable men who, acting on behalf of all, shall provide the widowed church with a pastor. An election held by any other method shall not be valid, unless it happens to have been effected by the common vote of all, without any flaw, as if by divine inspiration. If any men attempt to hold an election in violation of these procedures, they shall be deprived of the power of electing to the office.

We utterly forbid anyone to appoint an agent to act for him in the election unless he is absent, and unless on being duly summoned from the place where he is he is prevented by some lawful impediment from coming. If necessary he shall take an oath upon this matter, and then, if he wishes, he may authorize one of the assembly to act for him. We also pass censure upon secret elections, and decree that as soon as an election has been held, the result shall be solemnly announced.

XXV. *That an election which is effected by the secular power shall not be valid.*

If anybody presumes to agree to being elected by wrongfully making use of a secular authority, in violation of canonical liberty, he shall lose the benefit he has gained thereby and become ineligible, and cannot be elected to any office without a special dispensation. If any men presume to hold an election of this kind—which we declare to be void by the law itself—they shall be completely suspended from their offices and benefices for a period of three years, having first been deprived of the power to vote.

§ 22

A. Canon XXIX of the Fourth Lateran Council: Mansi, *Concilia*, XXII, 1015–18.

XXIX. *That no one may hold more than one benefice with the cure of souls attached.*

With great foresight it was forbidden in the Lateran Council[1] that anyone should receive more than one ecclesiastical office or parish church, in a manner contrary to what the sacred canons have laid down. Otherwise the giver would lose the power of giving and the recipient lose what he had received. But since, on account of the presumption and greed of certain persons, this decree has hitherto borne little or no fruit, we, being anxious to deal with the situation more plainly and explicitly, ordain by the present decree that if anybody receives a benefice which has the cure of souls attached to it, he shall by the law itself be deprived of any other such benefice he has already: and if perchance he strives to keep the first benefice, the second shall be taken from him also. The man in whose gift the first benefice lies may, once the incumbent has received another, freely bestow the benefice on anyone he sees is worthy to receive it. If he delays more than three months before bestowing it, not only shall the right of presentation devolve upon another, in accordance with the decree of the Lateran Council,[2] but he shall also be bound to make over to the church to which the benefice belongs, out of his own revenues, a sum equivalent to what he is agreed to have received from the benefice since it fell vacant. We decree that the same rule shall be observed concerning minor dignities [*personaius*], and we add that no one may presume to hold more than one office or minor dignity in the same church even if no cure of souls is attached to these. However, the Apostolic See may, when there is good reason to do so, make a dispensation for eminent and learned persons who ought to be honoured with greater benefices.

1. Canon XIII of the Third Lateran Council, 1179: Mansi, *Concilia*, XXII, 225.
2. Canon VIII of the Third Lateran Council, ibid., 222.

B. Canon XXXII of the Fourth Lateran Council: Mansi, *Concilia*, XXII, 1019.

XXXII. *That patrons shall allow clerics a sufficient portion.*

A practice which must be rooted out has sprung up in certain regions, whereby patrons of parish churches and certain other persons, claiming the churches' revenues completely for themselves, leave such a scanty portion for the priests appointed to serve them that the priests cannot be adequately maintained out of it. For we have learnt upon sure authority that in certain areas parish priests get only a fourth of a fourth, that is, a sixteenth, of the tithes for their maintenance. Hence it happens that in these areas almost no parish priest can be found who has even a slight knowledge of letters. Since, therefore, the mouth of the ox that threshes must not be muzzled,[1] and he who serves the altar ought to live by the altar: we decree that notwithstanding the common practice of a bishop or patron or any other person, an adequate portion must be assigned to the priests. Anyone who holds a parish church shall serve it in person and not through a vicar, in the manner which the care of the church demands, unless the parish church happens to be attached to a prebend or some other office. In that case we allow the holder of such a prebend or office, since he has to serve in a greater church, to take pains to keep in this parish church a suitable permanent vicar who has been canonically appointed. The vicar shall, as aforesaid, have a fitting portion of the revenues of this church: otherwise the office-holder shall know that he is deprived of it upon the authority of this decree and it shall be freely conferred upon another who is willing and able to carry out the above instructions. Again, we utterly forbid anyone fraudulently to bestow upon another person a pension for a benefice out of the revenues of a church which ought to enjoy the care of its own priest.

THE SCHOLASTIC METHOD OF PETER ABAILARD

§ 23. It would obviously be impossible to illustrate the intellectual revival of the twelfth century with any completeness in a general collection of texts of this size. One document, however, which can tell a surprising amount about it and add considerably to one's understanding of the word 'scholasticism', which is so widely used, is the Preface to Abailard's *Sic et Non*. It illustrates the critical method which, in the

1. Deuteronomy, xxv, 4.

course of the twelfth century, was widely adopted not only by theologians but by canonists also. The *Sic et Non*, compiled some time after 1120, consists of a collection of contradictory statements on particular questions assembled from the writings of the Fathers. In the body of the book there is no attempt to harmonize the contradictions, but the Preface contains hints as to how to do so. The *Sic et Non* was a syllabus from which Abailard intended that his students should work.

See C. H. Haskins, *The Renaissance of the twelfth century* (Cambridge, Mass., 1928), 353 foll.; J. G. Sikes, *Peter Abailard* (Cambridge, 1932), 76 foll.; J. Cotteaux, 'La conception de la théologie chez Abélard', R.H.E., 28 (1932), 788 foll.; G. Paré, A. Brunet and P. Tremblay, *La renaissance du XIIᵉ siècle: les écoles et l'enseignement* (Paris-Ottawa, 1933), 289 foll.; E. Gilson, *La philosophie au moyen âge* (1944), 280–1; J. de Ghellinck, *Le mouvement théologique du XIIᵉ siècle* (Bruges-Brussels-Paris, 1948), 65, 163 foll., 489 foll.

§ 23

Extracts from the Prologue to the *Sic et Non* of Peter Abailard: Migne, P.L., 178, 1339–49.

Although, amid so great a mass of verbiage, some of the sayings even of the saints not only seem to differ from but also actually to contradict one another, we must not be so bold as to judge those by whom the world itself must be judged, as it is written: 'The saints shall judge nations',[1] and, again, 'And you too shall sit in judgment'.[2] Let us not presume to denounce them as liars or despise them as mistaken, for the Lord said to them: 'He who listens to you, listens to me; he who despises you, despises me.'[3] Reflecting upon our own feebleness, let us suppose that we lack the gift of understanding rather than that they had no gift for writing, for it was said by the very Truth itself: 'It is not you who speak, but the Spirit of your Father, which speaks in you.'[4] Small wonder, then, that we should fail to understand these things, for the Spirit by means of which they were written and spoken and imparted to the writers is absent from us. A particular bar to understanding is the unfamiliar language and the different meaning of a great many identical words, since the same word is used sometimes with one and sometimes with another meaning. For as everyone has plenty of his own meaning, so also has he plenty of his own words. And since, as Cicero says,

1. Wisdom of Solomon, iii, 8. 2. Luke, xxii, 30. 3. Luke, x, 16. 4. Matthew, x, 20.

sameness is in all things the mother of satiety—in other words, it causes offence—it is necessary to vary the words in order to express the same thing. One must not lay bare, in common and ordinary words, all those things which (as St. Augustine says) are kept covered lest they be spoilt, and which give all the more pleasure for being sought out with greater industry and conquered with greater difficulty. Again, it is frequently necessary for words to be varied in accordance with the different natures of those to whom we are speaking: for it often happens that the proper meaning of the words is unknown or unfamiliar to some of them. If we wish to speak in order to teach them, as we must, we should follow their usage rather than aim at correctness of diction, even as Priscian, that prince of grammarians and instructor of speakers, teaches us . . . .

We should also, when any remarks of the saints are cast in our teeth as being opposed or foreign to truth, take great care that we are not being deceived by a false attribution or by corruption of the text itself. For a great many apocryphal writings were headed with the names of saints, that they might carry authority; and some even of the texts of the Holy Testaments were corrupted through the fault of the copyists. . . . Let us simply say that it is written in Matthew and John that the Lord was sacrificed at the sixth hour, but Mark says the third hour.[1] This was an error of the copyists, and 'the sixth hour' was originally written in Mark, but many thought the Greek letter was a gamma. . . . Small wonder, then, if, when even in the Gospels some corruptions occurred because of the ignorance of the copyists, the same thing should sometimes happen among the writings of the Fathers who came later, for they are of far slighter authority. So if perchance there appears to be something in the writings of the saints which is not in harmony with truth, as an act of devotion and proper humility and a due expression of that love which believes all things, hopes all things, bears all things and does not lightly suspect faults in those whom it embraces,[2] either we should suppose that that portion of the text is not faithfully translated or is corrupt, or we should confess that we do not understand it.

I think that we should no less consider whether these extracts produced from the writings of the saints are among those which were retracted by them in another place, and were corrected when the truth later became known, a thing which St. Augustine did on numerous occasions. We should also consider whether the saints were making a pronouncement according to the opinion of others rather than according to their own, just as the Preacher (Ecclesiastes) cites the discordant

1. Matthew, xxvii, 45; John, xix, 14; Mark, xv, 25.   2. 1 Corinthians, xiii, 7.

pronouncements of different men on a great many matters, so that, as St. Gregory bears witness in the fourth book of his Dialogues, he is rather regarded as a creator of confusion. We should, again, consider whether the saints left the matters in question in a spirit of inquiry rather than settle them with a definite decision. . . . From the testimony of St. Jerome, we know that the catholic doctors were in the habit of inserting among their own pronouncements in their commentaries even some of the worst opinions of heretics, since, striving after complete-ness, they delighted in including everything that the ancients had said. . . .

Again, some things in the Gospel are stated according to human opinion rather than the actual truth—as when Joseph is called 'the father of Christ' even by the mother of the Lord in accordance with the common opinion and practice, for she says: 'Your father and I have been seeking you, sorrowing'. . . .[1] Small wonder if the Holy Fathers sometimes propounded or even wrote down what they thought was true, but was not in fact true.

When different things are said about the same matter, it is necessary to discuss thoroughly what is intended as a binding precept and what as a dispensation relaxing the law or an exhortation to perfection, so that we may seek to resolve the conflict by taking into account the difference of intentions. If it is a commandment, is it general or par-ticular—addressed to all men in common or to some men especially? It is necessary to bear in mind the occasion and the reasons for dispensa-tions, because what is permitted at one time is often found to be pro-hibited at another; and things that are usually strictly commanded are sometimes modified by dispensation. It is especially necessary to take account of these points in considering what ecclesiastical decrees and canons have laid down. We can easily resolve a great many dis-putes if we can maintain that the same words have been used with different meanings by different authors.

A diligent reader will try to resolve disputes in the writings of the saints by all the aforesaid methods. But if it happens that there is such an obvious conflict that it cannot be resolved by any argument, then the authorities must be compared, and the one whose testimony is more robust and more fully confirmed should be preferred. . . . It is generally agreed that even the prophets sometimes lacked the gift of prophecy, and, out of the habit of prophesying, put about falsehoods by means of their own spirit when they thought that the spirit of prophecy was upon

1. Luke, ii, 48.

them. In order to preserve their humility, they were permitted more truly to understand which prophecies originated through the Spirit of God, and which through their own, and to understand that the Spirit which knows not how to lie or to be mistaken came to them as a gift—when it did come. The Spirit, when it is upon a man, just as it does not confer all gifts upon one person,[1] likewise does not enlighten the mind of the one whom it fills upon all matters, but reveals only so and so or only such and such, and, when it discloses one thing, hides another. St. Gregory points this out with clear examples in his first homily upon Ezekiel: that St. Peter, the very Chief of the Apostles, resplendent with so many miracles and gifts of the grace of God, even after the Lord had promised him that special outpouring of the Holy Spirit which teaches his disciples the whole truth, lapsed into error concerning the observance of circumcision and of certain other ancient rites. When he was weightily and salutarily corrected in public by his fellow-apostle Paul, he was not ashamed to give up this harmful deception.[2] Small wonder, then, when it is generally agreed that the very prophets and apostles were not altogether strangers to error, if, among the so numerous writings of the Holy Fathers, there appear to be certain things which have been propounded and written down erroneously for the reason set down above. But it is not seemly to reprove the saints as guilty of lying, if they sometimes think that some things are other than they really are and say so, not out of duplicity, but from ignorance. Nothing which is said out of love for any constructive purpose must be ascribed to presumption or sin, for it is well known that the Lord considers all things according to the intention behind them. . . .

The outstanding canonical authority of the Old and New Testaments is in a different category from the books of later writers. If anything in the Bible strikes you as absurd, it is not permissible to say: 'The author of this book did not uphold the truth', but that either the manuscript is false, or the translator made a mistake, or that you do not understand it. But if the little works of later men which are contained in innumerable books are thought to diverge from the truth (perhaps because they are not understood in the original sense), then the reader or listener is free to judge, and to approve what he likes and condemn what he dislikes and anything of that kind, unless the argument or account in the book is supported by sure reasons or by such canonical authority as will demonstrate that it was wholly so or could have been so. Otherwise, if somebody does not like it or does not want to believe

1. Cf. 1 Corinthians, xii, 28–30.   2. Cf. Acts, xv.

it, he cannot be blamed. So Augustine calls the canonical texts of the
Old and New Testaments such documents that it is heretical to proclaim that anything in them departs from the truth. . . .

After these preliminaries, we have decided to assemble various
sayings of the Holy Fathers dealing with particular questions, when they
occur to our memory, on account of a certain discord which there
appears to be between them, so that they may arouse inexperienced
readers to the most vigorous activity in seeking out the truth, and that
they may sharpen their wits by these inquiries. For assiduous and fre-
quent asking of questions is termed the first key to wisdom. That most
penetrating of all philosophers, Aristotle, exhorts scholars to take it up
with all their hearts, saying in his work 'ad aliquid': 'But perhaps it is
difficult to make confident pronouncements on matters like this, unless
they are frequently discussed. But it will be of some use to entertain
doubts about each of them'. For by doubting we come to inquiring
and by inquiring we perceive the truth—as the Truth himself says:
'Seek', he says, 'and you will find; knock and it will be opened to you.'[1]
Giving moral teaching by his own example, he wished to be found, in
about his twelfth year, sitting among the doctors and asking them
questions,—by asking questions he revealed himself to us in the guise of
a pupil, rather than by preaching showing himself a master, although
there is in him the full and perfect wisdom of God.

When any sayings of the Scriptures are cited, they rouse the reader
and entice him into seeking out the truth all the more effectively the
more the authority of the Scripture is commended. Hence we have
decided to preface this work of ours, which we have compiled by
gathering sayings of the saints into one volume, with the decree of
Pope Gelasius concerning authentic books, from which it shall be
known that we have not cited anything apocryphal here. And we have
added extracts from the Retractations of St. Augustine, from which it
shall appear that none of those things which he corrected by retracting
them have been included here.

THE AUTHENTICA HABITA

§ 24. The *Authentica Habita* was a pre-university charter—a general
privilege to the student class on imperial territory, and an important
basis for future privileges. It was issued by the Emperor Frederick I in

1. Matthew, vii, 7.

1158, probably because he saw the advantages to himself of encouraging the study of Roman law.

See H. Rashdall, *The universities of Europe in the middle ages*, ed. F. M. Powicke and A. B. Emden (Oxford, 1936), I, 145 foll., 180 foll.; H. Koeppler, 'Frederick Barbarossa and the Schools of Bologna: some remarks on the "*Authentica Habita*"', E.H.R., 54 (1939); F. M. Powicke, 'Bologna, Paris, Oxford: three *Studia Generalia*', in his *Ways of medieval life and thought* (London, 1949), 153 foll.; W. Ullmann, 'The medieval interpretation of Frederick I's Authentic "*Habita*"', in *L'Europa e il diritto romano: studi in memoria di Paolo Koschaker*, I (Milan, 1954); P. Kibre, *Scholarly privileges in the middle ages* (London, 1961), 10 foll.

See also below, Part III, no. 22.

§ 24

The *Privilegium Scholasticum* or *Authentica Habita* issued by the Emperor Frederick I at Roncaglia, November 1158: ed. Koeppler, 'Frederick Barbarossa and the schools of Bologna', 606–7; another text was edited by L. Weiland in M.G.H., Const., I (1893), 249.

Bishops, abbots, dukes, and all the judges and most eminent men of our sacred palace having diligently considered the matter, we grant this favour of our dutiful love to all scholars who are travelling for the sake of their studies, and especially to teachers of the divine and sacred laws: that they and their representatives may safely come to the places in which letters are studied and safely live in them. For we consider it fitting, since those who do good deserve our praise and protection, that we should with a certain particular love defend from all harm all those by whose knowledge the world is enlightened and the lives of subjects are moulded into obedience to God and to us, his servants. They all excite compassion, for they have made themselves exiles for love of knowledge; they reduce themselves from riches to poverty, expose their lives to every danger and suffer gratuitous bodily injuries, often at the hands of the lowest of men—a thing which must cause them serious annoyance.

We therefore decree by this general law, which is to be valid forever, that henceforth no one shall be so bold as to presume to do any injury to scholars or to cause them any loss on account of a debt incurred by another man from the same district, which, we have heard, has sometimes been done as the result of a depraved custom.

Be it known to all those who violate this sacred law, and also to all local authorities for the time being who fail to punish the crime, that a fourfold restitution of the goods that have been carried off shall be exacted from them, that the stigma of dishonour shall automatically attach to them, and that they shall be perpetually deprived of their office.

Moreover, if anyone presumes to bring suit against them on any matter, the scholars shall be allowed to choose whether he shall cite them before their own governor [*dominus*] or master or before the bishop of the city, for upon them we have conferred jurisdiction in this matter. If anybody attempts to cite the scholars before another judge, his case, even if it is a very good one, shall lapse because of this attempt.

We have ordered this law to be inserted among the imperial constitutions under the heading '*ne filius pro patre*', etc.

PRIVILEGES OF THE UNIVERSITY OF PARIS

§ 25. Gregory IX's Bull 'Parens scientiarum', issued in 1231, restated and extended the privileges already granted to the scholars of Paris. It also approved the use which the University had made of the weapon of ceasing to lecture in order to secure its demands and protect its privileges. It followed the 'great dispersal' which lasted from the spring of 1229 to the beginning of 1231. This, in turn, had resulted from a brawl between townsmen and gownsmen for which the civil authorities held the students responsible. In protest against the drastic action which the authorities took, the masters determined to suspend lectures.

See Rashdall, *Universities of Europe*, I, 334 foll.; Powicke, 'Bologna, Paris, Oxford', 173; Kibre, *Scholarly privileges*, 92 foll.

§ 25

The Bull 'Parens scientiarum' of Pope Gregory IX, April 13th, 1231: *Chartularium Universitatis Parisiensis*, ed. H. Denifle, I (1889), 136–9.

Bishop Gregory, servant of the servants of God, to his beloved sons, all the masters and scholars of Paris, greeting and the apostolic blessing.

May Paris, the mother of sciences, be famous in her riches like another Cariath Sepher or city of letters.[1] For she is great indeed; but she herself creates a desire for greater favours to be conferred on her teachers and pupils. She is like a special workshop for wisdom where seams of silver are made and there is also a place where gold is correctly manufactured, and hence the wise masters of eloquence forge golden collars inlaid with silver, and necklaces adorned with precious or rather priceless stones, and thus they beautify and honour the bride of Christ. There in Paris iron is extracted from the earth, for, when earthly frailty is shored up with strength, the breastplate of faith, the sword of the spirit and the rest of the armour of Christian knights, which prevails against the brazen powers, are formed from it. The stone melted by heat is turned into brass, for when stony hearts are kindled by the heat of the Holy Spirit they burn and become with their preaching the sonorous trumpets of the praise of Christ.

Hence there is no doubt that it would be gravely displeasing to God and to men if anyone should strive in any way to disturb these exceptional benefits in the city of Paris or should fail to oppose both vigorously and openly with all his might anyone who did so. Having assiduously listened to the lawsuits which have been referred to us as the result of a quarrel which has, at the instigation of the Devil, arisen at Paris and monstrously disturbed the University [studium], we have with the advice of our brothers decided that they should be settled by precautionary measures rather than by judicial sentence.

Concerning the constitution of the schools and scholars, we decree that hereafter, when any Chancellor of Paris is to be appointed, the masters shall be summoned, and when they are present on behalf of the corporation of scholars [universitate scolarium], the Chancellor shall at his installation swear before the Bishop or, if the Bishop command it, before the chapter of Paris, that he will grant only to worthy persons the licence to teach theology and the canon law [decreta] in good faith according to his conscience, at the proper time and place, and bearing in mind the situation in the city and the honour and reputation of the faculties; that he will not admit unworthy men, and that he will not make exceptions for either persons or nations. Before he grants a licence to anybody, he shall, within three months of the date of the application, make thorough inquiries of all the masters of theology present in the city and of other honourable and learned men through whom the truth may be known concerning the life, knowledge and eloquence and also the intentions of the candidate and his hopes of

1. Joshua, xv, 15–16; Judges, i, 12–13.

making progress and the other qualities which are to be sought in such people. Having thus inquired what is proper and expedient, he shall in good faith either grant or deny the licence asked for according to his conscience. Masters of theology and the canon law, when they begin to lecture, shall take an oath publicly that they will give faithful testimony on these points. The Chancellor shall swear that he will in no way disclose the recommendations of the masters to their detriment. The canons of Paris shall continue to enjoy the rights and liberty which they have had in incepting. The Chancellor shall also promise to examine masters in physic and arts and other faculties in good faith, and shall admit only the worthy, and reject the unsuitable.

Since untidiness can easily creep in where there is no order, we grant you the power to make prudent statutes and ordinances concerning the time and the manner of lecturing and disputing; on the regulation dress; on the burial of the dead; and on which of the bachelors must lecture, and when and on what subject they must do so. You may also assess the rents of lodging houses and put them out of bounds. We also empower you suitably to punish those who rebel against these statutes and ordinances by removing them from the society.

And if perchance the right to assess the rents of lodgings is withheld from you, or (which God forbid) some monstrous injury or offence is committed against you or any of your people, such as homicide or mutilation of a limb, unless satisfaction be made within fifteen days of the issue of a proper warning, it shall be lawful for you to suspend lectures until you receive suitable amends. And if any of your people happens to be imprisoned without due cause, it shall be lawful for you, if the wrong does not cease on the issue of a warning, to cease lecturing at once if you see that this is expedient.

We command the Bishop of Paris to punish the transgressions of offenders so that the honour of the scholars may be preserved and evil acts shall not remain unpunished: however, no innocent men shall be taken on the score that they have offended. If a plausible suspicion of anyone arises, let him be honourably arrested and later be released after giving a suitable security; the exactions of the jailers shall then end. But if the culprit has committed such a serious crime that imprisonment is necessary, the Bishop shall keep him in prison; the Chancellor shall be utterly forbidden to have his own prison. Moreover, we forbid that in future any scholar be arrested for contracting a debt, since this is forbidden upon canonical and lawful penalties. Neither the Bishop nor any official of his nor the Chancellor shall demand a money penalty for removing an excommunication or any other sentence; nor shall the Chancellor demand any oath, obedience or other pledge from the masters he is to license; nor shall he receive any payment or promise of payment for granting the licence, but shall be content with the oath mentioned above.

Moreover, the summer vacations shall not in future exceed one month; the bachelors may, if they wish to, continue their lectures during the vacation.

We expressly forbid scholars to go armed through the city; the corporation of scholars shall not defend disturbers of peace and of the University. Those who pretend to be scholars but do not attend the schools or acknowledge any master shall in no way enjoy the liberty of scholars.

We further ordain that masters of arts shall always give one lecture on Priscian and shall lecture on one book after another in an orderly fashion. They shall not use at Paris those books of natural philosophy which have on sure grounds been prohibited at a provincial Council until they have been examined and cleansed of every suspicion of error. Masters and students of theology shall strive to employ themselves in the faculty which they profess, and shall not parade as philosophers,— they shall content themselves with becoming learned in divinity. They shall not speak in the language of the people, nor confound the sacred language with the profane, but shall discuss in the schools only those questions which can be determined by means of theological books and the treatises of the Holy Fathers.

Furthermore, we have decided that the following steps must be taken to deal with the property of scholars who die intestate or fail to entrust others with ordering their affairs: that the Bishop and one of the masters appointed by the University to this task shall receive all the property of the deceased and, having deposited it in a safe and suitable place, shall fix a day on which the student's death shall be announced in his home town [patria]. Those who are to succeed to his property may then come to Paris or send there a suitable representative, and if they come or send somebody the property shall be restored to them, together with the security the student will have had to give. But if nobody appears, then the Bishop and the master shall bestow the goods for the soul of the deceased as they consider expedient, unless it happens that his heirs have for some good reason been unable to come. In that case they shall put off disposing of the goods until a suitable time.

The masters and scholars who, having suffered much damage and many wrongs, took an oath among themselves, disbanded the University and departed from the city of Paris, appear to be promoting not their own so much as the public welfare. We therefore, having carefully considered the needs and interests of the Church as a whole, wish and command that when privileges have been extended to the masters and scholars by our dearest son in Christ [Louis], the illustrious King of the French, and when the amends to be paid by their malefactors have been assessed, they may lawfully study at Paris, and shall not incur any stigma or be deemed disobedient on account of their absence or return.

To no man whatsoever shall it be lawful to offend against this our decree, statute and grant, or boldly to ignore its prohibitions and restraints. But if anyone attempts to do this, let him know that he will incur the wrath of Almighty God and that of St. Peter and St. Paul his apostles.

Given at the Lateran on the thirteenth of April, in the fifth year of our pontificate.

PART THREE

Emperors and Empire in Germany and Italy

CHAPTER I

The Ottonians and Salians

THE CORONATION OF OTTO THE GREAT

§ 1. In these chapters of his chronicle, the monk Widukind of Corvey describes the process by which Otto was chosen to succeed his father Henry as King of the Franks and Saxons, and how he was crowned at Aachen in 936. This passage contains a valuable account of the ceremonies which give expression to the German King's ideal of rulership, and of those symbolizing the policy which Henry had already begun—that of reducing the dukes to the position of royal servants.

See P. E. Schramm, 'Die Krönung in Deutschland bis zum Beginn des Salischen Hauses (1028)', Z.S.S.R., k.a., 24 (1935), 196 foll.; G. Barraclough, P. Joachimsen and H. Mitteis in *Mediaeval Germany, 911–1250*, ed. G. Barraclough (Oxford, 1938), I, 38–9, II, 98, 238; G. Barraclough, *Origins of modern Germany* (Oxford, 1947), 28; R. Folz, *Le souvenir et la légende de Charlemagne dans l'empire médiéval* (1950), 49 foll.; C. Erdmann, 'Königs- und Kaiserkrönung im Ottonischen Pontifikale', in his *Forschungen zur politischen Ideenwelt des Frühmittelalters* (Berlin, 1951); W. Ullmann, *Principles of government and politics in the middle ages* (London, 1961), Part II; W. Ullmann, 'Die Souveränitätsgedanke in dem mittelalterlichen Krönungsordines', *Festschrift für P. E. Schramm* (Wiesbaden, 1964).

§ 1

The coronation of Otto of Saxony at Aachen, August 7th, 936: Widukind of Corvey, *Res gestae Saxonicae*, II, i-ii, ed. P. Hirsch and H. E. Lohmann (Hanover, 1935), 63–7.

II, i. On the death of Henry, the father of his country and greatest and best of Kings, the entire Frankish and Saxon people chose as their head his son Otto, who had already been designated King by his father. Fixing a place for this election by all, they ordered it to be held

113

at the palace in Aachen, which is very near Jülich (named after its founder, Julius Caesar).

On arriving there, the dukes and chief governors, together with another group consisting of the principal soldiers, assembled at the church of Charles the Great. They placed their new leader on a throne erected there, and in their own fashion made him King by giving him their hands, vowing him loyalty and promising him aid against all his enemies.

Whilst the dukes and other magistrates were thus engaged, the supreme bishop [*pontifex maximus*] and the whole order of priests and all the people were waiting below in the church for the new King to come forward. When he did so, the Archbishop, dressed in linen and wearing a stole and chasuble, went to meet the King and touched the King's right hand with his left: in his own right hand he carried a wand. He went on into the middle of that holy place and then stopped and turned to the people, who were standing round about, for the church was circular and there were walks round it above and below, and hence he could be seen by all the people. 'Behold', he said, 'I bring you Otto, chosen by God, previously designated by the lord Henry, and now by all the princes made King. If you are content with this choice, show it by raising your right hands upwards'. At these words all the people raised their right hands skywards and with a loud cry appealed for success for their new leader. Then the Archbishop advanced with the King, who was dressed in a close-fitting tunic in the Frankish manner, to the altar, upon which had been placed the royal insignia—the sword and girdle, the military cloak with the armlets, and the staff with the sceptre and diadem.

At that time the supreme bishop was Hildibert, a Frankish monk, brought up and educated in the monastery of Fulda, of which he rose to be Abbot and from which he was deservedly promoted to the supreme dignity of the Archbishopric of Mainz. He was a man of marvellous sanctity and more than human wisdom, and distinguished in the study of letters. He is said to have received the inspiration to prophesy, among other gifts of grace. There had been a dispute between the Archbishops of Trier and Cologne about the King's consecration,— Trier was the older see and as good as founded by St. Peter, whilst Aachen belonged to the diocese of Cologne; and on these grounds they thought the honour of consecrating the King should be theirs. But they both gave place to Hildibert, whose benignity was known to everybody.

Hildibert, then, approaching the altar and picking up the sword and girdle from it, turned to the King and said, 'Receive this sword, with which you shall drive away all the enemies of Christ, barbarians and bad Christians, by the divine authority transferred to you and by all the power of the whole Frankish Empire, to establish a most enduring peace among all Christians.' Then he took up the armlets and cloak and put them on the King, saying, 'When these armlets hang from your shoulders you shall be apprised of the zeal for the faith with which you must burn, and of your duty to persevere in guarding peace, even unto the end.' Then, taking up the sceptre and staff, he said: 'You shall be advised by these symbols to exercise a fatherly discipline upon your subjects and first to extend the hand of mercy to the ministers of God and to widows and orphans; and may you never fail to be compassionate [*numquamque de capite tuo oleum miserationis deficiat*], that you may be crowned with an eternal reward both in the present and in the future.' After being anointed there with the holy oil and crowned with the golden diadem by the Archbishops Hildibert and Wicfried, when the whole consecration had been completed according to the law, Otto was led by these Archbishops to the throne, which was reached by a spiral staircase and was set up between two marble columns of wonderful beauty. Thence he could see and be seen by everybody.

II, ii. Then, when the divine lauds had been said and the sacrifice solemnly celebrated, the King went down to the palace, approached a marble table ornamented with royal magnificence, and sat down once more with the bishops and all the people. The dukes served them. Isilbert, Duke of the Lotharingians, under whose government Aachen lay, superintended everything. Evurhard took charge of the table, and Hermann Franco of the butlers. Arnulf was in charge of the order of knights and of choosing and pitching camps. Siegfried, the most noble of the Saxons, second only to the King, son-in-law to the late King and hence bound to Otto by a tie of relationship, acted at that time as regent of Saxony in case it should be attacked meanwhile by the enemy, and he kept with him the younger Henry, whom he was bringing up. After this, the King most joyfully dismissed the multitude, and with royal generosity honoured each of the princes with a suitable gift.

THE VICTORY AT LECHFELD

§ 2. This passage from Widukind's Chronicle is not only important as an account of the victory which decisively checked the Hungarian menace to the interior of Germany and greatly enhanced the prestige of Otto and his dynasty. Widukind also throws light on one of the various ways in which the title of Emperor was used in medieval Europe. He shows Otto acquiring the title of Emperor without as yet being crowned by the Pope or in any way relying on Rome for his title.

See P. E. Schramm, *Kaiser, Rom und Renovatio* (Leipzig-Berlin, 1929), I, 79 foll.; Barraclough, *Origins of modern Germany*, 37, 44; H. Beumann, *Widukind von Korvei* (Weimar, 1950), 83 foll., 228 foll.; Erdmann, 'Die nichtrömische Kaiseridee', in his *Forschungen*, 44 foll.; R. Folz, *L'idée d'empire en occident* (1953), 58 foll.; J. A. Brundage, 'Widukind of Corvey and the "non-Roman" imperial idea', M.S., 22 (1960).

§ 2

Otto the Great and his victory at Lechfeld, 955: Widukind of Corvey, *Res gestae Saxonicae*, Book III, chs. 46, 49, ed. P. Hirsch and H. E. Lohmann (Hanover, 1935), 127–9.

[*Widukind describes the Hungarian invasion of Germany in the summer of 955, the assembly of the Saxon, Frankish and Bavarian armies at Augsburg, and the early stages of the battle which began when the Hungarians crossed the river Lech and surrounded the German armies.—*ED.]

... The King saw that the battle was now going entirely in favour of the enemy and spoke to his comrades to exhort them in this manner: 'My soldiers, you can see for yourselves that we need stout hearts in such straits as these, for you are withstanding not a distant enemy but one who is actually upon us. I have made glorious use of your tireless hands and invincible swords and conquered everywhere outside my land and Empire: shall I now turn tail on my own ground and in my own Kingdom? They surpass us, I know, in numbers, but neither in weapons nor in valour—we know that for the most part they are quite without weapons and without the help of God, which is of the greatest comfort to us. They have only their own temerity to protect them: but God is our hope and defence. Let us blush to surrender to the enemy when we are lords of almost all Europe. If the end is at hand, my soldiers, it is better we die gloriously in battle than drag out our lives in slavery as subjects of the enemy or die by strangling like evil beasts. I would say more, my soldiers, if I knew how to increase the boldness and courage in your hearts with words. Let's start a better conversation —with the sword and not with the tongue!'

Saying this, and seizing his shield and the holy lance, he was the first to turn his horse towards the enemy, doing the duty of a very gallant soldier and an excellent commander [or Emperor—*optimi imperatoris*]. The bolder of the enemy resisted at first and then, when they saw their comrades turn and run, they were stunned, fell among our men and were slain. Some of the others, whose horses were weary, entered the nearest villages, and there, surrounded by armed men, were burnt to ashes with the walls; others swam across the near-by river, but the far bank gave way as they climbed up it, the river swept over them and they perished. That day their camps were invaded and all their prisoners recovered. On the second and third day the rest of the host was destroyed by the neighbouring cities so that none or very few escaped. But there has never been a bloodless victory over so savage a nation.

The King was glorified by a famous triumph and was called by his army father of his country and Emperor [*imperator*]. Decreeing that fitting honour and praise be offered to God on high in every church, and sending messengers to demand the same for his holy mother, the victor returned to Saxony with ceremony and the greatest rejoicing and was most gladly received by his people; for never had a King enjoyed such a victory for two hundred years before him.

LIUTPRAND'S MISSION TO BYZANTIUM

§ 3. Liutprand, the author of this passage, had formerly served the Kings of Lombardy, Hugh and Berengar, and, after a quarrel with Berengar, had taken service with the German King Otto, who created him Bishop of Cremona in 961. In 968 Otto entrusted Liutprand with a delicate embassy to the Emperor Nicephorus Phocas in Constantinople. In 960, Pope John XII had summoned Otto to defend Rome against his rebellious vassal Berengar, and Otto had entered Italy, defeated Berengar and his son Adelbert and obtained the imperial crown at the hands of Pope John. The power of Otto in Italy appeared to threaten the Byzantine territories of Apulia and Calabria, and his revival of the title of Roman Emperor could (like Charlemagne's title) be interpreted as an affront to the Byzantine Emperor. Liutprand was to try to establish friendly relations by negotiating for the marriage of Otto's son with a Byzantine princess. In the course of his mission he was forced to defend his master's right to the title of Roman Emperor (cf. on the same theme, Part I, nos. 6 and 7).

See P. E. Schramm, 'Kaiser, Basileus und Papst in der Zeit der Ottonen', H.Z., 129 (1923–1924); M. Lintzel, 'Die relatio de legatione Constantinopolitana', in his *Studien über Liutprand von Cremona* (Berlin, 1933); Barraclough, *Origins of modern Germany*, 50 foll.; W. Ohnsorge, *Das Zweikaiserproblem im früheren Mittelalter* (Hildesheim, 1947), 60–1; Folz, *L'idée d'empire*, 61 foll.; G. Ostrogorsky, *History of the Byzantine state* (Oxford, 1956), 258 foll.; P. Lamma, 'Il problema dei due imperi e dell'Italia meridionale', *Atti del terzo congresso internazionale di studi sull'alto medioevo* (Spoleto, 1959), 236 foll.

§ 3

Part of the report on his mission to Constantinople by Liutprand, Bishop of Cremona, ambassador of the Emperor Otto I to the Emperor Nicephorus Phocas, June 968: Liutprand, *Relatio de legatione Constantinopolitana*, chs. 4–7, ed. J. Becker (Hanover-Leipzig, 1915), 177–80.

[*Liutprand describes how he was led before the Emperor on the seventh of June, and the Emperor began:*]

'It had been our duty, or rather our desire, to receive you graciously and sumptuously, but the misconduct of your lord prevents us from doing so. For he has claimed Rome for himself by a most hostile invasion and forcibly deprived Berengar and Adelbert of their land in violation of law and right. Some Romans he has put to the sword, others he has hanged, blinded or banished; and, furthermore, he has tried to subject the cities of our Empire to himself by murder or arson. And now, because his wicked design has failed, under the cloak of peace, he sends us you, the instigator and inspirer of this evil, as a *catascopos*, that is, a spy.'

I answered him: 'My lord has not invaded the city of Rome with violence or tyranny, but has freed it from the yoke of a tyrant, or rather tyrants. Did not the effeminate rule over it?[1] and, worse still, did not harlots do so? I think your power, or rather that of your predecessors, was asleep. They have been Emperors in name only—not in reality. If they were mighty and if they were Emperors of the Romans, why did they leave Rome in the power of harlots? Were not some of the most holy Popes exiled, others so afflicted that they could not even meet their everyday expenses or obtain alms? Did not Adelbert send abusive letters to the Emperors Romanus and Constantine, your predecessors?

1. Isaiah, iii, 4.

Did he not rob and pillage the churches of the most holy apostles?
Which of you Emperors was inspired by godly zeal to avenge this
ignoble crime and restore the holy Church to its proper condition?
You neglected this, but not so my lord, who, 'rising up from the ends
of the earth'[1] and coming to Rome, bore off the ungodly and restored
to the vicars of the holy apostles all their power and honour. And
afterwards he executed, beheaded, hanged and exiled all rebels against
himself and the Apostolic Lord, as perjurers, profaners, torturers of
their Apostolic Lords, robbers, in accordance with the decrees of the
Roman Emperors, Justinian, Valentinian, Theodosius and others; and
had he not done so, he would have been impious, unjust, cruel and a
tyrant. It is plain that Berengar and Adelbert had become his vassals
and received the Kingdom of Italy at his hands by means of the golden
sceptre: and they swore an oath of loyalty in the presence of servants of
yours, who are still alive and active in this city. And because at the
devil's prompting they have treacherously violated the oath, he has
justly deprived them of the Kingdom as deserters and rebels against
himself—as you would do to any subjects of yours who subsequently
rebelled against you.'

'But', said the Emperor, 'Adelbert's knight tells a different story.'
I said to him: 'If he says otherwise, any of my knights, at your command, will prove my story is true in a duel tomorrow.' 'Supposing', he
said, 'your lord has, as you say, been justified in doing this. Now
explain why he has attacked the frontiers of our Empire with fire and
the sword. We were friends, and were thinking of making our alliance
indissoluble by arranging a marriage'.

'The land', I said, 'which you say is part of your Empire is shown to be
part of the Kingdom of Italy both by the inhabitants and by the
language. Moreover, the Lombards have held it in their power; and
Louis, Emperor of the Lombards and Franks, delivered it from the hands
of the Saracens, of whom he struck down a great number. But Landulf,
too, Prince of Benevento and Capua, subjected it for seven years to his
power. It would never, to this day, have emerged from servitude to him
or his successors had not the Roman Emperor with an immense gift of
money bought the friendship of our King Hugh. That was why he
married the bastard daughter of our King, the same Hugh, to his
nephew and namesake. And, I think, you account it not graciousness but
impotence on the part of my lord that, for so many years after his
acquisition of Italy and Rome, he should allow you to keep it. This

1. Jeremiah, vi, 22.

I

bond of friendship, which you say you wanted to form by a marriage, we regard as a ruse and an artifice; you demand a truce, which you cannot reasonably demand nor we concede. But my lord has sent me to you that falsehood may be rooted out and truth revealed—so that, if you wish to give the daughter of the Emperor Romanus and the Empress Theophana to my lord his son the august Emperor Otto in marriage, you shall declare it to me on oath, and I will swear to you that my lord will carry out and observe such and such conditions in return for these favours. But my lord has now given you, his brother, the best pledge of friendship, since he has abandoned all of Apulia that was subject to his power, on my intercession—on whose instigation, you say, the evil was done. All the people of Apulia will bear witness to this.'

THE IMPERIALISM OF OTTO III

§ 4. Extracts 4A and B illustrate different aspects of the ambitious attempts made by the Emperor Otto III (983–1002) to assert and elaborate on his imperial title and to make his dominion over Italy a reality. Extract 4B tells something of the relationship which existed between Otto and his leading ecclesiastical servants. Probably composed by Bishop Leo of Vercelli, it indicates the terms on which Otto III conferred the eight counties of the Pentapolis upon the Roman church when it was ruled by his former teacher, Gerbert of Aurillac, now Pope Sylvester II. This imperial Diploma is also interesting for its rejection of the Donation of Constantine (see above, Part I, no. 4).

See Schramm, *Kaiser, Rom und Renovatio*, I, 110 foll., 140, 161 foll.; Barraclough, *Origins of modern Germany*, 59 foll.; Folz, *L'idée d'empire en occident*, 76 foll.; M. Uhlirz, *Jahrbücher des deutschen Reiches unter Otto II und Otto III*, II (Berlin, 1954), 332 foll., 353 foll.; W. Ullmann, *The growth of papal government in the middle ages* (London, 1962), 238 foll.

§ 4

A. The imperialism of Otto III: Thietmar (Ditmarus) of Mersebourg, *Chronicon*, IV, ch. 47, ed. R. Holtzmann (Berlin, 1955), 184, 186.

[*In the year 1000.*] The Emperor, wishing in his own time to restore ancient Roman custom, which had now largely died out, did many things to which different people reacted differently. He sat alone at a semi-circular table in a place higher than the others. Being uncertain where the bones of the Emperor Charles rested, he secretly tore up the floor and gave orders to dig in the place where he thought they lay, until they were found, upon the royal throne. Removing a golden cross, which was hanging from the neck, and also part of the clothing, which was still undecayed, he put back the rest with great reverence. And what need have I to record all his journeys to and fro through all his bishoprics and counties? Having set in good order everything beyond the Alps, he visited the Roman Empire and came to the fortresses of Romulus, where he was received with great ceremony by the Pope and his fellow bishops.

B. The Donation of Otto III to the Roman church, January 18th–23rd, 1001: Schramm, *Kaiser, Rom und Renovatio*, II, 66–7; previously edited by T. Sickel, in M.G.H., Dip., II (Hanover, 1893), 819–20.

In the name of the holy and indivisible Trinity, Otto, the servant of the apostles, and, by the will of God our saviour, Emperor Augustus of the Romans.

We proclaim that Rome is the head of the world and we bear witness that she is the mother of all churches, but that, owing to the negligence and ignorance of the Popes, her glorious titles have long been obscured.

For the Popes not only sold property which lay outside the city and alienated it from the house of St. Peter by means of certain frauds, but also (a thing painful to repeat) they gave for money to all men in common any property which they owned in this our royal city, that they might err with still greater abandon, and plundered St. Peter and St. Paul, even to their very altars, and instead of restoring them they only created disorder. Having thrown the papal laws into confusion and degraded the Roman church, some of the Popes went to such lengths as to attach the best part of our Empire to their apostolic dominion. Not inquiring what and how much they have lost by their own fault, and not caring how much they have squandered by wilful frivolity, but abandoning their own property (as they themselves have depleted it) they have moved on to that of others, and especially to ours and that of our Empire, as if they were visiting their own guilt upon it.

Such are the tales which they have devised, whereby John the Deacon of the Maimed Fingers drew up a decree in letters of gold and faked great age for it by falsely ascribing it to Constantine the Great.

There are also stories in which they say that a certain Charles[1] bestowed our public property on St. Peter. We answer, however, that this Charles could not lawfully give anything, since he had already been put to flight, deprived of his Empire, beggared and made as nothing by a better Charles.[2] Therefore he gave away what he did not own,—or gave it (as he undoubtedly could give it) as one who had gotten it ill and had no hope of keeping it for long.

Rejecting, therefore, these fictitious decrees and fantastic writings, we, out of our own generosity, give to St. Peter things which belong to us: we are not granting him things which really belong to him as if they are ours. For even as, for love of St. Peter, we have chosen our teacher the lord Silvester and, God willing, ordained and created this most serene man Pope: so, for love of the lord Pope Silvester, do we make gifts to St. Peter out of our public property, so that the teacher may have something to offer our Prince Peter on behalf of his pupil.

We therefore offer and donate to St. Peter eight counties for love of our teacher the lord Pope Silvester, so that, to the honour of God and St. Peter and to his and our salvation, he may have and hold them and rule them for the prosperity of his apostolic dominion and of our Empire. We have granted him these to rule: Pesaro, Farro, Senigallia, Ancona, Fossombrone, Cagli, Iesi and Osimo—so that no man may ever dare to disturb him and St. Peter or trouble him with any form of trickery.

If anyone presume to do so, he shall lose all he has and St. Peter shall receive his goods.

That all men may observe it forever, we have signed this decree with our own hand, which, with God's assistance, will long be victorious; and we have ordered it to be signed with our seal, that it may be valid for him and his successors.

The signature of the lord Otto, invincible Emperor Augustus of the Romans.

IMPERIAL CORONATION ORDO C

§ 5. The imperial coronation Ordo C, which very likely dates from the early eleventh century and was first used at the coronation of Henry II in 1014, symbolizes the hierocratic relationship between Pope and

1. Charles the Bald.
2. Carloman, son of Louis the German, whose intervention forced Charles the Bald to leave Italy in 877.

Emperor which as yet existed only in the mind of the Popes and their supporters, but which the Papacy would attempt to translate into reality later in the century. It stands as a revealing contrast to the Donation of Otto (extract 4B, above) and even to the account of the royal coronation ceremony furnished by Widukind (extract 1, above).

See E. Eichmann, *Die Kaiserkrönung im Abendlandes* (Würzburg, 1942); Ullmann, *Growth of papal government*, 253 foll., with references.

§ 5

Part of Imperial Coronation Ordo C: *Liber Censuum*, ed. P. Fabre and L. Duchesne (1901), I, 1*–6*; W. Ullmann, *The growth of papal government in the middle ages* (London, 1955 edn.), 458–465; now ed. R. Elze, *Die Ordines für die Weihe und Krönung des Kaiser und der Kaiserin* (Hanover, 1960), 35 foll.

How the Roman Emperor must be crowned.

The Roman form of service for blessing the Emperor, when he receives the crown from the lord Pope in the church of St. Peter at the altar of St. Maurice.

At day break on Sunday the Emperor-elect and his wife go down to Santa Maria Transpadina, by Terebintum, where he is honourably received by the prefect of the city and the count of the Lateran palace, and his wife by the judge delegate and the treasurer. He is then led through the portico, with all the clergy of the city dressed in cloaks, chasubles, dalmatics and tunics, carrying thuribles and chanting 'Behold, I send my angel', up to the platform at the head of the steps in front of the bronze doors of Santa Maria in Torre. There sits the lord Pope upon his seat, with the bishops, cardinals, deacons and other orders of the Church standing around him. Then the Emperor-elect, his wife and all his barons, both clerical and lay, kiss the feet of the lord Pope. The Queen and her guides having retired to one side, the Emperor-elect swears fealty to the lord Pope in this manner:

'In the name of Our Lord Jesus Christ, I, N., King and future Emperor of the Romans, promise and swear fealty by these Gospels in the presence of God and St. Peter the apostle to you, N., vicar of St. Peter the apostle, and to all who succeed you canonically; and I promise to be the protector and defender of all the interests of this holy Roman church, of you and of your successors, as far as God will aid me, to the best of my knowledge and ability, and without deceit and ill will. So help me God and these holy Gospels.'

Then the chamberlain of the lord Pope shall receive the cloak of the Emperor-elect, which he is to keep for himself. Then the lord Pope asks him three times if he wishes to be at peace with the Church, and when he has three times answered 'I do', the lord Pope says 'I give you peace, as the Lord gave it to his disciples', and kisses his forehead and chin (which must be shaven), both his cheeks and finally his mouth. Then the lord Pope rises and three times asks him if he wishes to be a son of the Church, and when he has three times answered 'I do', the lord Pope says 'And I receive you as a son of the Church', and takes him under his mantle, and he kisses the lord Pope's breast. And the Pope takes the Emperor-elect by the right hand and his chancellor supports him on the left. The Emperor-elect is led by the right hand by the lord Pope's archdeacon and so enters by the door of bronze, with the clergy of St. Peter chanting 'Blessed be the Lord God of Israel', as far as the door of silver. There the lord Pope leaves him praying, and the Queen follows at a slow pace with her guides as far as the silver door. The Emperor-elect, having finished his prayers, rises, and the Bishop of Albano says this first prayer over him: 'O God, in whose hand lie the hearts of kings, incline your merciful ears to our humble prayers and inspire our prince, your servant, N., with wisdom. May he drink deep of your counsel, be pleasing to you and rule over all kingdoms. Through Our Lord.'

Then the lord Pope enters the church of St. Peter, with its clergy singing the responsory 'Peter, do you love me?' When this is done, the lord Pope gives the blessing. Then he sits upon the seat prepared for him on the right hand side of the Rota. When the Bishop of Albano has finished his prayer, the Emperor-elect enters and sits upon this seat: the archpriest and archdeacon of the cardinals lead him here and sit by him to teach him how to answer the lord Pope in the examination. The lord Pope makes the examination in this manner. Seven bishops shall sit on his right hand, in their order, the German bishops shall sit on the right of the Emperor-elect, and the cardinals and other orders of the Church shall be seated. The lord Pope says:

'The ancient law of the holy fathers teaches and ordains that if anyone is chosen to command, he must first be most diligently examined with all love concerning his faith in the Holy Trinity, and be questioned about certain matters or habits suitable to his royal position, according to the saying of the apostle "Lay hands hastily on no man".[1] The law

1. 1 Timothy, v, 22.

also prescribes that the ordinand shall first receive instruction on how to conduct himself when raised to his great place, so that it may be justifiable to lay hands upon him. By this authority and commandment, then, we ask you, most beloved son, in sincere love, if you will be willing to devote all your wisdom to the service of God, to the limits of your ability?'

He answers: 'I wish to obey and consent to this in all things with all my heart.'

Q. 'Do you wish to curb yourself of all evil habits and to change them wholly into good, with God's assistance, as far as you are able?'

A. 'As far as I can, I do.'

Q. 'Do you wish, with God's help, to preserve a proper moderation?'

A. 'As far as I can, I do.'

[*The examination in morals proceeds on these lines, and is followed by a number of leading questions designed to establish the orthodoxy of the Emperor-elect's beliefs.*—ED.]

Then the lord Pope goes to the sacristy and puts on his pontifical vestments, as far as the dalmatic, and seats himself dressed in this. Meanwhile the Bishop of Portua, standing in the middle of the centre Rota, says over the Emperor-elect the prayer 'Ineffable God, maker of the world' and the others, as at the anointing of the King. When the prayer is finished, the Emperor-elect goes to the choir of St. Gregory with the archpriest and archdeacon of the cardinals, whom he must treat as his teachers throughout the service of unction. They dress him in the amice, alb and girdle, and take him to the lord Pope in the sacristy, and there the Pope makes him a clerk and grants him the tunic, dalmatic, pluvial and mitre, and the shoes and sandals which he is to use in his coronation, and thus clad he stands before the lord Pope. . . .

Once all this has been done, the attendants shall dress the lord Pope in the chasuble and pall, and, putting on his mitre, he shall set forth, with the various orders preceding him in the usual fashion. After him shall go the Emperor-elect, with his guides, and his wife shall follow him as far as the tomb of St. Peter. Then the precentor and the choir sing the Introit and the Kyrie eleison and fall silent. The lord Pope goes up to the altar and after the confession he gives peace to the deacons and shakes the censer. After this he goes up to the throne. Meanwhile, the Emperor-elect and his wife prostrate themselves before the tomb of St. Peter and the archdeacon recites the litany. When this is done, the pluvial only is removed from the Emperor-elect. The Bishop of Ostia shall anoint him with the blessed oil on the right arm and between the shoulders, and say: 'O Lord God Almighty, from whom all power and rank are derived, we beg you with humble and devout prayers to favour this servant of yours in his imperial office, so that nothing done in past or future may hinder the man appointed to rule the Church under your sway, and so that he can justly rule the people subject to him given the inspiration of your Spirit and so that he may always fear you in everything he does and ever strive to please you. Through Our Lord.' Then follows the prayer: 'May God, the Son of God, Jesus Christ Our Lord, who was anointed by the Father with the oil of exultation, by this infusion of the holy oil pour forth the blessing of the Holy Spirit upon your head and cause it to penetrate to the inmost depths of your heart, so that by means of this visible and tangible gift you may deserve to receive things invisible and, having ruled justly upon earth, to reign eternally with him who, being alone without sin, lives as King of Kings and is worshipped with God the Father in the unity of the same Holy Spirit.'

.   .   .   .

After this the lord Pope descends from his seat and goes to the altar of St. Maurice with the Emperor-elect and the Queen following, and the lord Pope stands on the threshold of the entrance to the altar, with the Emperor-elect standing before him in the middle of the Rota, the Queen on the right of the Emperor-elect, and six bishops of the Lateran palace standing near by on the Rotae which are set there, with the seventh one serving the lord Pope at the altar. Then the first and second oblationary shall take up the crowns of the Emperor-elect and the Queen from the altar of St. Peter and put them on the altar of St. Maurice.

Then the lord Pope shall give the ring to the Emperor-elect and say: 'Receive the ring, the symbol of the holy faith, the very foundation of kingship, the increase of power by which you shall learn to triumph over and drive back your enemies, to destroy heresies, to unite your subjects and bind them together in adherence to the catholic faith. Through Our Lord.' The prayer after giving the ring: 'O God, from whom all power and rank is derived, favour your servant in his office and may you reward him throughout his tenure of it and may he strive continually to please you. Through Our Lord.'

Here he girds him with the sword and says: 'Receive this sword, conferred on you with the blessing of God; and with this may you succeed in resisting and expelling all enemies of your own and of the Church of God and in guarding the realm entrusted to you and in

protecting the fortresses of God with the aid of the invincible victor
Our Lord Jesus Christ, who lives and reigns with God and the Holy
Spirit, ever world without end. Amen.' The prayer after giving the
sword: 'O God, who with your providence govern things heavenly
and earthly together, favour our most Christian King, that all the
strength of his enemies may be broken by the prowess of the spiritual
sword and utterly crushed by his army. Through Our Lord.'

Here the Emperor-elect shall be crowned. The archdeacon shall
take the crown from the altar of St. Maurice and offer it to the lord Pope.
When the lord Pope places it on the head of the Emperor-elect, he shall
say this prayer: 'Receive the symbol of glory in the name of the Father
and of the Son and of the Holy Spirit, so that, spurning the ancient
enemy and spurning the infection of every vice, you may so love
justice and prudence and conduct yourself so mercifully that you may
receive the crown of the eternal Kingdom from Our Lord Jesus Christ
in the company of the saints: for he lives and reigns as God with the
Father and Holy Spirit, ever world without end. Amen.'

.   .   .   .

Here the lord Pope shall give the sceptre of Empire and say: 'Receive
the sceptre, the emblem of royal power, the straight wand of kingship,
the wand of virtue by which you shall well govern yourself and with
royal courage defend from evil men the Holy Church and the
Christian people entrusted to you by God, discipline the wicked, give
peace to the righteous and with your aid direct them to the straight
path that they may be able to follow it: so that from the temporal you
may reach the eternal Kingdom, with the aid of him whose Kingdom
and Empire shall endlessly endure, ever world without end. Amen.'
The prayer after giving the sceptre: 'O Lord, the source of everything
good and creator of all progress, grant, we beg, to your servant N. the
office of ruling well which he has earned and see fit to confirm the
honour which you have offered him. Honour him before all the kings
of the earth, enrich him with fruitful blessings, and establish him firmly
upon the throne of his Kingdom. Visit him with offspring, grant him
long life, may justice always arise in his time, that he may be happily
and joyfully glorified in the eternal Kingdom, through Our Lord.'

GUARANTEES TO HOLDERS OF BENEFICES

§ 6. Benefices were slower to become heritable in the Empire than in

France. The process by which they did so was, however, speeded up by the action of Conrad II (1024–1039). He pursued a new policy of backing his sub-vassals against the greater lords, their immediate superiors, by—among other things—guaranteeing them comparative security in their benefices. The edict translated here was issued by Conrad in his capacity as King or head of the feudal hierarchy in Lombardy, after a revolt of the sub-vassals or *valvassores* of Milan and the surrounding territories against their immediate lords. Conrad pursued a similar policy in Germany, though not apparently by an explicit law.

See J. W. Thompson, *Feudal Germany* (Chicago, 1928), 70, 311; H. Mitteis, *Lehnrecht und Staatsgewalt* (Weimar, 1933), 399 foll.; H. Mitteis, 'German feudalism', in Barraclough, ed. *Mediaeval Germany*, II, 239–40; Barraclough, *Origins of modern Germany*, 79–80; F. L. Ganshof, *Feudalism* (New York, 1961), 134–5; M. Bloch, *Feudal Society* (London, 1961), 197–9.

§ 6

The *Edictum de Beneficiis Regni Italici*, issued by Conrad II of Germany, May 28th, 1037, ed. L. Weiland in M.G.H., Const., I (1893), 90–1.

In the name of the holy and indivisible Trinity. Conrad, by the grace of God Emperor Augustus of the Romans.

1. We would have it known to all loyal subjects of the holy Church of God and of ourselves, both present and future, that, for the purpose of reconciling lords and vassals so that they may live forever in mutual harmony and serve us and their lords devoutly, loyally and with perseverance, we have decreed and firmly ordained: that no vassal of a bishop, abbot, abbess, margrave, count or any other person who now holds or shall come to hold or has in the past unjustly lost a benefice taken from our public property or from the estates of a church, whether he be one of our greater sub-vassals [*valvassores*] or one of their vassals, may lose his benefice unless he has been convicted of a definite offence and save in accordance with the decrees of our predecessors and the judgment of his peers.

2. Should a dispute arise between lord and vassal, and the vassal's peers decide that he should lose his benefice, and the vassal say that this was done unjustly or out of prejudice, he shall keep his benefice until the lord and the vassal whom he is accusing and the vassal's peers come before us and the case is justly decided in our presence. And if the peers

are accused of failing their lord in judgment, the accused vassal shall keep his benefice until he and his lord and his peers come before us. The lord or the accused vassal, whichever of them has decided to come to us, shall give notice to the other contending party six weeks before beginning the journey. This rule shall be observed where our greater sub-vassals are concerned.

3. Cases involving the lesser sub-vassals in the Kingdom shall be determined either before their lords or before our representative.

4. We further ordain that when any vassal, great or small, has departed this life, his son shall have his benefice. If he has had no son, but has left a grandson by a male child, the grandson shall likewise have the benefice so long as he meets the obligation of the greater sub-vassals to provide their lords with weapons and horses. If the deceased has left no grandson in the male line, but has a legitimate brother on his father's side, and if this man has offended his lord and wishes to make amends to him and become his vassal, then he may have the benefice which was his father's.

5. Furthermore we utterly forbid any lord to exchange the benefices of his vassals or make them into leasehold or precarial tenures without their consent.[1] Let no man dare to deprive them unjustly of the property which they hold by right of ownership, either by royal charter [*preceptum*] or by a proper perpetual lease [*libellum*] or by life tenure [*precaria*].

6. We wish to receive the forage from the castles which our predecessors used to receive. But we ask for nothing which they did not receive.

7. If anyone infringes this decree, he shall pay 100 pounds in gold, one half to our treasury and the other to the man he has injured.

The signature of the most serene lord Conrad, Emperor Augustus of the Romans.

The Chancellor Cadolo has witnessed this in the place of Hermann the Arch-chancellor.

Given on May 28th, indiction five, in the one thousand and thirty-eighth year of Our Lord's incarnation.

In the lord Conrad's thirteenth year as King and his eleventh as Emperor. Done at the siege of Milan: happily amen.

---

1. 'nullus senior de beneficio suorum militum cambium aut precariam aut libellum sine eorum consensu facere presumat'. *Precaria* is defined in Du Cange's *Glossarium* as an agreement 'by which a man receives an allod or estate from a church for use during his lifetime on payment of an annual rent', and *libellus* as one whereby 'an estate is granted in perpetual lease [*emphyteusis*], a form of contract or agreement once common in dealing with ecclesiastical estates'.

See also Bloch, *Feudal Society*, 164–5.

CHAPTER II

The Investiture Contest

LAY INVESTITURE

§ 7. The documents in this section mark phases in a developing struggle for ultimate supremacy within a Christian society conceived as a Church—a struggle between royal power and priestly authority in general and Emperor and Pope in particular, for its effects were most far reaching in the Empire, where the Emperor depended heavily on the power to appoint and invest bishops. From the mid-eleventh century, the Papacy was assuming the leadership of a movement designed to free the clergy of all control by laymen.

Extract 7 below is an attack by Humbert of Moyenmoutier, Cardinal Bishop of Silva Candida, on the practice whereby laymen invested bishops with ring and staff. This was the outward and visible sign of royal control over episcopal appointments. Humbert's treatise, which denied the validity of all acts carried out by bishops who had bought their sees, was completed and published about the year 1058. Humbert and Peter Damiani were perhaps the most eminent of the reformers at Rome before Hildebrand acceded to the Papacy as Gregory VII (1073). Humbert's treatise may have strongly influenced the decree of 1059 designed to protect papal elections from lay interference, whether by the Emperor or by the Roman aristocracy (see above, Part II, no. 6).

Extract 8 consists of the other reforming decrees issued by Pope Nicholas II in 1059 and is included here to show how the attacks on lay investiture formed part of a wider programme for improving the discipline of the clergy.

For general accounts of the development of the Investiture Contest in Germany, see Thompson, *Feudal Germany*, chs. III, VI and VII; Barraclough, *Origins of modern Germany*, chs. V and VI. On the ideals and theories of Gregory VII, M. Pacaut, *La théocratie: l'église et le pouvoir au moyen âge* (1957), ch. III; Ullmann, *Growth of papal government*, ch. IX.

Other letters of Gregory VII are translated in E. Emerson, *The correspondence of Pope Gregory VII* (New York, 1932).

On Cardinal Humbert and his influence as a reformer, and on the general question of lay investiture, see H. Halfmann, *Cardinal Humbert, sein Leben und seine Werke mit besonderer Berücksichtung seines Traktates 'Libri tres adversus simoniacos'* (Göttingen, 1883); C. Mirbt, *Die Publizistik im Zeitalter Gregors VII* (Leipzig, 1894), 463 foll.; A. Scharnagl, *Der Begriff der Investitur in den Quellen und der Literatur des Investiturstreites* (Stuttgart, 1908), 15 foll.; R. W. and A. J. Carlyle, *A history of mediaeval political theory in the west*, IV (Edinburgh-London, 1922); A. Michel, *Humbert und Kerullarios* (Paderborn, 1924–1930); A. Fliche, *La réforme grégorienne* (Louvain-Paris, 1924–1937), I, 265 foll.; P. Schmid, *Der Begriff der kanonischen Wahl in den Anfängen des Investiturstreits* (Stuttgart, 1926), 113 foll.; J. P. Whitney, *Hildebrandine Essays* (Cambridge, 1932), 23 foll., 29 foll., 120 foll.; A. Michel, *Papstwahl und Königsrecht oder das Papstwahl-Konkordat von 1059* (Munich, 1936); Z. N. Brooke, 'Lay investiture and its relation to the conflict of Empire and Papacy', P.B.A., 25 (1939); A. Fliche in Fliche-Martin, *Histoire de l'Église*, VIII (1946), 15 foll.; A. Michel, 'Die folgenschweren Ideen des Kardinals Humbert und ihr Einfluss auf Gregor VII', S.G., 1 (1947); J. Haller, 'Pseudo-Isidors erstes Auftreten im deutschen Investiturstreit', S.G., 2 (1947); G. Tellenbach, *Church, state and Christian society at the time of the Investiture Contest* (Oxford, 1940), 108 foll.; A. Michel, 'Humbert und Hildebrand bei Nikolaus II (1059–1061)', H.J., 72 (1953); H. G. Krause, *Das Papstwahldekret von 1059 und seine Rolle in Investiturstreit*, S.G., 7 (1960); Ullmann, *Growth of papal government*, 265 foll.

§ 7

Part of the attack on lay investiture by Cardinal Humbert of Silva Candida: *Libri III adversus simoniacos*, III, chs. vi and vii, ed. F. Thaner in M.G.H., L.L., I (1891), 205–6.

VI. *On the staffs and rings given by the hands of lay authorities.*

The supreme bishops who must be venerated throughout the world have decreed at the dictation of the Holy Spirit that [*in episcopal elections* —Ed.] the choice made by the clergy shall be confirmed by the decision of the metropolitan, and the request of laity and people by the consent of the prince. But everything is in fact done in a perverted order, in rejection of the holy canons and in utter contempt of the whole

Christian religion, and the first things come last and the last first. For the lay authority comes first in electing and confirming, and then, willy-nilly, the consent of laity, people and clergy follows, and the metropolitan's decision comes last of all. Men preferred by this means are not to be numbered among the bishops, because they have been installed in a topsy-turvy manner and because what ought to be done to them last is in fact done first, and done by men who have no business with it.

For how can it belong to lay persons to dispose of the mysteries of the Church and dispense pontifical or pastoral grace in the form of crooked staffs and rings, on which the whole consecration of a bishop chiefly depends, from which it proceeds and by which it is completed? For crooked staffs are curved and hooked at the top to draw and pull in, pointed and barbed below to wound and drive away, and they designate the pastoral care which is handed over with them. The shape admonishes the pastors to be upright and moderate and temper the inflexibility of their thoughts and actions for the sake of drawing and attracting the flock of God to themselves, but in such a way that they always come back to themselves and never turn away their mind's eye from self-examination. The end of the staff indicates that they shall strike fear into the undisciplined by stern reproof and, if they persist, thrust them from the Church by the ultimate sentence. The apostle points briefly to all these things when he says: 'We ask you to censure the unruly, to comfort the feeble-minded, to support the weak and to be patient with all men'.[1]

Again, the ring bears the sign of heavenly secrets, which charges the preachers, together with the apostle, to set apart the secret wisdom of God and to speak it among the perfect,[2] but to withhold it like a sealed letter from the imperfect, who cannot yet have solid food, but only milk. Like friends of the bridegroom, they are charged to show unceasing loyalty to his bride the Church and to commend it to others.

Whoever therefore invests a man with staff and ring undoubtedly claims all the authority of a pastor by taking this upon himself. Once these have been handed over, how can the clergy, the people and the laity or the metropolitan who is to perform the consecration decide freely about such prelates, when these have already been given to them? What remains to them but compliance? A man who has already received ring and staff bursts violently in upon clergy, laity and people, ready to rule them before they know, seek or ask for him. He ap-

1. 1 Thessalonians, v, 14.   2. 1 Corinthians, ii, 6.

proaches the metropolitan to judge him, not to be judged by him: he does not ask and receive his decision, he merely demands and extorts a service from him, in the form of prayer and unction, which is all that remains to the metropolitan. For why should he return to the metropolitan the staff and ring which he already bears? Because they were given him by a lay person? But baptism is not to be repeated even if a layman has given it, though if the child lives prayer and unction are to be supplied by a priest. Without these, if the child does not live, it can undoubtedly enter the Kingdom of Heaven—though without being washed by water no one can do so. Hence it is plain that the whole office of a bishop has been given in the ring and staff, for without initiation with these and without their authority no one can act as a bishop, since it is generally agreed that episcopal authority was bestowed upon the holy apostles without the visible act of unction, but simply by the acceptance of pastoral responsibility, which is visibly shown and given in the ring and staff. I ask therefore why the ring and staff are returned to the metropolitan, unless it be so that the things of the Church may be sold afresh under this form of transaction or donation; that the original sale may be ratified by the metropolitan and his suffragans; or indeed that the presumptuous act of ordination by a layman may be disguised under cover of clerical regulations?

If this never happens and never has happened, anyone may give me the lie. Most serious is that we are not merely hearing stories of such things being done in the past: we see them done and know that they are usual in our own times. For did not the princes of this world once sell the things of the Church, and do they not do so still under the false name of investiture, and do not the metropolitans do likewise in the course of consecration?

VII. *Of the time of the Ottos, of the designs of the Emperor Henry and of the malice of the King of France.*

Not to mention earlier centuries, many can remember the fury of bartering which spread through Germany, the Gauls and the whole of Italy from the time of the Ottos to that of Henry, son of Conrad, Emperor of august and holy memory.[1] He in his time did remove some of the sacrilege both from himself and from the ecclesiastical persons of the Empire entrusted to him, though much of it was rife; and he wanted to remove it all. Kept by untimely death from fulfilling this dearest wish of his heart, he was translated, as we believe, to the King-

1. Henry III, b. 1017, d. 1056, succeeded his father Conrad II as sole ruler of Germany 1038, crowned Emperor 1046.

dom of Eternal Life either for this intention alone or for the purity of his outlook, though there were many other good deeds for which to praise him. But his contemporary and namesake,[1] the destroyer of western France, the tyrant of God, like a son of damnation and an Antichrist, opposes Christ and ceases not to assault and battle with his grace in every part of his realm. . . .

§ 8

The reforming decrees of Pope Nicholas II, 1059: Mansi, *Concilia*. XIX, 897–9.

Bishop Nicholas, servant of the servants of God, to all catholic bishops and all the clergy and people, most loving greeting and the apostolic blessing.

Being obliged by our vigilant rulership of the world to care diligently for all men, making provision for your salvation, we are concerned to inform you of the decrees canonically enacted in the Council recently celebrated at Rome in the presence of a hundred and thirteen bishops under our unworthy presidency: for we wish you to carry them out for the sake of your own salvation and we order you to do so by the apostolic authority.

I. First, it is established in the sight of God that it shall lie in the power of the cardinal bishops to elect the Bishop of Rome: so that, if anyone is enthroned in the Apostolic See without their having first agreed to it and canonically elected him, and without the consent of the other religious orders and of clergy and laity, he shall be regarded not as a Pope or Apostolic Pontiff but as an apostate.

II. That on the death of the Bishop of Rome or of any other city no one may presume to invade his property, but it shall be kept intact for his successor.

III. That no one shall hear Mass said by a priest whom he knows without doubt to be keeping a mistress or a woman in his house. Hence the holy Council has decreed this article, upon pain of excommunication:

If any priest, deacon or subdeacon publicly takes a mistress or refuses to leave one he has already taken, in spite of the decree of our predecessor the most holy Pope Leo of blessed memory on the chastity of the clergy, on behalf of Almighty God, by the authority of the blessed

1. Henry I, b. 1008, d. 1060, succeeded his father as King of France 1031.

apostles Peter and Paul, we utterly forbid him to sing Mass or to read the Gospel, Epistle or Mass, or to remain in the presbytery for the divine offices with those who obey this decree or to accept any duty from the Church until, God willing, we have given a decision on the case.

IV. We further decree that those priests, deacons and subdeacons who have obeyed Pope Leo and kept their chastity shall eat and sleep together as Christian clerks are obliged to do according to the churches to which they have been assigned: and they shall hold all income from the churches in common. We ask and advise them to strive above all to adopt the apostolic, that is the communal, way of life.

V. Again, that first fruits and tithes and the offerings of the living and the dead shall be faithfully handed over by laymen to the churches of God and shall be at the disposal of the bishop. Those who withhold them shall be cut off from communion with the holy Church.

VI. That no clerk or priest may obtain a church, either with or without payment, through laymen.

VII. That no one may take the habit of a monk in the hope or promise of becoming an abbot.

VIII. No priest may hold two churches at the same time.

IX. That no one is to be assigned or promoted to any ecclesiastical office by means of the heresy of simony.

X. That laymen may not judge clerks of any order.

XI. That no one may take a wife of his own kin unto the seventh generation or so far as there is any traceable relationship.

XII. That no layman who has a wife and a mistress at the same time may communicate with the Church.

XIII. That no layman may be promoted to any ecclesiastical rank without preliminary—i.e., unless he has first put off his worldly habit and been tested by prolonged association with clergymen.

You shall therefore keep these and other statutes of the holy fathers faithfully and with Christian reverence if you wish to enjoy the peace, communion and blessing of the holy Roman church and the Apostolic See.

THE 'DICTATUS PAPAE'

§ 9. The much discussed *Dictatus Papae* is a collection of statements of papal prerogative included in the register of Pope Gregory VII. Accord-

K

ing to the widely accepted opinion of Father G. B. Borino, the *Dictatus Papae*—which simply means 'writings of the Pope'—were the headings of an index to a collection of canons relating to the primacy of the Roman church.

On the *Dictatus Papae* in general and various aspects of them, see Fliche, *La réforme grégorienne*, II, 189 foll.; E. Voosen, *Papauté et pouvoir civil à l'époque de Grégoire VII* (Gembloux, 1927), 118–19 and *passim*; K. Hofmann, *Der Dictatus Papae Gregors VII* (Paderborn, 1933); H. X. Arquillière, *Saint Grégoire VII: essai sur sa conception du pouvoir pontifical* (1934), 130 foll.; G. B. Borino, 'Un ipotesi sul "*Dictatus Papae*" di Gregorio VII', A.D.R.S., 67 (1944); Fliche in Fliche-Martin, *Histoire de l'Église*, VIII, 79 foll.; K. Hofmann, 'Der *Dictatus Papae* Gregors VII als Index einer Kanonessammlung?', S. Kuttner, '*Liber canonicus:* a note on "*Dictatus Papae*" ch. 17', and P. E. Schramm, '*Sacerdotium* und *Regnum* im Austausch ihrer Vorrechte', all in S.G., 2 (1947); Pacaut, *La théocratie*, 74 foll.; W. Ullmann, '*Romanus pontifex indubitanter efficitur sanctus:* "*Dictatus Papae*" 23 in retrospect and prospect', S.G., 6 (1959–1961); Ullmann, *Growth of papal government*, 291 foll.

§ 9

The *Dictatus Papae* from the Register of Pope Gregory VII, 1075: E Caspar, *Das Register Gregors VII*, I (Berlin, 1920), 202–7.

The dictate of the Pope.

I. That the Roman church was founded by God alone.

II. That only the Bishop of Rome is by law called universal.

III. That he alone may depose or reinstate bishops.

IV. That his legate may preside over all the bishops in council, even should he be of inferior rank, and may pronounce sentence of deposition against them.

V. That the Pope may depose persons in their absence.

VI. That, among other things, we must not stay under the same roof with persons whom he has excommunicated.

VII. That he alone may establish new laws to meet urgent needs of the time, found new dioceses [*novas plebes congregare*] or make a canonry into an abbey; and, on the other hand, divide a rich bishopric and combine poor ones.

VIII. That he alone may use the imperial insignia.

IX. That the Pope is the only man whose feet shall be kissed by all princes.

X. That his title alone shall be read out in churches.

XI. That this title is unique in all the world.[1]

XII. That he may depose Emperors.

XIII. That for urgent reasons he may transfer bishops from one see to another.

XIV. That he may ordain a clerk from any church, wherever he wishes.

XV. That one ordained by him may hold a commanding but not a subordinate position in another church, and must not accept higher rank from any other bishop.

XVI. That no council may be called 'general' without his commandment.

XVII. That no chapter or book may be recognized as canonical without his authority.

XVIII. That no sentence of his may be retracted by anyone, and he is the only one who can retract it.

XIX. That he must not be judged by anyone.

XX. That no one shall dare to condemn one who appeals to the Apostolic See.

XXI. That the more important lawsuits of any church must be referred to the Apostolic See.

XXII. That the Roman church has never erred, nor, as witness Scripture, will it ever do so.[2]

XXIII. That the Bishop of Rome, if he has been canonically ordained, is undoubtedly sanctified by the merits of St. Peter, on the testimony of St. Ennodius, Bishop of Pavia, with the support of many holy Fathers—as it says in the decrees of the blessed Pope Symmachus.[3]

XXIV. That by his commandment and with his permission, subordinate persons may bring accusations.

XXV. That he may depose and reinstate bishops without summoning a council.

XXVI. That no one may be regarded as a catholic if he is not in agreement with the Roman church.

XXVII. That the Pope can absolve the subjects of the wicked from their fealty to them.

---

1. Philippians, ii, 9.   2. Cf. Luke, xxii, 32.

3. See *Decretales pseudo-Isidorianae*, ed. P. Hinschius (Leipzig, 1863), 666: Ennodius, *Libellus pro synodo*, ed. W. Hartel in C.S.E.L., VI (1882), 295.

HENRY IV'S ATTACKS ON GREGORY VII

§ 10. Extracts 10A and B show some of the arguments used on behalf of Henry IV at the outbreak of the struggle which came to be known as the Investiture Contest. Both letters were possibly written by Gottschalk of Aachen, a theologian who rose to be chief royal chaplain and provost of Aachen. 10A was written at or after the Council of Worms of January 1076 where the King and bishops declared the election of Pope Gregory VII null and void and called on him to abdicate. 10B forms part of a circular letter issued by Henry IV summoning the bishops to a further meeting at Pentecost 1076. Both letters have been seen as early attempts to formulate a 'dualistic' as opposed to 'hierocratic' theory of the relationship between lay and clerical power.

On the authorship and chronology, see K. Hampe, 'Heinrichs IV Absagebrief an Gregor VII vom Jahre 1076', H.Z., 138 (1928); C. Erdmann and D. von Gladiss, 'Gottschalk von Aachen im Dienste Heinrichs IV', D.A.G.M., 3 (1939).

On the theory contained in the letters, Fliche, La réforme grégorienne, II, 291 foll., III, 50 foll.; Voosen, Papauté et pouvoir civil, 286 foll.; J. Lecler, 'L'argument des deux glaives dans les controverses politiques du moyen âge', R.S,R. 21 (1931), 307–8; H. X. Arquillière, Saint Grégoire VII, 141 foll.; Fliche in Fliche-Martin, Histoire de l'Église, VIII, 135–6; Ullmann, Growth of papal government, 345 foll.

On the theory of the two swords in general, see the literature cited above, Part II, extracts 9A and B; for theories of the two swords, see also below, Part III, nos. 20A and 35.

§ 10

A. Henry IV's attack on Gregory VII, January 1076: Die Briefe Heinrichs IV, ed. C. Erdmann (Leipzig, 1937), 15–17.

Henry, King by no usurpation but by the holy ordinance of God, to Hildebrand, now no Apostolic Pontiff but a false monk.

You have earned this greeting by the disorder you have created: for you have spared no estate within the Church, and brought disorder, not honour, and curses, not blessings, upon all.

To select from the many only a few points of conspicuous importance: not only have you not scrupled to touch the rulers of Holy Church, archbishops, bishops and priests, although they are the Lord's anointed, but you have even trampled them underfoot like slaves who know not what their master does.[1] By treating them thus, you have won yourself vulgar acclaim. You have decided that they all know nothing and you alone know everything, and have sought to use your knowledge not to build but to destroy,[2] so that on these grounds we may believe that St. Gregory, whose name you have claimed for yourself, was prophesying about you when he said: 'The mind of the prelate is often exhilarated by the abundance of his subjects and he thinks he knows more than everybody else when he sees that he has more power than they!'[3]

And we have borne with all this, striving to maintain the honour of the Apostolic See. But you interpreted our humility as fear and were bold enough to squeeze out the royal power granted to us by God, which you dared to threaten to take away from us: as if we received our Kingdom from you, and as if Kingship and Empire lay in your hand and not in God's.

Our Lord Jesus Christ called us to kingship: he did not call you to priesthood. For these were the steps in your ascent: by cunning—which is abomination to a monk—you got money, by money favour, by favour arms, by arms you invaded the seat of peace, and from the seat of peace you shattered peace by arming subjects against prelates, whilst you, who had no vocation, taught that our bishops, though called by God, were to be despised; whilst you stole for laymen their ministry over priests, so that laymen may depose and condemn those who have received them as pupils from the hand of the Lord by the laying-on of the hands of bishops.

You have touched me, anointed as I am to rule (however unworthy), although the tradition of the holy fathers teaches that I am to be judged by God alone and asserts that I am not to be deposed for any crime save—which God forbid—for straying from the faith. For the wisdom of the holy bishops entrusted the judgment and deposition even of Julian the Apostate not to themselves but to God alone. And the true Pope, St. Peter himself, proclaims 'Fear God, honour the King';[4] but you, because you fear not God, dishonour in me the appointed of him.

Hence St. Paul, who did not spare even an angel from heaven if he preached other things, made no exception for you, who teach other things on earth. For he says: 'If I or even an angel from heaven preach anything other than what we have already preached to you, let him be

1. Psalms, cv, 15; John, xv, 15.   2. 2 Corinthians, x, 8, xiii, 10.
3. *Liber regulae pastoralis*, Bk. II, ch. 6, in Migne, P.L., 77, 35.   4. 1 Peter, ii, 17.

anathema'.[1] And therefore come down, condemned by this anathema, by the judgment of all our bishops and by our own judgment, and leave the Apostolic See which you have claimed. Let another ascend to the throne of St. Peter, one who will not commit violence under cover of religion but will teach the sound doctrine of St. Peter.

I, Henry, King by the grace of God, with all our bishops, say to you: Come down, come down!

B. Extract from Henry IV's circular to the bishops in the Empire, summoning them to a Council at Worms, at Pentecost (May 15th, 1076): ibid., 18–19.

. . . Hear that he we call Hildebrand, who wears a monk's costume and is called an Apostolic Pontiff, is holding the Apostolic See, not with the care of a pastor, but with the violence of an invader, and from the seat of peace bursting the bonds of the one catholic peace, which is plain for you to see. To select a few points from the many: he has usurped both kingship and priesthood for himself behind God's back. In this he has defied the holy ordinance of God, which wanted the two things, kingship and priesthood, to exist from the beginning as two and not as one, as the Saviour himself gave us to understand at the time of his passion through the symbol of the sufficiency of the two swords. When it was said to him, 'Master, here are two swords', he answered 'It is enough',[2] and by calling this duality enough he meant that a spiritual and a carnal sword must be wielded in the Church, and that everything harmful must be cut away by them. He taught that every man was to be compelled by the priestly sword to obey the king for the sake of God, and by the royal sword to drive away the enemies of Christ abroad and to obey the priesthood at home. So each should extend love to the other, and kingship should not be deprived of the respect of priesthood nor priesthood of the respect of kingship. You yourself know—if you have wished to know—how the frenzy of Hildebrand has thrown this ordinance of God into confusion. For in his opinion no one can become a priest unless he has begged for his priesthood from his highness Hildebrand. And he has striven to deprive me of my Kingdom, though God called me to it and did not call him to priesthood, for he sees that I want to reign as of God and not of him, since he did not appoint me King; and he is threatening to take away both my Kingdom and my soul, although he gave me neither.

1. Galatians, i, 8.   2. Luke, xxii, 38.

THE EXCOMMUNICATION OF HENRY IV

§ 11. Gregory's first sentence excommunicating Henry IV was issued at the Lenten synod in Rome in February 1076, after Roland, a clerk of Parma, had announced the decision of the council at Worms, since ratified by another assembly of bishops at Piacenza. The sentence was a practical application of some of the principles formulated in the *Dictatus Papae* (above, Part III, no. 9). The document raises the question of the relationship between the excommunication and the suspension or deposition of Henry IV.

See Fliche, *La réforme grégorienne*, II, 283 foll.; Voosen, *Papauté et pouvoir civil*, 258 foll.; Arquillière, *Saint Grégoire VII*, 144 foll; Fliche in Fliche-Martin, *Histoire de l'Église*, VIII, 136–7; A. Fliche and H. X. Arquillière, 'Grégoire VII, à Canossa, a-t-il réintegré Henri IV dans sa fonction royale?', S.G., I (1947), 4 (1952); Ullmann, *Growth of papal government*, 299 foll.

§ 11

Gregory VII's first excommunication of Henry IV, February 14th–20th, 1076: *Das Register Gregors VII*, ed. E. Caspar (Berlin, 1920–1923), I, 270–1.

The excommunication of Henry, King of the Germans.

St. Peter, Prince of Apostles, we beg you to lend us your ears and to hear me, your servant whom you have from childhood and even to this day delivered from the hands of the wicked who hated and still hate me for my loyalty to you. You, and my lady the mother of God, and St. Paul, your brother among all the saints, are witnesses that your holy Roman church dragged me against my own will to its helm, that I had no plan to seize your throne by violence, that I would sooner end my life as a monk than seize your place by worldly cunning for the sake of worldly glory. And so I think it was by your grace, and not by my works, that it has pleased and still pleases you that the Christian people entrusted specially to you shall especially obey me because I have been made your deputy. By your grace I have the power given by God to bind and to loose in heaven and on earth.

Strengthened, therefore, by your trust in me, for the honour and protection of your church, on behalf of God Almighty, Father, Son and Holy Spirit, by your power and authority I forbid King Henry, son of the Emperor Henry, who has rebelled with unheard-of insolence against your church, to govern any part of the Kingdom of the Germans or of Italy; and I absolve all Christians from any oaths to him which they have already taken or shall take in the future and I forbid anyone to serve him as if he were King. For it is right that one who seeks to detract from the honour of your church shall himself lose the honour which is accorded him. And because he has refused to obey as a Christian and has not returned to God, whom he has deserted by associating with excommunicated men, by spurning the warning which (as you are my witness) I issued for his own salvation, and by withdrawing from your church in an attempt to sunder it apart: in your place I bind him with the chain of anathema, and so bind him by virtue of your trust in me that the nations may know without doubt that you are Peter and upon your rock the son of the living God built his church and the gates of hell shall not prevail against it.[1]

CANOSSA AND FORCHEIM

§ 12. This account of Henry's submission to Gregory at Canossa and of the German princes' election of an anti-King, Rudolf of Rheinfelden, Duke of Swabia, on their own initiative was written by a Saxon chronicler hostile to Henry IV. Bruno's history of the Saxon war was prepared about 1082, when he was in the service of Wernher, Bishop of Merseburg, one of the bishops who had been hostile to Henry IV from the beginning of the Investiture Contest. According to one theory, it was designed to justify the coronation of Hermann of Salm, who in 1081 succeeded Rudolf as anti-King. Rudolf's electors tried, in opposition to Henry, to establish the revolutionary principle that the monarchy was elective and not hereditary. It was far from being accepted immediately. Bruno's account of Canossa differs in important respects from the official papal version.

See Fliche, *La réforme grégorienne*, II, 303 foll., 357 foll.; Arquillière, *Saint Grégoire VII*, 161 foll., 394 foll.; Barraclough in Barraclough, ed. *Mediaeval Germany*, I, 56 foll.; P. Joachimsen, 'The Investiture Contest and the German constitution', in Barraclough, ed., *Mediaeval Germany*, II; Fliche in Fliche-Martin, *Histoire de l'Église*, VIII, 140 foll.; Fliche, 'Grégoire VII à Canossa'; Arquillière, 'Grégoire VII à Canossa'; W. Berger, 'Gregor VII und das deutsche Designationsrecht', S.G., 2 (1947).

1. Matthew, xvi, 18.

§ 12

The submission of Henry IV to the Pope at Canossa, 1077, and the election of Rudolf of Swabia as anti-King at Forchheim, March 13th–15th, 1077: Bruno, *De Bello Saxonico*, chs. 90–1, ed. H. E. Lohmann (Leipzig, 1937), pp. 84–6.

Henry, wandering in Italy, uncertain in his mind, did not know what action to take, for he was afraid of losing his Kingdom whatever he did. For he knew that, unless he came in supplication to the Apostolic Pontiff and were absolved by him from the sentence, he would certainly not receive back his Kingdom. But he feared that, if he did come as a suppliant to make amends, the Pope would take away his Kingdom for the enormity of his crimes or bind him twice over with the chains of the apostolic power for his disobedience. Thus, with his many worries, he was torn between different courses of action. Though he had no doubt that he was and would be lost either way, nevertheless he chose the course in which he thought there was some hope; and he came to the Apostolic Pontiff barefoot and in woollen garments, saying that he loved the heavenly more than the earthly Kingdom and so he would humbly undertake whatever penance the Pope wished to impose upon him. The Apostolic Pontiff, rejoicing at such humility on the part of such a man, ordered him not to put on the royal insignia until he allowed him to, since the contrition of his heart, and hence also the base clothing by which he showed it outwardly, were more acceptable to Almighty God. He must avoid living or speaking with excommunicated persons lest, having been cleansed by the grace of God at his conversion, he were made filthier than before by contact with others. Having promised to do both these things, Henry was dismissed after being absolved from this sentence and repeatedly warned not to lie to God, because, if he did not fulfil his promises, not only would the original chains not be removed, but other tighter ones would be added.

When he returned to his own people and began to exclude them from his company, they started to create a great disturbance, saying that if he now thrust from him those by means of whose wisdom and virtue he had hitherto held his Kingdom, the Apostolic Pontiff would be able neither to restore it to him nor to get him another. His mind was changed by these and other such words and through the wicked counsel of evil men he returned to his usual ways. He placed on his head the golden diadem and in his heart he kept the anathema stouter than steel. He joined the communion of the excommunicate and, wretch that he was, was thrust out from that of the saints. Now he made it clear to everyone that his assertion that he loved the heavenly more than the earthly Kingdom was untrue. Had he remained obedient for a little time, he could have kept the present Kingdom on earth in peace and at some time come into eternal possession of a heavenly Kingdom. Now for his disobedience he would not obtain his beloved Kingdom without great toil, and would not receive it without a great change in his whole way of life.

Meanwhile the Saxons and Swabians assembled at Forchheim, and delegates from other regions were also present, and indicated that their people would approve anything concerning the commonwealth which they decreed in a proper manner. The legate of the Apostolic Pontiff[1] was also there to confirm with the supreme apostolic authority all profitable measures taken by our countrymen concerning the Kingdom. Out of the many whom they proposed for election as being of a worthy character, the Saxons and Swabians in unison eventually chose Rudolf, Duke of the Swabians, as their King. But when they had to approve him as their King individually, some of them wanted to impose certain conditions whereby they would raise him as King above them provided that he made them a special promise that their wrongs would be righted. Duke Otto, for example, refused to make Rudolf his King unless he promised to restore him the honour unjustly removed from him. Many others drew attention to their own particular cases and wanted Rudolf to promise to set them right. Realizing this, the legate of the Apostolic Pontiff forbade it and—pointing out that Rudolf was to become King, not of certain individuals only, but of them all—asserted that it was enough for him to promise to be just to everybody. The legate said, moreover, that if the election were preceded by a series of individual promises in the way in which they had begun, it would appear not to be honest, but tainted rather with the poisonous heresy of simony. Nevertheless, a special exception was made for certain particular abuses, which Rudolf was obliged to put right because they had wrongfully flourished: he promised that he would not give bishoprics, either for money or out of favour, but would allow each church to elect one of its own people as the canons ordain. It was then agreed there by common consent, and confirmed by the authority of the Bishop of Rome, that the royal power should not henceforth pass to anyone by inheritance as had previously been the custom: but that the King's son,

1. There were in fact two legates present: Bernard, a cardinal-deacon, and Bernard, Abbot of St. Victor, Marseilles.

even if he were outstandingly suitable, should become King by spontaneous election rather than by right of succession. If the King's son
were not worthy, or if the people did not want him, the people should
have the power to make the man they wanted King.

Having lawfully decreed all these things, they conducted Rudolf,
their chosen King, with great honour to Mainz and stood by him
reverently and steadfastly, as it soon appeared, until he was consecrated
King. He was consecrated by Siegfried, Archbishop of Mainz, with the
presence and support of a multitude of others, on March 26th in the
year of Our Lord 1077.

THE REFORM OF THE CHURCH

§ 13. These decrees of a council held at Rome in 1078 by Gregory VII
provide further illustration of the papal programme for reforming the
morals of the clergy and for freeing them from all lay control or influence.

On the question of lay investiture, see the authorities listed above,
Part III, no. 7.

§ 13

Disciplinary decrees of the Roman council, November 19th, 1078: *Das
Register Gregors VII*, ed. E. Caspar (Berlin, 1920), II, 402–6.

1. If any knight or member of any other order or profession has
received or invaded or in the future receives estates of the Church from
any king or lay prince, or takes them from any bishops, abbots or other
rulers of churches against their will, or holds such estates with the
vicious or corrupt connivance of their governors, he shall lie under excommunication unless he restores these estates to the churches concerned.

. . . .

3. Since we have understood that lay persons invest with churches
in many regions, contrary to the ordinances of the holy fathers, and
that numberless disturbances have arisen in the Church as a result, and
that the Christian religion has been trodden underfoot, we decree that
no clergyman may receive investiture of a bishopric, abbey or church
from the hands of an Emperor or King or any other lay person, male or

female. And if one should so presume, let him know that the investiture is, by the apostolic authority, null and void, and that he lies under excommunication until he makes proper satisfaction.

4. If any bishop has sold prebends, archdeaconries, priorships or any other ecclesiastical office, or disposed of these in a manner contrary to the ordinances of the holy fathers, he shall be suspended from office. For it is fitting that, as he received his bishopric for nothing, he should also distribute the offices of that bishopric without receiving payment.

5. We pronounce null and void all those appointments which are influenced by bribes or entreaties or by offering obedience to anyone, and those appointments which are not carried out according to the canon laws with the common consent of clergy and people and are not approved by those to whom consecration belongs. For those who are so appointed do not enter by the door, that is, through Christ, but, as the Truth itself bears witness, break in like thieves and robbers.[1]

.   .   .   .

7. By the apostolic authority we forbid laymen to possess tithes, which are shown by canonical authority to have been granted for religious uses. No matter from whom they received them, even bishops or kings, let them know that, unless they return them to the Church, they are committing the crime of sacrilege and running the risk of eternal damnation.

.   .   .   .

11. If anyone misappropriates the estates of St. Peter, the Prince of Apostles, in any place or fails to reveal them when he knows of their existence, or fails to render to St. Peter the service which is due on their account, let him know that he is incurring the wrath of God and the holy apostles for his sacrilege. Whoever is detected in this crime must lawfully restore this patrimony of St. Peter and pay a fourfold penalty out of his own property.

12. If any bishop be persuaded by bribes or entreaties to connive at fornication on the part of priests, deacons or subdeacons, or at the crime of incest being committed within his diocese, or fail to attack this with his official authority when he has sure knowledge that it has been committed, he shall be suspended from his office.

1. John, x, 1.

GREGORY VII TO HERMANN OF METZ

§ 14. The second of Gregory VII's letters to Hermann, Bishop of Metz, elaborates and develops to the full some of the principles already stated in the *Dictatus Papae* (see above, Part III, no. 9). It was designed to rally Gregory's partisans in Germany by affirming the power of the Apostolic See to excommunicate Henry IV and by asserting the superiority of clerical to lay power in general. It illustrates the use made by Gregory, not only of biblical arguments, but also of historical precedent and of the canon law. The theory of the origins of kingship contained in this letter has been much discussed.

See Fliche, *La réforme grégorienne*, II, 389 foll.; Voosen, *Papauté et pouvoir civil*, 158 foll., 243 foll.; C. H. McIlwain, *The growth of political thought in the west* (New York, 1932), 206 foll.; Fliche in Fliche-Martin, *Histoire de l'Église*, VIII, 179 foll.

§ 14

The letter of Gregory VII to Hermann, Bishop of Metz, March 15th 1081: *Das Register Gregors VII*, ed. E. Caspar (Berlin, 1920–1923), II, 546–62.

Bishop Gregory, servant of the servants of God, to his beloved brother in Christ Hermann, Bishop of Metz, greeting and the apostolic blessing.

We hear that you are ready to undergo both trouble and danger for the defence of the truth, and we have no doubt that this is a gift of God. For in his ineffable grace and marvellous compassion he never allows his chosen ones to fall profoundly into error, to be shaken to the roots or to be overthrown: rather he makes them stronger than before, after he has subjected them to some useful test at a time of persecution, and even after they have fallen into some confusion.[1] Among the feeble, fear drives one man to fly more disgracefully than his fellows, and likewise, among the strong, a manly heart inspires one to act more bravely than another, to move forward with greater ardour: and so we are anxious to exhort you to rejoice in being among the leaders of the army of the Christian religion the more fervently for your certain knowledge that these are the men closest to the victor, God, and the most deserving.

1. This may refer to the fact that Hermann was one of the bishops who, at the Council of Worms, had declared Gregory VII deposed.

You have asked to be aided and fortified, as it were, by writings of
ours against the frenzy of those who wickedly babble that the authority
of the holy and Apostolic See could not excommunicate King Henry, a
man who defied the law of Christ, ruined churches and Empire and
made and sided with heretics, and that it could not absolve anyone
from an oath of fealty to him. It seems unnecessary for us to write anything because so many perfectly clear examples of this can be found in
the pages of the Holy Scriptures. We do not think that those who, to
their own damnation, are shamelessly detracting from and contradicting
the truth have, in their ignorance or in the wretched frenzy of their
desperation, enlisted these examples in their defence. There is nothing
surprising in their behaviour, since it is usual with the rejected to strive
to defend others like themselves for the protection of their own
iniquity, for they think nothing of getting themselves damned for
their lies.

To select a few of the many points: everybody knows the words of
our Lord and Saviour Jesus Christ, who says in the Gospel: 'You are
Peter and upon this rock I will build my church, and the gates of hell
shall not prevail against it; and I will give you the keys of the kingdom
of heaven; and whatsoever you shall bind on earth shall be bound in
heaven also, and whatsoever you shall loose on earth shall be loosed in
heaven also.'[1] Are kings excepted here, and are they not among the
sheep which the son of God entrusted to St. Peter?[2] Who, I ask, thinks
that he is exempted from the power conferred on Peter by this universal grant of binding and loosing, save perhaps the unhappy wretch
who will not carry the yoke of the Lord, but takes up the Devil's
burden, and refuses to be numbered among the sheep of Christ? By
shaking off from his proud neck the power divinely granted to St.
Peter, he gains no liberty, however wretched: for the more a man
refuses out of pride to bear this yoke, the heavier the burden that he
carries to his own damnation at the Day of Judgment.

The holy fathers have with great reverence accepted and supported
this institution of the will of God, this mainstay of the government of
the Church, this privilege conferred at the beginning by heavenly
decree on St. Peter the Chief of the Apostles and so ratified; and in
General Councils and in other acts and writings they have called the
holy Roman church the Universal Mother. They have accepted its
teachings in support of the faith and in exposition of the holy religion
and likewise its judgments, agreeing, as with one spirit and one voice,

1. Matthew, xvi, 18–19.   2. John, xxi, 17.

that all the more important matters and affairs of great moment and the judgments pronounced by all churches ought to be referred to it as the mother and the head; that there is no appeal from it; and that its judgments cannot and must not be retracted or rebutted by anyone. Hence St. Gelasius the Pope, supported by divine authority, writing to the Emperor Anastasius, instructed him as follows how and what he ought to think concerning the primacy of the holy and Apostolic See: 'If it is appropriate for the faithful to submit to all priests in general who rightly deal with things divine, then how much more must they give support to the bishop of this see, who, even by the supreme divine will, was to surpass all other priests, and whom the Church has obediently honoured with universal loyalty. Hence you in your wisdom may clearly observe that no one by any human measure can make himself so privileged or so widely acknowledged as the one whom the words of Christ have set before all, and whom the venerable Church recognizes and has always devoutly proclaimed as primate.'[1] Again, Pope Julius, writing to the eastern bishops, says, concerning the power of the holy and Apostolic See: 'Brothers, you should have spoken of the holy Roman and apostolic church with courtesy and not with derision, since our Lord Jesus Christ himself fittingly addressed it and said: "You are Peter, and upon this rock I will build my church, and the gates of hell shall not prevail against it; and I will give you the keys of the kingdom of heaven." For it has the power granted by unique privilege to open and close the gates of the kingdom of heaven to anyone it pleases.'[2] And if a man is given power to open and close heaven, is it unlawful for him to judge the things of the earth? Far from it. Do you remember what the most blessed apostle Paul says: 'Do you not know that we shall judge angels? How much more, then, things of this life!'[3] And St. Gregory the Pope ordains that kings who presume to infringe the decrees of the Apostolic See shall fall from their office and writes in these words to a certain Senator, an abbot: 'If anyone, be he king, priest, judge or other lay person, is aware of the existence of this our charter but tries to contravene it, he shall lose his power and honour and know that he is answerable at the judgment of God for the wicked act he has committed; and unless he restores the things which he has evilly taken away, and shows remorse for his unlawful acts by a fitting penance, then he shall be set apart from the most holy body and blood

---

1. See above, Part II, no. 1A.
2. *Decretales Pseudo-Isidorianae*, ed. P. Hinschius (Leipzig, 1863), 464.
3. 1 Corinthians, vi, 3.

of our Lord and Redeemer Jesus Christ and be liable to severe punishment at the eternal judgment.'[1]

Now if St. Gregory, that most gentle doctor, decreed that kings who violated his statutes concerning one single hospice were not only deposed but also excommunicate and damned at the eternal judgment, then who—save, perhaps, somebody like Henry—will blame us for deposing and excommunicating him? He not only defies the apostolic judgments, but also does his utmost to trample on the mother church and most impiously and wickedly to plunder and destroy all his Kingdom and its churches. We have learnt this from St. Peter in his letter about the ordination of Clement, in which he says: 'If anyone befriends those to whom he'—that is, Clement,—'will not speak, then he himself makes one of those who want to destroy the Church of God; and though he seem to be with us in the body, he is against us in mind and soul, and is a much more formidable enemy than those who are outside and are openly hostile. For he commits his hostilities under cover of friendship and so disperses and ruins the Church.'[2] Note then, dearest brother: if St. Peter judges so severely one who merely befriends or converses with persons from whom the Pope is estranged on account of their deeds, then how harshly will he condemn the actual man from whom he is estranged because of his deeds!

But to return to the point. Shall not the office created by laymen, even by those who knew not God, be subjected to the office created to his own honour by the providence of God Almighty and mercifully given to the world? The son of God, just as he is firmly believed to be God and man, is likewise recognized as supreme priest, head of all priests, sitting at the right hand of the Father and always interceding for us.[3] He scorned a worldly kingdom, the pride of the sons of the world, and of his own free will came to the priesthood of the Cross. Who does not know that kings and dukes originated from those who, being ignorant of God, strove with blind greed and insufferable presumption to dominate their equals, that is their fellow men, by pride, violence, treachery, murder and almost every other crime at the instigation of the Prince of the World, that is, the Devil? And when they try to force the priests of the Lord to follow them, can kings not best be compared to him who is head over all the children of pride?[4] The Devil, tempting the Supreme Bishop, the head of priests, the son of the most high, and

---

1. Ed. L. M. Hartmann in M.G.H., Epp., II, 376–8.
2. *Decretales Pseudo-Isidorianae*, ed. cit., 36.
3. Romans, viii, 34.   4. Job, xli, 25.

promising him all the kingdoms of the world, said to him: 'I will give
you all these, if you fall down and worship me'.[1] Who doubts that the
priests of Christ are held to be the fathers and teachers of kings and
princes and of all the faithful? Is it not wretchedly foolish for a son to
try to subject a father, or a pupil his teacher, to himself, and to put him
in his power by imposing sinful undertakings upon him, when he
believes that he can be bound and loosed by him not only on earth but
in heaven also? As St. Gregory reminds us in the letter he addressed to
the Emperor Maurice, the Emperor Constantine the Great, lord of all
kings and princes in almost all the world, clearly realized this, and, at
the holy Council of Nicea, took his seat below all the bishops and would
not presume to pronounce any judgment upon them. Rather he called
them gods, and decreed that they were not subject to his jurisdiction,
but that he had to follow their decision.[2] And Pope Gelasius, when
persuading the Emperor Anastasius not to be offended at having the
truth conveyed to him, added that: 'There are two powers, august
Emperor, by which this world is ruled from the beginning: the consecrated authority of the bishops, and the royal power. In these matters
the priests bear the heavier burden because they will render account,
even for rulers of men, at the divine judgment'; and, after a few other
things, he goes on to say: 'You know that in these matters you must
follow their judgment without wanting to subject them to your will.'[3]

Fortified by such precepts and authorities, many of the bishops have
excommunicated kings or Emperors. If we need some specific example
involving the person of a prince, St. Innocent the Pope excommunicated the Emperor Arcadius, because he had consented to the expulsion
of St. John Chrysostom from his diocese.[4] Another Bishop of Rome
deprived a King of the Franks of his kingdom, not for his sins, but because he was unfit to wield such power, and put Pippin, father of the
Emperor Charles the Great, in his place, and absolved all the Franks
from the oath of fealty which they had taken to the deposed King.[5] The
holy Church often uses its authority to do this, when it absolves
vassals from the oaths they have taken to bishops who are being deprived of pontifical rank by apostolic authority. And St. Ambrose
(who, although he was a saint, was not Bishop of the Universal
Church) excommunicated the Emperor Theodosius the Great and

---

1. Matthew, iv, 9.   2. Ed. P. Ewald in M.G.H., Epp., I (1891), 318.
3. See above, Part II, no. 1A.   4. Pope Innocent I in 404—Migne, P.L., 20, 629-32.
5. For the deposition of King Childeric III on the authority of Pope Zachary, *circa* 750,
see above, Part I, no. 2.

thrust him out of the Church for a fault which did not seem so grave to other priests. And in his writings Ambrose shows that the priestly office is even more superior to the royal power than gold is to silver, for he writes at the beginning of his book on pastoral duties: 'Brothers, the honour and exalted dignity of a bishop is quite beyond any comparison. If you compare it with the splendour of kings or the diadems of princes, this will be far feebler than comparing the base metal, lead, with the splendour of gold—for you see the heads of kings and princes bowed below the knees of priests, and they think that if they kiss their right hands they can take part in their prayers'; and a little later: 'Brothers, you must know that we have set all these things down so as to show that nothing is found in this world more excellent than priests or more exalted than bishops'.[1]

You ought to remember, brother, that greater power is granted to an exorcist, when he is appointed a spiritual Emperor to cast out demons, than can ever be assigned to any layman for the purpose of worldly dominion. For, alas! demons rule all the kings and princes of the earth who do not lead a Christian and godfearing life as they should, and they oppress them with miserable enslavement. For such men do not want authority for the honour of God and the welfare of souls, like Christian priests, who are led on by the love of God: these men strive to dominate others in order to flaunt their insufferable pride, and fulfil the wanton desires in their minds. Of them St. Augustine says in his first book on Christian doctrine: 'If anyone strives to dominate those who are his natural equals, that is, his fellow men, it is insufferable pride.'[2] Moreover, exorcists, as we said, hold of God an Empire over demons—how much more then, over those who are subject to demons and limbs of Satan! If mere exorcists are above them, then how much more are priests above them!

Moreover, every Christian king, when he comes to the end of his life, must beg like a poor wretch for the help of a priest, that he may escape from the dungeon of hell, may struggle from darkness to light and may appear at the judgment of God released from the chains of his sins. And who,—even among laymen, let alone among priests,—who, being on the point of death, has ever begged for the assistance of an earthly king for the salvation of his soul? What king or Emperor can, by virtue of the office he is charged with, snatch any Christian by holy baptism away from the power of the Devil, number him among the

1. Ambrose, *De dignitate sacerdotali*, ch. 2, in Migne, P.L., 17, 569–70.
2. Augustine, *De doctrina christiana*, ch. 23, in Migne, P.L., 34, 27.

sons of God and protect him by holy anointing? And—for this is the greatest thing in the Christian religion—which of them can with his own mouth make the body and blood of the Lord? To which of them is given the power of binding and loosing in heaven and on earth? From this we can clearly deduce how much greater is the power of the priestly office. What king or Emperor can ordain any clerk in the holy Church, let alone depose him for any offence? For, in ecclesiastical orders, greater power is needed to depose than to ordain. For bishops can ordain other bishops, but in no way can they depose them without the authority of the Apostolic See. Little intelligence, then, is needed to understand that priests have precedence over kings. And if kings ought to be judged by priests for their sins, then who is more entitled to judge them than is the Bishop of Rome?

All in all, good Christians deserve the title of King much more than do bad princes. For good Christians vigorously rule themselves, by seeking the glory of God, but bad princes, being their own worst enemies, tyrannically oppress others, seeking their own and not the things that are God's:[1] the first are the body of the true King, Christ;[2] the second, the body of the Devil. The first govern themselves that they may eternally reign with the supreme Emperor; but the power of the second leads to their being consumed in everlasting damnation with the Prince of Darkness, who is King over all the sons of pride.[3]

There is no wonder that bad bishops should side with a wicked king, whom they love and fear for the honours they have evilly gained through him—no wonder that they should sell God at a low price by simoniacally ordaining anybody they like. For just as the chosen are indissolubly united to their head, so also are the rejected lastingly leagued with him who is the head of all evil, especially against the good. But we should not rail against the wicked: rather should we groan, weep and lament for them, that Almighty God may snatch them from the traps in which Satan holds them prisoner,[4] and may at last lead them through the dangers to a knowledge of the truth.

So much for kings and Emperors who, puffed up with worldly glory, reign, not for God, but for themselves. But because it is our duty to give advice to everyone according to the rank or office in which he functions, we are concerned, with God's help, to provide Emperors, kings and other princes with the weapons of humility, so that they can hold back the billows of their pride which surge like the sea. For we know that men in authority are particularly liable to be filled with

1. Philippians, ii, 21.   2. 1 Corinthians, xii, 27.   3. Job, xli, 25.   4. 2 Timothy, ii, 26.

pride by worldly glory and worldly preoccupations, so that, seeking their own glory, and always forgetting to be humble, they wish to out-do their brothers. It would benefit Emperors and kings especially if, when their souls aspire to great heights and to the pursuit of unparal-leled glory, they found some means of humbling themselves and realized that what gave them joy was rather to be feared. They should carefully consider how dangerous and how fearful are the imperial and royal office, of which very few holders are saved, and those who by God's mercy do attain salvation are not glorified in the holy Church by the decision of the Holy Spirit as much as are many of the poor. In all authentic writings, from the beginning of the world down to our own times, we cannot find even as many as seven Emperors or kings whose lives were as remarkable for their Christianity or as resplendent with miracles as those of the countless mass of men who have despised the world—although we believe that more than seven of them did find salvation by the mercy of Almighty God. For what Emperor or king was famous for miracles like St. Martin, St. Antony or St. Benedict (to say nothing of the apostles and martyrs)? What Emperor or king ever raised the dead, cleansed the leprous or gave sight to the blind? The holy Church praises and venerates the Emperor Constantine of holy memory and Theodosius and Honorius, Charles and Louis as lovers of justice, propagators of the Christian religion and defenders of churches; but it does not say that they were so resplendent with glorious miracles. How often has the holy Church decreed that churches or altars should be dedicated to the names of kings and Emperors, or that Masses should be celebrated in their honour? Kings and other princes ought to be afraid lest their delight in being set above other men in this life should result in their being plunged the more deeply into everlasting fire. Hence it is written: 'The mighty shall suffer mighty torments.'[1] For they shall render account to God for all men whom they have had subject to their government. As even an ordinary Christian has no little trouble in guarding his one soul, immense is the toil that awaits those who are chiefs over many thousands of souls. Moreover, if the judgment of the holy Church severely punishes the sinner for killing even one man, then what will happen to those who have delivered many thousands to death for the sake of honour in this world? They may verbally accept the blame for the slaughter of many, but still they rejoice in their hearts at this enhancement of their so-called honour, and would not have what they did undone and feel no

1. Wisdom of Solomon, vi, 7.

grief at having driven their brothers into Hades. And if they do not repent with their whole heart, and will not forego the things acquired or retained by human bloodshed, their repentance cannot in the sight of God bear its proper fruit. Hence the terrible fact, which they must repeatedly recall, that, as we said before, since the beginning of the world very few kings out of the innumerable mass of them in the various kingdoms of the earth have been found to. be saints: whereas in one single bishopric, that is the Roman, since the time of St. Peter the apostle, fully one hundred in the continuous succession of bishops have been numbered among the most holy. The reason for this is that the kings and princes of the earth, seduced (as aforesaid) by vain-glory, put their own interests before things spiritual, whilst Christian bishops despise empty glory and put the things that are God's before all things of the flesh. Kings and princes readily punish those who offend against them, but are indifferent to men who sin against God; but the bishops quickly forgive those who sin against them, and do not lightly spare offenders against God. Kings and princes, too much devoted to worldly activities, set little value on the spiritual; but bishops, assiduously thinking of heaven, despise all earthly things.

Therefore all Christians who wish to reign with Christ must be admonished not to try to reign with an ambition for worldly power. They should rather keep in mind the admonition of the most holy Pope St. Gregory, in his book of pastoral duties, that 'We must maintain and follow the principle that even a virtuous man should come to rule only if he is forced, whilst one who lacks virtue should not do so, even under pressure.'[1] Now, if the Godfearing come very timidly and only under pressure even to the Apostolic See, in which those who are correctly ordained are made better by the merits of St. Peter the apostle, then with what fear and trembling should one accede to a royal throne, on which even good and humble men deteriorate—as witness the example of Saul and David! For what we have said about the Apostolic See is contained in the decrees of St. Symmachus the Pope, though we may know it by our own experience: 'He,'—that is, St. Peter,—'has transmitted to his successors a perpetual endowment of merits with a patrimony of innocence'; and, a little later: 'Who doubts the sanctity of one who is raised up by so high an office? For if his own merits are not adequate, his predecessor in this place will lend him a sufficient quantity. For St. Peter either raises to these heights men who are already famous, or else he himself glorifies those who are so promoted.'[2]

1. Gregory, *Liber regulae pastoralis*, I, ch. 9, in Migne, P.L., 77, 22.
2. *Decretales Pseudo-Isidorianae*, ed. cit., 666.

Hence those whom the holy Church of its own free will upon mature deliberation summons to government or Empire, not for passing glory, but for the salvation of many, should humbly obey and always bear in mind what St. Gregory says in the same book of pastoral duties: 'A man who scorns to be like his fellows becomes like a rebel angel. Thus did Saul become swollen with pride at the height of his power, when once he had had the merit of humility. For humility he was promoted and for pride rejected, as the Lord bore witness when he said: "Did I not appoint you head over the tribes of Israel because you were little in your own eyes?" ';[1] and a little further on: 'Strange to say, Saul seemed great to the Lord when he was little to himself; but when he seemed great to himself, he was little to the Lord.'[2] Let kings take care to remember what the Lord says in the Gospel: 'I seek not my own glory',[3] and 'The man who wants to be first among you shall be the servant of all'.[4] Let them always put God's honour before their own; let them maintain and defend justice by preserving to each man his rights; let them not walk in the counsels of the ungodly,[5] but always be willing to associate with Christian men. Let them not try to subject the holy Church to themselves like a servant girl; let them rather strive to give due honour above all to the eyes of the Church, that is, the priests of the Lord, by acknowledging them as teachers and fathers. For if we are ordered to honour our fathers and mothers in the flesh,[6] then how much more must we honour our spiritual fathers? And if he who curses his carnal father or mother must pay the penalty of death,[7] then what punishment does he deserve who curses his spiritual father or mother? Let carnal love not seduce them into putting their own sons in charge of the flock for which Christ shed his blood, if they can find others who are better and more useful than they, lest by loving a son more than God they inflict the greatest harm upon the holy Church. For clearly one who fails to provide as best he can for something which so vitally affects the interests of the holy Church is proved guilty of not loving God and his neighbour as behoves a Christian. For if a man neglects this virtue, love, then no good act he does will bring him salvation. Those who humbly do these things and continue to love God and their neighbour as they should may count on the mercy of him who says: 'Learn from me, for I am gentle and humble of heart'.[8] If they

---

1. 1 Kings, xv, 17.   2. Gregory, *Liber Regulae Pastoralis*, II, ch. 6, Migne, P.L., 77, 35.
3. John, viii, 50.   4. Mark, x, 44.   5. Psalms, i, 1.
6. Deuteronomy, v, 16.   7. Exodus, xxi, 17.   8. Matthew, xi, 29.

humbly imitate him, then they shall cross over from the passing realm of slavery to the eternal kingdom of true freedom.

Given on the fifteenth of March.

THE PEACE OF WORMS, 1122

§ 15. The Peace of Worms, a Concordat between the Emperor Henry V and Pope Calixtus II, was an important if by no means completely satisfactory attempt to end the disputes between Emperor and Pope, in so far as they were concerned with the question of lay investiture. In this compromise solution the parties tried to distinguish the material aspects of a church from the spiritual.

See Scharnagl, *Der Begriff der Investitur*, 122 foll.; Thompson, *Feudal Germany*, 145 foll.; Mitteis, 'German Feudalism', in Barraclough, ed. *Mediaeval Germany*, II, 242–4; Brooke, 'Lay investiture'; Fliche in Fliche-Martin, *Histoire de l'Église*, VIII, 376 foll., with a bibliography of German works; Barraclough, *Origins of modern Germany*, 129 foll.; on the question of the *regalia* mentioned in the Concordat, I. Ott, 'Der Regalienbegriff im 12 Jahrhundert', Z.S.S.R., k.a., 35 (1948); Ullmann, *Growth of papal government*, 407 foll.

§ 15

The Peace of Worms between the Emperor Henry V and Pope Calixtus II, September 23rd, 1122: ed. L. Weiland in M.G.H., Const., I (1893), 159–161.

The Emperor's Privilege.

In the name of the holy and indivisible Trinity, I, Henry, by the grace of God Emperor Augustus of the Romans, for the love of God and the holy church of Rome and the lord Pope Calixtus, and for the health of my soul, renounce to God and to Peter and Paul his holy apostles and to the holy catholic Church all investiture by ring and staff, and I grant that in all churches in my Kingdom and Empire there may be canonical election and free consecration.

2. I restore to the holy church of Rome all the property and *regalia* of St. Peter which have been removed from it from the beginning of this dispute to the present day, whether in my father's time or in my own,

and which I now have in my possession; and I will loyally help to restore those which are not in my possession.

3. I will on the advice of the princes and according to justice restore all the property of all other churches, of the princes and of other persons, both clergy and laity, which has been lost in the late war and which I now have in my possession; and I will loyally help to restore anything not in my possession.

4. I give true peace to the lord Pope Calixtus and the holy church of Rome and to all who are or have been on its side.

5. I will loyally assist the holy church of Rome whenever it asks for aid; and whenever it makes a complaint to me, I will render to it its due.

All these things are done with the advice and consent of the princes whose names are written below:

Adelbert, Archbishop of Mainz; Frederick, Archbishop of Cologne; Hartwig, Bishop of Ratisbon; Otto, Bishop of Bamberg; Bruno, Bishop of Spires; Hermann, Bishop of Augsburg; Godebald, Bishop of Utrecht; Odalric, Bishop of Constance; Erlholf, Abbot of Fulda; Duke Henry; Duke Frederick; Duke Simon; Duke Pertolf; Margrave Theobald; Margrave Engelbert; Godfrey, Count Palatine; Otto, Count Palatine; Count Berengar.[1]

I, Frederick, Archbishop of Cologne and Arch-chancellor, have witnessed this.

The Pope's Privilege.

I, Bishop Calixtus, servant of the servants of God, grant to you, my beloved son Henry, by the grace of God Emperor Augustus of the Romans, that elections of bishops and abbots of and belonging to the Kingdom of Germany may take place in your presence so long as there is no simony or violence; and if any dispute arises between parties, you shall, following the advice and decision of the metropolitan and other bishops of the province, lend aid and support to the sounder party. The chosen candidate shall receive the *regalia* from you by the sceptre and he shall perform the service he owes you by law on account of them.

2. In the other parts of the Empire the entrant shall receive the *regalia* from you by the sceptre within six months of being consecrated and shall perform the service he owes you by law on account of them.

---

1. i.e. Henry VIII, Duke of Bavaria; Frederick II, Duke of Swabia; Simon I, Duke of Upper Lotharingia; Theobald, Margrave of Vohburg; Engelbert I, Margrave of Istria; Godfrey of Swabia, Count Palatine of Lotharingia; Otto I of Wittelsbach, Count Palatine of Bavaria; Berengar of Sulzbach, Count of Bavaria.

Nothing known to belong to the church of Rome shall be included therein.

3. I will lend you aid as my office requires whenever you complain to me and ask for assistance.

4. I give true peace to you and to all who are or have been on your side at the time of the late dispute.

CHAPTER III

The Reign of Frederick I

§ 16. This document embodies an important concession made by Frederick I to Henry the Lion, Duke of Bavaria and Saxony. It helped to increase Henry's power within the dominion he was building up by his conquests of the Slav lands to the north-east of Germany. Since the accession of Lothar of Supplinburg to the Duchy of Saxony in 1106, a series of military campaigns with clerical collaboration had been launched against Wendish territory. In 1147, Henry the Lion had attacked Mecklenburg and Pomerania. His ambitions had collided with those of Hartwig, Archbishop of Bremen, who had appointed his candidate to the long-vacant sees of Oldenburg and Mecklenburg without reference to Henry. In 1154, Frederick sided with Henry the Lion.

According to Giesebrecht, the document issued in 1154 was not completed by Frederick's signature. It was more in the nature of a promise, which was only carried into effect at a more suitable time, in 1160.

See W. von Giesebrecht, *Geschichte der deutschen Kaiserzeit*, V (Brunswick, 1880), 36, 353; A. Hauck, *Kirchengeschichte Deutschlands*, IV (Leipzig, 1913), 210; A. L. Poole in C.M.H., V (1926), 353–6, 397–400; Thompson, *Feudal Germany*, Part II, on the general question of eastern colonization; A. Brackmann, 'The national state', in Barraclough, ed. *Mediaeval Germany*, II, 294–7; Barraclough, *Origins of modern Germany*, 176, 186–7, and 258 foll. on eastern colonization; W. Ullmann, 'Reflections on the mediaeval Empire', T.R.H.S. (1964).

§ 16

Privilege granted by Frederick I to Henry the Lion and his successors, drawn up at Goslar, 1154: ed. L. Weiland in M.G.H., Const., I (1893), 206–7.

In the name of the holy and indivisible Trinity. Frederick, by the gracious favour of God King of the Romans.

As we have by the grace of God risen to the supreme office of King, it is fitting that we should widen and extend the fame, honour and worship of him from whom all power derives, so that all things may minister to his glory, even as all things are derived from his grace.

Therefore let all men present and future know how we have commanded our beloved Henry, Duke of Saxony, to found, establish and build in the province beyond the Elbe which he holds by our generosity bishoprics and churches to extend the Empire of Christendom. We have also granted him freedom to endow these churches out of the property of the realm, in accordance with his own wishes and with the extent of the lands. That he may attend more earnestly and faithfully to this matter, we grant to him and to all who shall succeed him in this province the investiture of the three bishoprics of Oldenburg, Mecklenburg and Ratzeburg, so that anyone who is to be promoted to a bishopric there may receive what belongs to the King in it from Henry's hands as if they were ours. We further add that if he can by his own efforts establish bishoprics in the surrounding provinces in which the Christian religion is not yet observed, he may wield the same power therein.

That the authority of this our grant may stand firm and unshaken throughout all future ages, we have confirmed this charter with our own hand, as appears below, and have ordered our seal to be placed upon it.

These things were done with the assent of the following princes of the realm: Wichmann, Archbishop of Magdeburg; Bruno, Bishop of Hildesheim; Hermann, Bishop of Verden; Wicher, Bishop of Brandenburg; Bertold, Bishop-elect of Zeitz; Wicbald, Abbot of Corvey; Margrave Conrad; Margrave Albert; the Count Palatine Frederick; the Landgrave Ludwig.[1]

THE ESTABLISHMENT OF THE DUCHY OF AUSTRIA

§ 17. These documents further illustrate the relationship between Frederick I and the greater princes of Germany, whose powers he was prepared to increase on the strict understanding that they were recog-

1. i.e. Conrad of Wettin, Margrave of Meissen; Albert the Bear, Margrave of Brandenburg; Frederick VI, Count Palatine of Saxony; Ludwig II, Landgrave of Thuringia.

nized as deriving from him. On his accession it was essential for Frederick to win the support of his cousin, Henry the Lion of the house of Welf. Henry was claiming the Duchy of Bavaria from his stepfather, Henry Jasomirgott of the house of Babenberg, uncle to Frederick. In 1152–1154, Jasomirgott had refused to answer summonses to Frederick's court and been formally deprived of the Duchy. But it was in practice impossible to eject him without compensation. The account by Otto of Freising of the Diet at Ratisbon in 1156 and the text of the *Privilegium Minus* show how this was achieved, and how extensive powers were formally conceded to the new Duke of Austria. Austria was once more detached from Bavaria—the two had been united under Leopold IV, half-brother of King Conrad III, in 1139.

The *Privilegium Minus* is so called to distinguish it from a later forgery, the *Privilegium Maius*, issued by Rudolf IV, 'Archduke Palatine' of Austria (1358–1365), and claiming even greater powers for the Duke. The authenticity of the *Privilegium Minus* has also been questioned, though not conclusively.

See W. Levison, 'Otto von Freising und das Privileg Friedrichs I für das Herzogtum Oesterreich', N.A., 34 (1909); Barraclough in Barraclough, ed. *Mediaeval Germany*, I, 104 foll.; T. Mayer, 'The state of the Dukes of Zähringen', ibid., II, 194, 198–9; Mitteis, 'German feudalism', ibid., II, 247–8, with references to German literature on the *Privilegium Minus*; A. W. A. Leeper, *A history of mediaeval Austria* (Oxford, 1941), 252 foll.; K. J. Heilig, 'Ostrom und das deutsche Reich um die Mitte des 12 Jahrhunderts', in T. Mayer, K. J. Heilig and C. Erdmann, *Kaisertum und Herzogsgewalt im Zeitalter Friedrichs I* (Leipzig, 1944); T. Mayer, 'Friedrich I und Heinrich der Löwe', ibid., 419 foll.; Barraclough, *Origins of modern Germany*, 175–6; K. Hampe, *Deutsche Kaisergeschichte in der Zeit der Salier und Staufer* (Leipzig, 1949), 147 foll.

§ 17

A. The establishment of the Duchy of Austria: Otto of Freising, *Gesta Friderici I Imperatoris*, Bk. II, ch. 55, ed. G. Waitz and B. von Simson (Hanover-Leipzig, 1912), 160–1.

As it was now the middle of September, princes assembled at Ratisbon and for some days awaited the arrival of the Emperor.

Then the Emperor met his uncle on the field—for Henry Jasomirgott was encamped in tents near by, two German miles away—and all the great lords and magnates joined them. Then the scheme which had long been kept secret was made public. This, as I recall, was the essence of the agreement. The elder Henry [Henry Jasomirgott] resigned the Duchy of Bavaria to the Emperor by means of seven banners. These were handed to the younger Henry, and he with two banners restored the Eastern Marches and the counties belonging to them of old. Then, by the decision of the princes, the Emperor made the Marches into a Duchy, together with these counties, which they call the Three Counties; and he conferred it by two banners, not only on Henry [Jasomirgott] himself, but on his wife also. He confirmed this with his privilege so that none of his successors could violate or change it. These things were done in his fifth year as King and second as Emperor.

B. The establishment of the Duchy of Austria: the *Privilegium minus*, issued by Frederick I at Ratisbon, September 17th, 1156: ed. W. Erben in his *Das Privilegium Friedrich I für das Herzogtum Österreich* (Vienna, 1902), 137–40; previously ed. L. Weiland, M.G.H., Const., I, 221–3.

In the name of the holy and indivisible Trinity. Frederick, by the gracious favour of God Emperor Augustus of the Romans.

Our imperial authority must step in to ensure that there can be no doubt about what has been enacted here, even though a physical act of exchange can suffice to make an exchange valid, and even though acts lawfully performed cannot be undone by any form of opposition.

Therefore let the present and all future generations of all loyal subjects of Christ and our Empire know that, supported by the favour of him who sent peace from heaven to men upon earth, at a general court held at Ratisbon at the Nativity of the Virgin, in the presence of many Christian and catholic princes, we resolved the dispute and controversy over the Duchy of Bavaria which had long raged between our most beloved uncle Henry, Duke of Austria, and our dearest nephew Henry, Duke of Saxony, in this wise: the Duke of Austria resigned to us the Duchy of Bavaria, which we immediately granted as a benefice to the Duke of Saxony, whilst the Duke of Bavaria resigned to us the March of Austria with all his rights in it and with all the benefices which the late Margrave Leopold used to hold of the Duchy of Bavaria.

Lest in this transaction the honour and glory of our most beloved uncle should appear to be diminished in any way, on the advice and decision of the princes, with Ladislaus, the illustrious Duke of Bohemia, publishing the sentence and all the princes approving it, we have converted the March of Austria into a Duchy and have granted this Duchy with all its rights as a benefice to our uncle Henry and his most noble wife Theodora. We ordain, by a law to be valid forever, that they and their children after them, whether male or female, may have the said Duchy of Austria and hold it of the realm with a hereditary right therein. But if our aforesaid uncle the Duke of Austria and his wife die without children, they will be free to bequeath this Duchy to anyone they wish.

We further decree that no person, great or small, may presume to exercise any jurisdiction within the dominion of the Duchy without the consent or permission of the Duke.

The Duke of Austria shall not for his Duchy be obliged to perform any service to the Empire other than that of answering the summons to courts which the Emperor arranges in Bavaria. He need not join the imperial army, unless the Emperor has summoned one to enter kingdoms or provinces near to Austria.

That this our imperial law may stand firm and inviolate forever, we have ordered this charter to be drawn up and our seal to be placed upon it, having called in suitable witnesses, whose names are as follows: Pilgrim, Patriarch of Aquileia; Eberhard, Archbishop of Salzburg: Otto, Bishop of Freising; Conrad, Bishop of Passau; Eberhard, Bishop of Bamberg; Hartmann, Bishop of Brixen; Hartwig, Bishop of Ratisbon; [Albert], Bishop of Trent; the Lord Welf; Duke Conrad, the Emperor's brother; Frederick, son of King Conrad; Henry, Duke of Carinthia; Engelbert, Margrave of Istria; Albert, Margrave of Staden; the Margrave Diepold;[1] Hermann, Count Palatine of the Rhine; Otto, Count Palatine, and his brother Frederick; Geberhard, Count of Sulzbach; Rudolf, Count of Swinshud; Engelbert, Count of Halle; Geberhard, Count of Burghausen; the Count of Peutten; the Count of Pilsting and many more.

The seal of the lord Frederick, invincible Emperor of the Romans.

I, the Chancellor Rainald, have witnessed this in place of Arnold, Archbishop of Mainz and Arch-chancellor.

Given at Ratisbon on September 17th, indiction four, in the year of Our Lord's Incarnation 1156, in the reign of the lord Frederick, Emperor Augustus of the Romans; happily in Christ amen; in the fifth year of his reign as King and his second year as Emperor.

---

1. Diepold of Cham, Margrave of Vohburg.

THE FALL OF HENRY THE LION

§ 18. The Gelnhausen charter records the trial and downfall of the most formidable of the German dukes under Frederick Barbarossa, Henry the Lion, and the partition of his Duchy. The immediate occasion of the trial was a quarrel which arose out of the restoration of Ulrich, Bishop of Halberstadt, to his see under the terms of the peace treaty concluded by Frederick I and Pope Alexander III in 1177. The charter demonstrates the mechanism of a trial according to feudal and to customary law; it shows how the political map of Germany was changed by the dismemberment of the great Welf territories and the substitution for them of smaller duchies; and it suggests the existence of a recognized estate of princes in Germany.

See F. Güterbock, *Der Prozess Heinrichs des Löwen* (Berlin, 1909); J. Haller, 'Der Sturz Heinrichs des Löwen', A.U., 3 (1911); K. Hampe, 'Heinrichs des Löwen Sturz in politisch-historischer Beurteilung', H.Z., 109 (1912); H. Niese, 'Der Sturz Heinrichs des Löwen', H.Z., 112 (1914); R. Moeller, 'Die Neuordnung des Reichsfürstenstandes und der Prozess Heinrichs des Löwen', Z.S.S.R., g.a., 39 (1918); A. L. Poole in C.M.H., V (1926), 401 foll.; H. Mitteis, *Politische Prozesse des früheren Mittelalters in Deutschland und Frankreich* (Heidelberg, 1927), 48 foll.; Barraclough in Barraclough, ed. *Mediaeval Germany*, I, 76 foll., 102 foll., 110; O. von Dungern, 'Constitutional reorganization and reform under the Hohenstaufen', ibid., II, 229 foll.; Mitteis, 'German feudalism', ibid., II, 249 foll., 273–4, with further references; C. Erdmann, 'Der Prozess Heinrichs des Löwen', in Mayer *et al.*, *Kaisertum und Herzogsgewalt*, with bibliography; Barraclough, *Origins of modern Germany*, 188–90, with further references; E. E. Stengel, 'Zum Prozess Heinrichs des Löwen', in his *Abhandlungen und Untersuchungen zur mittelalterliche Geschichte* (Cologne, 1960).

§ 18

The Gelnhausen charter, 1180: ed. F. Güterbock in his *Die Gelnhäuser Urkunde und der Prozess Heinrichs des Löwen* (Hildesheim-Leipzig, 1920), 24–7; previously ed. L. Weiland, M.G.H., Const., I, 385–6.

In the name of the holy and indivisible Trinity. Frederick, by the gracious favour of God Emperor Augustus of the Romans.

Since human memory is fallible and cannot suffice for a mass of things, the divine Kings and Emperors our predecessors have deemed by their authority that things which long lapses of time once used to remove from men's knowledge should be noted down in writing.

Hence the whole body of loyal subjects of the Empire, both present and future, shall know how Henry, late Duke of Bavaria and Westphalia, had severely repressed the liberty of the churches of God and of the nobles of the Empire by seizing their property and diminishing their rights.

Hence, on the urgent complaint of the princes and of a great many noblemen, he was summoned before us, but scorned to present himself to Our Majesty; and for this contumacy was sentenced by the princes and by the Swabians of the same status as he to be outlawed by us; but still he did not cease to attack the churches of God and the rights and liberty of princes and nobles. For the injuries done to them, for his repeated disregard of us, and especially because he is manifestly guilty of high treason and has failed to appear when summoned to a hearing before us by three lawful edicts under feudal law and has sent no one to answer for him, he has been judged contumacious.

Hence he has been deprived of the Duchies of Bavaria and of Westphalia and Angaria and of all the benefices which he held of the Empire by the unanimous sentence of the princes in a solemn court held at Würzburg, and these have been added to our estates.

We, having deliberated with the princes, by their collective advice have divided in two the Duchy which is called that of Westphalia and Angaria; and, considering how our beloved Prince Philip, Archbishop of Cologne, has deserved the privilege of the Emperor's favour for furthering and upholding the honour of the Imperial Crown without hesitating to spend of his property or endanger his person, we have, by a lawful deed of gift and with imperial generosity, conferred a part of the Duchy upon the church of Cologne—that is, the part which used to extend into the Bishopric of Cologne and throughout the whole Bishopric of Paderborn, with all rights and jurisdiction therein, that is, with counties, advowsons, rights of protection [*conductus*], manors, messuages, benefices, servants, tenements and all things belonging to that Duchy. We asked for a decision from the princes as to whether this was lawful, and the sentence was pronounced and ratified by the collective approval of the princes and of all the court: and our beloved kinsman Duke Bernard, to whom we have granted the remainder of the Duchy, also gave his public consent, and we then with the imperial banner solemnly invested the aforesaid Archbishop Philip with the portion of the Duchy which was conferred upon his church.

We therefore confirm to the church of Cologne and our oft-mentioned Prince-Archbishop Philip and to all his successors this lawful donation and investiture by Our Majesty; and, wishing this to remain to them in every future age, by imperial decree we forbid anyone to be so foolhardy as to infringe or in any way violate it; and we confirm and authenticate this our decree by the present privilege sealed with the golden bull of our excellency, noting down the witnesses who were present at this act.

They were the following:

Arnold, Archbishop of Trier; Wichmann, Archbishop of Magdeburg; Conrad, Archbishop of Salzburg; Siegfried, Archbishop-elect of Bremen; Conrad, Bishop of Worms; Rudolf, Bishop of Liége; Bertram, Bishop of Metz; Arnold, Bishop of Osnabrück; Conrad, Abbot of Fulda; Adolf, Abbot of Hersfeld; Lothar, Provost of Bonn; Ludwig, Count Palatine of Saxony and Landgrave of Thuringia; Bernard, Duke of Westphalia and Angaria; Godfrey, Duke of Lorraine; Frederick, Duke of Swabia; Otto, Margrave of Brandenburg; Theoderic, Margrave of Lusatia; Dedo, Count of Groitzsch; Siegfried, Count of Orlamünde; Robert, Count of Nassau; Emicho, Count of Liningen; Engelbert, Count of Berg; Theoderic, Count of Hofstade; Gerard, Count of Nürburg; Henry, Count of Arnsberg; Hermann, Count of Ravensberg; Henry, Count of Cuijk; Wernher, Count of Witgenstein; Widikind of Waldeck; Frederick of Anfurde; Hartmann of Büdingen; Wernher of Boland; Conrad the Butler; Henry, Marshal of Bappenheim; Sibot of Groitzsch the Chamberlain and many others.

The signature of the lord Frederick, invincible Emperor of the Romans.

I, Godfrey, Chancellor of the Imperial Palace, have witnessed this in place of Christian, Archbishop of Mainz and Arch-chancellor of Germany.

These things were done in the year of the Lord's incarnation 1180, indiction thirteen, in the reign of the lord Frederick, invincible Emperor of the Romans, in his twenty-ninth year as King and twenty-sixth as Emperor; happily amen.

Given at a solemn court at Gelnhausen in the territory of Mainz on the thirteenth of April.

THE IMPERIALISM OF
FREDERICK I AND HIS ITALIAN POLICY

§§ 19–23. The following extracts are taken mainly from the chronicle of the reign of Frederick I compiled by Otto of Freising and his continuator Rahewin. They are included here to illustrate the methods by which Frederick I asserted his fiscal and administrative prerogatives and the independence of his Empire against both the Papacy and the increasingly powerful communes of northern Italy.

The chronicle was an 'official' history, though both authors recognized the desirability of being objective and Rahewin included original documents in his text (as in 20) in a conscious effort to be impartial. Otto, born about 1110 and Bishop of Freising from 1137 until his death in 1158, was maternal uncle to Frederick I. Rahewin, a canon of Freising, was at one time Otto's chaplain.

For general accounts of Frederick's imperialism and of his Italian policy, see G. von Below, *Die italienische Kaiserpolitik des deutschen Mittelalters* (H.Z. supplement 10, 1927); M. Bloch, 'L'empire et l'idée d'empire sous les Hohenstaufen', R.B.C.C., 30 (1928–1929); F. Kern, *Kingship and law in the middle ages* (Oxford, 1939), 65 foll.; H. Koeppler, 'Frederick Barbarossa and the Schools of Bologna', E.H.R., 54 (1939); Barraclough, *Origins of modern Germany*, 167 foll.; Folz, *L'idée d'empire*, 110 foll., with bibliography at 244–5; H. J. Kirfel, *Weltherrschaftsidee und Bündnispolitik: Untersuchungen zur auswärtigen Politik der Staufer* (Bonn, 1959), with bibliography.

A complete translation of the chronicle of Otto and Rahewin, with a bibliography, has been published as *The deeds of Frederick Barbarossa*, by C. C. Mierow and R. Emery (New York, 1953).

FREDERICK I AND THE IMPERIAL TITLE

§§ 19–20. These passages contain official theories of the origins of Frederick I's Empire, which he was determined to represent as independent of any grant made either by the people of Rome (19) or by the Pope (20).

In the 1140s, a vigorous communal movement, modelling itself on the ancient Roman republic, had sprung up in Rome, and the heresiarch Arnold of Brescia had associated himself with it. By the treaty of Constance, of March 1153, Frederick had undertaken to recover and defend the temporal power of which the Popes had been deprived by the commune, in exchange for which the then Pope (Eugenius IV) had agreed to crown him Emperor in Rome. When Frederick approached Rome in 1155, during the pontificate of Adrian IV, the Senate still hoped to reach an agreement with him, and demanded that he should recognize Rome as the source of his authority. Extract 19 consists of the speech which Otto attributed to Frederick in reply to a deputation from the city of Rome.

See G. W. Greenaway, *Arnold of Brescia* (Cambridge, 1931), 134 foll.; Folz, *L'idée d'empire*, 106 foll., 208–10.

The next group of extracts (20) records the dispute which arose out of Adrian IV's use of the ambiguous term *beneficium* to describe the imperial coronation, in a letter presented by the papal legates at the imperial Diet of Besançon in 1157. One of the legates involved was Rolando Bandinelli, the future Pope Alexander III. Eskil, Archbishop of Lund, the subject of the letter, had been returning from Rome, where he had had an important privilege confirmed. By this privilege, the Swedish bishoprics had been subordinated to Eskil, contrary to earlier concessions made by Innocent II to the German see of Hamburg-Bremen in 1133. After the papal legates had returned to Rome from Besançon, Adrian IV sent a letter to the German bishops asking them to persuade the Emperor to see reason. Extract 20B is taken from the letter in which the German bishops replied to Adrian, reporting what the Emperor had said in answer to them. They called this 'worthy of a Catholic prince'.

See E. Jordan, *L'Allemagne et l'Italie aux XIIe et XIIIe siècles* (1939), 57 foll.; W. Ullmann, 'Cardinal Roland and Besançon', M.H.P. (1954); W. Ullmann, 'The pontificate of Adrian IV', C.H.J., 11 (1955), with bibliography; M. Pacaut, *Alexandre III: étude sur la conception du pouvoir pontifical dans sa pensée et dans son œuvre* (1956), 79 foll.; M. Maccarrone, *Papato e impero dalla elezione di Federico I alla morte di Adriano IV (1152–1159)* (Rome, 1959), 132 foll., 159 foll.

On the theory of the two swords in general (see 20A) see the literature cited above, Part II, no. 9. For theories of the two swords, see also above, Part III, no. 10, and below, Part III, no. 35.

§ 19

Frederick I's speech on receiving an embassy from the people of Rome,

1155: Otto of Freising, *Gesta Friderici I Imperatoris*, Bk. II, ch. 30, ed. G. Waitz and B. von Simson (Hanover-Leipzig, 1912), 136–9.

'We have heard much about the wisdom and fortitude of the Romans; more, indeed, about their wisdom. We are utterly astonished at hearing from you words which are blunted with swelling arrogance rather than sharpened with wisdom. You point out how noble your city was in ancient times: you praise to the skies the condition of your divine republic in the old days. I know that perfectly well, and, if I may use the words of your own writer, 'there was *once* virtue in this republic'.[1] I say 'once'; and I wish we could say 'there is virtue now' truthfully as well as readily. Your Rome, or rather our Rome, has experienced changes of circumstance. She could not alone escape the fate ordained by eternal law by the maker of all things for all who live beneath the moon. What shall I say? It is well known how the best part of your nobility was transferred from this city of ours to the royal city of the east, and for how many years the hungry Greekling sucked at the bosom of your delights. Then came the Frank, truly noble both in name and in reality, who snatched away the nobility which still remained to you. Do you wish to know the ancient glory of your Rome and the dignity of the Senatorial office, to see its array of tents and the powers and discipline of the order of knights, and their fine indomitable courage as they advance into battle? Behold our commonwealth! All those things are to be found among us. All of them have come down to us, together with the Empire. The Empire did not come to us naked, but clad in its own virtue; it brought with it its own adornments. With us are your Consuls, with us is your Senate, with us are your soldiers. The Frankish lords will have to govern you with their counsel, and the Frankish knights to drive harm from you with their swords.

You boast that I was summoned by you, that you made me first a citizen and then a prince, that I received from you what was yours. I leave it to you and to any wise man to judge how irrational and devoid of truth this unprecedented argument is. Let us consider the deeds of modern Emperors: did not our divine princes Charles and Otto tear the city, together with the whole of Italy, from the Greeks and Lombards and add it to the Frankish dominions? It was not handed over by anyone as a favour, but conquered by their skill and courage. This is shown by Desiderius and Berengarius, your tyrants, of whom you boasted and on whom you depended as princes.[2] We have learnt from

1. From Cicero's first oration against Catiline, ch. 1.
2. Desiderius, King of the Lombards, defeated and deprived by Charlemagne, 774; Berengarius II, King of Italy, defeated and captured by Otto the Great, 963.

a true account that they were not only subdued and captured by our
Franks, but even grew old and ended their lives in bondage to them. The
fact that their ashes were buried in our country is the clearest demonstra-
tion of this. But you say: 'You came at my summons.' I admit that I was
summoned. But give us the reason why! You were being battered by
enemies and could not be freed either by your own hand or by the
effeminate Greeks. The skill of the Franks was called in by your own
invitation. I would call it an entreaty rather than a summons. In your
wretchedness you appealed to the happy, in your weakness to the
strong, in your impotence to the powerful, in your anxiety to the care-
free. I came after being summoned in that strain, if it ought to be called
a summons. I made your prince my vassal and transferred you into my
power, even unto this day. I am the lawful owner. Let him who can
'snatch the club from the hand of Hercules'.[1] Will the Sicilian you trust
in do that? Let him look at earlier examples. The hand of the Franks or
Germans has not yet lost its power. If God allows and his life lasts, he
too will be able some day to test his own foolhardiness.

You demand your rights, which you say I must render you. I for-
bear to point out that the prince ought to prescribe laws for the people,
not the people for the prince. I will not remind you that an owner about
to enter upon his estate ought not to allow any condition to be imposed
to his prejudice. Let us argue reasonably. You propose, it seems to me,
to exact three oaths. I will answer concerning each one.

You say that I must swear to observe the laws of the Emperors, my
predecessors, confirmed to you by their privileges, and also to observe
your good customs. You then add that I should swear to protect the
country even at the risk of my life. I will answer these two points together. Either what you ask is just, or it is unjust. If it is unjust, it is not
yours to ask or mine to grant. If it is just, I acknowledge that I want to
do this because I ought and ought to because I want to. Hence it will
be unnecessary to impose an oath on me to do my willing duty and my
dutiful will. Why should I trespass upon your rights, when I desire to
preserve his own even for the least of men? Why should I not defend
the country—and especially the seat of my Empire—even at the risk of
my life, when I have contemplated restoring its frontiers as far as I am
able, not without weighing up that particular danger? Denmark,
recently subdued and restored to the Roman world, has learnt this; and
perhaps more provinces and more kingdoms would have felt it had this
present affair not stood in the way.

1. Macrobius, *Saturnalia*, Bk. V, iii, 16.

I pass to the third point. You assert that I should personally swear to pay you a certain sum of money. This is abominable. You, Rome, make demands of your prince like a sutler of a pedlar. With us, such payments are demanded of captives. Am I then held in captivity? Do the chains of the enemy weigh upon me? Do I not sit in splendour, surrounded by a large and valiant troop of soldiery? Shall a Roman Prince be forced against his will to supply money to anyone rather than to give it? Hitherto I have been accustomed to give royally and splendidly of my own, to whom I pleased, and as much as was fitting, and especially to those who had deserved well of me. For even as lesser men are expected to give obedience, even so do the great dispense well-earned favours. Why should I deny to my own citizens this usage which I took over from my divine parents and have observed in other places? Why should I not make the city happy at my entrance? But it is right to deny all things to those who make unjust demands.'

§ 20

An incident at the imperial Diet of Besançon, 1157: Rahewin, continuator of Otto of Freising, *Gesta Friderici I Imperatoris*, Bk. III, ed. cit.

A. Bk. III, chapters 9–11; ed. cit., 174–9.
[*From the letter read by the papal legates to the Diet: this begins by rebuking the Emperor Frederick for failing to punish the brigands who had assaulted and captured Eskil, Archbishop of Lund, on his way across imperial territory from a visit to the Apostolic See.*—ED.]
'We have no idea of the cause of this dissimulation and neglect, since our conscience does not accuse us of having offended the glory of Your Serenity in any matter. We have loved you with a sincere love and treated you with due kindness and goodwill as a most dear and special son of ours and a most Christian prince, and we have no doubt that you are solidly grounded by the grace of God on the rock of the apostolic faith.
'For you ought, most glorious son, to recall to mind how joyfully and gladly your mother the holy church of Rome received you the other year, with what heartfelt affection she treated you, what unlimited dignity and honour she conferred upon you, and how by most willingly conferring the emblem of the Imperial Crown upon you she sought to nurture Your Supreme Highness in her most kindly bosom

and did nothing which she knew would clash with the royal will, even in the smallest particular.

'And we have no regrets at having gratified your wishes in all things: indeed, had Your Excellency received even greater benefits [*beneficia*] at our hands (if such were possible) we had had good reason to rejoice, reflecting how we and the Church of God could be benefited and made greater by you.

'But now, since you appear to be ignoring and passing over this heinous crime, notoriously committed as an insult to the universal Church and to your Empire, we suspect and fear that you have been induced to do so because you have, at the instigation of some perverse troublemaker, conceived some indignation or rancour (which God forbid) against your most merciful mother the holy church of Rome and against ourselves. . . .'

This letter was read and the Chancellor Rainald[1] presented it carefully in a faithful enough translation. The princes who were present were seized with great indignation, for there was considerable asperity running throughout the letter and it seemed outwardly to be even now opening the way to future trouble. All were particularly incensed at hearing it said (among other things) in this letter that the Emperor's unlimited dignity and honour had been conferred on him by the Roman Pontiff; that the Emperor had received the emblem of the Imperial Crown at his hands; and that the Pope would have had no regrets had the Emperor received even greater benefices [*beneficia*] at his hands, reflecting how the church of Rome could be benefited and made greater by him. The audience were driven to a strict understanding of these words and to believing this interpretation of their meaning because they knew that some of the Romans were audaciously asserting that our Kings had hitherto held the Empire of the City of Rome and the Kingdom of Italy by gift of the Popes. They had set this out not only in words but also in writings and pictures and handed it down to posterity. Hence, over a picture of this kind in the Lateran palace, these words concerning the Emperor Lothar appear:

'The King appears before the gates and first swears to do his duty to the City. Then he becomes the Pope's vassal and takes the crown which he gives him.'

This picture and the inscription over it had been reported to the prince by imperial vassals when he was in Rome a year or two before, and it had violently annoyed him. It is said that, after making a friendly

1. Rainald of Dassel, Archbishop of Cologne.

complaint about it, he had received Pope Adrian's agreement to the removal of the inscription and the picture, lest such an empty thing should give cause for dispute and disagreement to the greatest men in the world.

All these things were taken in conjunction, and the clamour and disturbance amongst the lords of the realm at such an extraordinary embassy grew greater and greater, and it was said that one of the papal legates had asked (as if to add fuel to the fire): 'From whom does he have his Empire, if not from the lord Pope?' The fury at this remark reached such a pitch that one of them, Otto, Count Palatine of Bavaria, as it was said, drew his sword and threatened the legate with death. But Frederick, by his own authoritative presence, quelled the tumult, gave the legates a safe-conduct and ordered them to be taken to their lodgings and to set out upon their way at dawn. He added in his orders that they were not to stray here or there on to the lands of bishops or abbots, but to return to Rome by the direct route without turning to left or right. And whilst they went back having accomplished nothing, what the Emperor had done was prudently announced by letter throughout the whole breadth of the realm, as follows:

'Since the might of God, from which all power in heaven and on earth is derived, has entrusted us, the anointed of God, with ruling the Kingdom and the Empire and has ordained that peace shall be preserved for churches by imperial weapons, it is with the deepest grief that we are forced to complain to you, our affectionate lord, that causes of discord, seeds of evil and pestilential poisons are being scattered abroad from the head of the holy Church, on whom Christ set the mark of his peace and love. We fear that unless God prevents it the whole body of the Church will be corrupted, its unity will be split and a rupture will take place between kingship and priesthood. . . .'

[*The letter then gives the imperial version of what had occurred at the Diet of Besançon*—ED.]

'Kingship and Empire are bestowed on us through election by the princes by God alone, who during the passion of Christ his son subjected the world to the two swords necessary to rule it.[1] The apostle Peter taught the world the doctrine: "Fear God. Honour the King."[2] Therefore, if anyone says that we received the Imperial Crown as a benefice [*pro beneficio*] from the lord Pope, he is contravening the edict of God and the doctrine of Peter and is guilty of lying. Because we have hitherto striven to tear out of the hands of the Egyptians the

1. Luke, xxii, 38.   2. I Peter, ii, 17.

honour and liberty of churches, which has long been weighed down by the yoke of unjust servitude, and because we intend to preserve for them all the rights attached to their offices, we ask the whole company of you to feel great pain at such gross affronts to us and to the Empire. We hope, moreover, that your sincere and undivided loyalty will not allow the honour of the Empire, which has stood forth splendid and untarnished from the foundation of the City of Rome and the establishment of the Christian religion down to your own times, to be diminished by such an unprecedented innovation and such a presumptuous boast. For you know without a shadow of doubt that we would rather incur the risk of death than the stigma of allowing such confusion to arise in our own times.'

B. Bk. III, chapter 17: ed. cit., 187–9. Extract from a further letter of Frederick I to the bishops of Germany.

'There are two means by which our Empire ought to be ruled: the holy laws of the Emperor, and the good customs of our predecessors and fathers. We have no wish and no power to overstep the limits which these set upon the Church; we will reject anything which is at odds with them. We gladly show due reverence to our father; but we regard the free crown of our Empire as a benefice [*beneficium*] from God alone. We acknowledge that the first vote in the election belongs to the Archbishop of Mainz, and the remaining votes to the other princes in due order; the anointing as King to the Archbishop of Cologne; and the supreme anointing, that is, as Emperor, to the Supreme Pontiff. "Anything over and above this has evil origins".'[1]

c. Bk. III, chapter 23: ed. cit., 195–7. Extract from a letter presented by the papal legates to the Emperor at Augsburg, June 1158.

'Your anger, it is said, was roused by the use of a certain word, "*beneficium*", which should not have stirred the heart of any lesser person, let alone that of so great a man. Admittedly this word "*beneficium*" is used by some people with a meaning different from the original one. But it ought now to be understood in the sense in which we used it and which it is well known to have carried since it was invented. For this word is composed of "*bonum*", good, and "*factum*", deed; and "*beneficium*", with us, means, not a fief, but a good deed. It is found to have that meaning throughout the entire body of Holy Scripture, where we are said to be guided and nurtured "*ex beneficio Dei*": not by

1. Matthew, v, 37.

feudal means, but by his blessings and good deeds. And Your Majesty will readily acknowledge that we have placed the emblem of the imperial office upon your head in such a good and honourable fashion that all may judge it to be a good deed.

'Certain persons have tried to twist this word and another, in the phrase "we have conferred on you the emblem of the Imperial Crown", away from its proper sense and into another. They have not done so for a just reason, but out of their own wilfulness and at the suggestion of those who do not like the royal power and the Church to be at peace. For by saying "we have conferred" we simply mean, as stated above, "we have placed". . . .'

THE LOMBARD CITIES

§ 21. This is a concise sketch, from the point of view of a German visitor, of the character of the developing Lombard cities with whose independence Frederick I had to come to terms, if he could not curtail or destroy it.

On the cities in general, and on Milan in particular, see C. W. Previté-Orton in C.M.H., V (1929); A. Visconti, *Storia di Milano* (Milan, 1937), Part III, ch. 1; Jordan, *L'Allemagne et l'Italie*, 62 foll.; also, recently, G. L. Barni and G. Franceschini in G. Treccani degli Alfieri, *Storia di Milano*, IV (Milan, 1954); G. L. Barni, '*Cives* e *rustici* a Milano alla fine del XII secolo e all' inizio del XIII', R.S.I., 69 (1957); A. Bosisio, 'Crema ai tempi di Federico Barbarossa (1152–1190)', A.S.L. (1960); E. Sestan, 'La città comunale italiana dei secoli XI–XIII nelle sue note caratteristiche rispetto al movimento comunale europeo', *XIᵉ Congrès International des Sciences Historiques, Rapports*, III (Stockholm, 1960), with references.

§ 21

The cities of Lombardy in the mid-twelfth century: Otto of Freising, *Gesta Friderici Imperatoris*, Bk. II, chs. 13–15, ed. cit., 116–18.

After describing Italy and its Lombard invaders:

The Lombards, however, have abandoned their barbaric savagery, perhaps because they married natives and begot children who derived something of the mildness and wisdom of the Romans from the blood of their mothers and from the properties of the country and climate. Even now they retain the elegant Latin speech and polished manners. In the government of their cities and the service of their commonwealth they still copy the skilful methods of the ancient Romans. They are so eager for freedom that they recoil from excess of power and are ruled by the will of consuls rather than of dictators [*imperantes*]. And as it is known that there are three estates among them, consisting of captains, vavasours and people, consuls are chosen, in order that arrogance may be suppressed, not from one estate alone, but from every estate; and, lest they be seized with a lust for power, they are changed nearly every year. Hence it happens that almost all the land is divided between the cities, and they all compel their bishops to dwell among them, and it is almost impossible to find any noble or magnate, even in so wide an area, who does not obey the orders of his city. The cities are accustomed to call their territories *contadi* [*comitatus*], from their own power to threaten them [*comminari*]. To have the means to subdue their neighbours, they do not scorn to promote to knighthood and to offices of various ranks young men of inferior condition, and workers engaged in low, even in manual trades, whom other peoples thrust out like the plague from the freer and more honourable pursuits. Hence it happens that they far surpass all other cities in the world in wealth and power.

They are helped to this position not only, as we have said, by their industrious habits, but also by the absence of their Princes, who usually stay on the other side of the Alps. In one respect, however, they forget their ancient nobility and do retain some traces of barbaric impurity, since, although they boast of living by the laws, yet they fail to obey them. For they scarcely ever receive their Prince with the respect which as subjects they ought willingly to show him; nor do they obediently accept what he has ordained in accordance with the whole body of the laws, unless he brings up a large force of soldiers and they are compelled to feel his authority. The result is often that, although a citizen ought to be moulded by the law and an enemy coerced with arms according to the laws, they frequently entertain in a hostile fashion the man whom they ought to receive as their own gentle Prince, even though he is merely asking for his own rights. Hence the commonwealth suffers in two ways—one, that the Prince is distracted by having to raise an army to reduce the citizen to obedience; and the other, that the citizen is forced to obey his Prince with considerable loss of his own property. The people must be condemned for their foolhardiness, but the Prince must by the same token be exonerated in the sight of God and man because he has no choice in the matter.

Among the cities of this people, Milan now holds first place. It lies between the Po and the Alps. The Ticino and the Adda rise in the Alps and flow into the Po, and between them is a very fertile arc of land like an island, and as Milan is set in the middle [*media posita*] of this it is well named *Mediolanum*, although some people think that it was called *Mediolanum*, 'half wool', by its founders because of a monstrous sow, which had bristles on one side and wool on the other. This city, as we said, enjoys greater fame than the others, not only because of its size and plentiful supply of valiant men, but also because it has sub-jected to its authority two neighbouring cities which lie on the same arc of land, Como and Lodi. Moreover, as often happens in this un-certain life when we are flattered by fortune smiling upon us, Milan, elated by success, has swollen with such bold arrogance that not only does she not shrink from attacking her neighbours but she has even dared recently to incur the displeasure of the Prince, having no fear of His Majesty. Later, I will briefly disclose the reasons why this situation arose.

Meanwhile, I think that something ought to be said about the claims of the royal power. There is an ancient custom, which has come down to our own day from the time when the Roman Empire devolved upon the Franks, that whenever the Kings decide to enter Italy they send experienced members of their household before them to go the rounds of all the cities and towns and seek out the things which are due to the royal fisc and are called by the locals 'forage' [*fodrum*]. Hence it happens that when the Prince appears a great many cities, towns and fortresses which try to resist these claims, either by completely denying them or by not meeting them in full, are razed to the ground to give proof of their insolence to posterity. Another right is likewise said to have originated in ancient custom, i.e. that when the Prince enters Italy all offices and magistracies must be vacated and all things be dealt with at his behest according to lawful ordinances and to the judgment of men learned in the law. The judges of the land are said to recognize that he has such extensive authority that they think it right to supply for royal use a part of all the necessities which the land pro-duces: oxen and seeds which are fit for the cultivation of the soil are excepted, but of anything else which is useful to his soldiers the Prince may have as much as is needed.

THE DIET OF RONCAGLIA, 1158

§§ 22–23. In 22A, Rahewin describes or reconstructs the proceedings at the imperial Diet of Roncaglia in November 1158, at which the regalian rights of the King-Emperor were defined with the assistance of a group of Roman lawyers from Bologna. The speeches of Frederick and the Archbishop of Milan, with their numerous quotations from Sallust and Justinian, may simply be idealized versions of what the two men ought to have said, rather than accurate reports of what they did say. But they give some idea of the aura with which Frederick liked to surround himself.

22 B is a version of the Roncaglian decree defining regalian rights not found in Rahewin's chronicle.

23 consists of the feudal legislation issued at Roncaglia in 1158. The decrees included here, up to the clause prohibiting the division of duchies, marches and counties, had already been enacted at a previous court held at Roncaglia in December 1154. They indicate the challenges which were then being offered to feudalism in northern Italy and the steps taken by Frederick to prevent its being undermined.

See G. Blondel, 'Les droits régaliens et la constitution de Roncaglia', *Mélanges Paul Fabre* (1902); P. W. Finstenwalder, 'Die Gesetze des Reichstags von Roncaglia', Z.S.S.R., g.a., 51 (1931); G. Deibel, 'Die finanzielle Bedeutung Reichs-Italiens für die staufischen Herrscher des zwölften Jahrhunderts', ibid., 54 (1934); T. Mayer, 'Die Ausbildung der Grundlagen des modernen deutschen Staates im hohen Mittelalter', H.Z., 159 (1938–1939), 468 foll.; Koeppler, 'Barbarossa and the Schools of Bologna', 580 foll.; I. Ott, 'Der Regalienbegriff im 12 Jahrhundert', Z.S.S.R., k.a., 35 (1948), 272 foll.

Specifically on the feudal legislation, see Mitteis, *Lehnrecht und Staatsgewalt*, 613 foll., and in Barraclough, ed. *Mediaeval Germany*, II, 248–9.

The privilege to scholars on imperial territory also issued at Roncaglia in 1158 is included as Part II, no. 24.

§ 22

A. The imperial Diet of Roncaglia, 1158. Rahewin, continuator of Otto of Freising, *Gesta Friderici I Imperatoris*, Bk. IV, chs. 4–9, ed. cit., 236–41.

The Emperor's speech on the fourth day of the Diet:

'Since the ordinance of God, from which all power in heaven and on earth is derived,[1] has decreed that we should stand at the helm of the Roman Empire, with good reason do we pursue the things which are known to belong to that position so far as we can with God's approval. We are aware that it is the duty of the Imperial Majesty to control the wicked and troublesome by our vigilant efforts and through the fear of punishment, and to raise up the good and nourish them in peace and tranquillity. But we likewise know what rights and honour have been accorded to the supreme excellency of the King by the authority of divine and human laws. But we who bear the name of King wish to have an Empire governed by law which sets out to preserve for everyone his rights and liberty rather than to grow insolent from lack of restraint (as in the saying, "to do everything with impunity, that is to be a king") and to transform the duty of ruling into arrogance and despotism.[2] With God's help we will not change our ways with our fortune. We will take care to maintain our Empire by the same skills as originally created it.[3] Nor will we by our apathy permit anyone to detract from its glory and excellence.

'Since, then, we may acquire fame either in war or in peace, and it is pointless to ask whether it is better to protect the country with arms or to guide it with laws, since each requires the aid of the other,[4] now that the tumults of war have been stilled by the favour of God let us turn our attention to the laws of peace. You know that the civil laws have been brought to perfection by our gracious acts, that they have been ratified and approved by the conduct of those who use them, and so they have force enough; but you also know that the laws of the kingdoms, in which earlier usages have later been obscured by discontinuance, need a light shone upon them by imperial measures and by your wisdom.[5] Whether, then, our law or yours is being reduced to writing, in making it we must take care that it be honourable, just, feasible, necessary, profitable and appropriate to the time and place; and when we establish the law both we and you must exercise very careful foresight, since once the laws have been passed nobody will be free to judge them: it will be necessary to judge *by* them.'

A eulogistic speech delivered by the Archbishop of Milan in reply to this ends:
'As for us, your loyal subjects, you in your wisdom are pleased to take advice from your people concerning the laws, rights and honour of the

1. Cf. Romans, xiii, 1–2.
2. Cf. Sallust, *Catilinae Coniuratio*, ch. 6, and *Bellum Iugurthinum*, ch. 31.
3. Sallust, *Catilinae Coniuratio*, ch. 2.
4. Ibid., chs. 1, 3.
5. Cf. preamble to the *Institutes* of Justinian.

Empire. Know, then, that all the rights of the people in establishing laws have been made over to you. Your will is law, in accordance with the saying: "What the Prince has decided has the force of law, since the people have granted to and conferred upon him all their sovereignty [*imperium*] and power [*potestas*]. For anything that the Emperor has established by letter or judicially decided or commanded by edict is generally recognized as law."[1] Moreover it is natural that the profits from a thing should accrue to the man who incurs the losses therefrom:[2] i.e. that you should govern everybody, since you bear the burden of looking after us all.'

When this was completed, the court, which that day had continued till the evening, was adjourned. Some people even sang of the Emperor's acts publicly in songs of praise.

On the days which followed, in a full and solemn court, the Emperor, devoting himself to judging and dispensing justice from morning till evening, carefully listened to the complaints and appeals of rich and poor alike. He had four judges with him, Bulgarus, Martin, James and Hugh, eloquent and Godfearing men and most learned in the law, of which they were doctors in the city of Bologna, where they taught many pupils. With these and other legal experts from different cities he heard, discussed and decided business. Seeing the great number of persons carrying crosses,—for the Italians have a custom that when they have a complaint they bear a cross in their hands,—and taking pity on them, the Emperor said he was astonished at the wisdom of the Latins: for although they were remarkably boastful of their knowledge of the laws, they were found to be very great transgressors of them; and from this mass of people 'hungering and thirsting after justice'[3] it was clear how determined was their pursuit of it. Acting on God's advice, he appointed a judge for each diocese—not a man from the same city, but from the court or from other cities, changing people round lest, if a citizen were set in authority over his fellows, he might easily be diverted from the truth either by favouritism or by enmity. And so it was accomplished that out of such a multitude of plaintiffs hardly anyone was left who did not rejoice at having obtained, from the lawsuit, either complete victory, or at least his rights, or a suitable agreement with his opponent.

Then the Emperor earnestly discoursed of the claims of the royal

1. Justinian, *Institutes*, Bk. I, *titulus* ii, section 6.
2. Justinian, *Digest*, Bk. L, *titulus* xvii, section 10.
3. Matthew, v, 6.

power and of the *regalia*, which had long ago died out in the Empire either through the audacity of usurpers or through the neglect of the Kings. At this the bishops, the lords and the cities, since they could find no excuse for not doing so, with one voice and by common consent restored the *regalia* to the hands of the Prince, and the Milanese were the first to resign them. Asked what these rights were, they assigned to him duchies, marches, counties, consulates, mints, tolls [*thelonea*], forage, waggon tolls [*vectigalia*], port dues [*portus*], transit tolls [*pedatica*], mills, fisheries, bridges, all profits derived from the flowing of rivers, and the yield, not only of the annual land tax, but also of the poll tax on their own persons.

And when all these things had been assigned to the fisc, their previous owners were treated with such generosity that if anyone could show by lawful deeds that he held any of these rights by gift of the Kings, he was even now to hold it in perpetuity as an imperial benefice and in the name of the Kingdom. But from those who had intruded upon the *regalia* without any right but only out of presumption, some 30,000 talents were added to the public revenues every year.

Furthermore, everybody pronounced and acknowledged that the Emperor had the right to appoint mayors [*podestà, potestates*], consuls and other magistrates with the consent of the people in all the cities—men who, being both loyal and prudent, would know how to uphold the Prince's honour and the rights due to the citizens and their own country.

Oaths were taken by all the cities that all these things would be accepted and observed in good faith and without deceit, and pledges were given to please the Emperor. Then they swore to a common peace—that no city would attack another city and no man another man unless ordered to do so by the Prince.

B. A further definition of regalian rights: ed. L. Weiland in M.G.H., Const., I (1893), 244–5.

Regalia are these things: the right to military service [*arimannie*]; public ways; navigable rivers and things which make them navigable; port dues [*portus*]; bank dues [*ripatica*]; the waggon dues [*vectigalia*] commonly called tolls [*tholonea*]; mints; the proceeds of fines and penalties; vacant property; property taken by law from the unworthy (save where this has been specially granted to certain persons); the property of those who contract incestuous marriages and that of condemned and outlawed persons, as stipulated in the new decrees; the dues which consist of paying direct and indirect taxes on men or land and of supplying land and water transport [*angariarum et parangariarum et plaustrorum et navium prestationes*]; extraordinary assemblies of the host summoned at the royal behest; the power of appointing magistrates for the administration of justice; silver mines; palaces in the usual cities; revenues from fisheries and salteries; the property of those who commit the crime of treason [*maiestas*]; one half of any treasure found without assistance on imperial or church land; if the Emperor has given assistance, the whole of the treasure belongs to him.

§ 23

The feudal constitutions issued by Frederick I at Roncaglia, 1158: ed. L. Weiland in M.G.H., Const., I (1893), 247–9.

Frederick, by the grace of God Emperor of the Romans and always Augustus, to all the subjects of our Empire.

It is fitting that the Emperor should apply his skill to caring for the commonwealth and to discovering what best suits his subjects, so that the realm may contrive to profit and the estate of each man may be perpetually preserved intact. Hence, when we sat in judgment at the general court of Roncaglia, according to the custom of our predecessors, we received serious complaints from the chief men of Italy, both from governors of churches and from other loyal men of the realm, that their vassals had without permission from their lords pledged and sold the benefices and fiefs which they held of them (sometimes conspiring to disguise the sale as a lease). Hence the lords were losing the services due to them, the honour of the Empire was suffering and our military levy was falling below its full strength.

Having therefore taken the advice of bishops, dukes, margraves and counts, and likewise of judges palatine and other noble lords, we have determined by this edictal law which, God willing, will be valid for ever: that it shall be lawful for no man to sell or pledge the whole or any part of a fief, or in any way to alienate it or bestow it for the salvation of his soul, without the permission of the overlord to whom the fief is known to belong. The Emperor Lothar published a law merely providing that this should not happen in the future; but we, providing for the greater profit of the realm, annul and declare void by this present decree not only all unlawful alienations in the future, but also any that

N

have been perpetrated in the past. No lapse of time shall act as a bar to this; a *bona fide* buyer may bring an action against the seller of a fief to recover the price. Furthermore—to thwart the cunning manœuvres of those who receive a payment and, under the pretext of investiture, which they say is allowed to them, sell fiefs and transfer them to others —we utterly forbid anyone to devise that or any other fiction in order to circumvent this our decree. Upon our authority, the buyer and seller who are found to have concluded such unlawful agreements shall be liable to lose the fief, and it shall freely revert to the lord. A notary who knowingly draws up a deed on these lines shall forfeit his office, lose a hand and be liable to loss of civil rights [*infamia*].

Again, if any feudatory over 14 years of age by his own carelessness or neglect allows a year and a day to pass without seeking investiture of the fief from his own lord, he shall lose the fief when this period has elapsed and it shall return to the lord.

We firmly decree, both in Italy and in Germany, that if anyone, when a levy of troops has been publicly announced, is summoned by his lord to this levy and fails without cause to come within the proper time, and refuses to send a substitute acceptable to his lord, and does not pay his lord one-half of the revenue from the fief for one year, he shall lose the fief which he holds of a bishop or other lord, and the lord of the fief shall be fully empowered to convert it to his own use.

Again, henceforth no duchy, margravate or county shall be divided. But any other fief may be divided if the partners in it so wish, provided that all who have a portion of the fief which has been or is to be divided do fealty to the lord; and provided also that no vassal be compelled to have more than one lord for one fief, and provided that no lord transfer a fief to another without the consent of the vassals.

Moreover, if the son of a vassal offends his lord, his father, when called upon by the lord, shall bring his son to make amends to the lord or else cut his son off from him; otherwise he shall be deprived of his fief. But if the father wishes to bring him to make amends and the son refuses, he shall not succeed to the fief on his father's death, unless he has first made amends to the lord. The vassal shall act likewise on behalf of all members of his household.

We also decree that if a vassal has another vassal enfeoffed to him, and the vassal's vassal offends his lord's lord, he shall be deprived of his fief unless he did this in the service of another lord whom he genuinely had before, and the fief shall revert to the lord from whom he immediately held it, unless, on being required to do so, he is prepared to make amends to the overlord whom he has offended. If the intermediate lord, on being called upon by his lord, fails to require the man to make amends to the overlord whom he has offended, he shall lose his fief.

Again, should there be a dispute between two vassals over a fief, the lord shall have jurisdiction over it and the dispute be decided by him. But should a dispute arise between a lord and vassal, it shall be decided by the peers of his court who have been sworn in by the lord upon their duty of fealty to him.

We have also decreed that, in every oath of fealty, fealty to the Emperor shall expressly be reserved.

THE PEACE OF CONSTANCE

§ 24. The Peace of Constance of June 1183 represents the final compromise between Frederick I and the cities of the Lombard League. This League had been formed in 1167 (in succession to the League of Verona, of 1164) to defend the rights of the cities against the German imperial government.

In addition to the general authorities cited above, before no. 19, see W. Lenel, 'Der Konstanzer Frieden von 1183 und die italienische Politik Friedrichs I', H.Z., 128 (1923); H. Kauffmann, *Die italienische Politik Kaiser Friedrichs I nach dem Frieden von Konstanz, 1183–89* (Greifswald, 1933); Jordan, *L'Allemagne et l'Italie*, 139–42; Hampe, *Deutsche Kaisergeschichte*, 206 foll.

§ 24

The Peace of Constance concluded by the Emperor Frederick I with the Lombard League, June 25th, 1183, ed. L. Weiland in M.G.H., Const., I (1898), 411–18.

The Privilege of the Emperor.

In the name of the holy and indivisible Trinity. Frederick, by the gracious favour of God Emperor Augustus of the Romans, and Henry VI his son, King Augustus of the Romans.

The Emperor in his serene and gentle mercy has always been used to dispense grace and favour to his subjects in such a way that, although he can and must discipline criminal excesses with sternness and severity, nevertheless he strives still more earnestly to rule the Roman Empire calmly, peacefully and mercifully, and to recall rebels in their insolence to due loyalty and properly loyal obedience. Hence let all loyal subjects of the Empire both present and to come know that we, with our usual gracious kindness, extending the compassion which is rooted in us to the loyal and devoted Lombards who at one time offended us and our Empire, have received them, their League and their adherents into the fullness of our grace. We have graciously forgiven all the offences and misdeeds by which they roused us to indignation, and we consider them, for that loyal and devoted service which we believe we shall undoubtedly receive from them, worthy to be counted among our beloved and loyal subjects. Therefore we have ordered our peace, which we have graciously granted them, to be confirmed by this present charter and corroborated by the seal of our authority. It runs as follows:

1. We, Frederick, Emperor of the Romans, and our son Henry, King of the Romans, grant in perpetuity to you, the cities, places and persons of the League, the *regalia* and your customs both within and outside each city: that is, to Verona and its castle and suburbs, and to the other cities, places and persons of the League. This means that in each city you may have everything that you have and have had up to this day, and outside the city you may without opposition claim all the customary rights that you claim and have claimed of old: that is over forage, woods, pastures, bridges, waters and mills that you have or have been accustomed to have of old; in military service, in the fortification of the city, in jurisdiction both within and outside it both in criminal cases and in actions for money, and in other things which affect the interests of cities.

2. We wish the *regalia* which have not been granted to you to be judged in this manner: there shall be chosen men of the city and of the diocese, men of good judgment who shall be considered suitable for this purpose and who are not seized by any personal and particular prejudice either against the city or against Our Majesty; and they, together with the bishop of the place, shall swear that they will in good faith and without fraud seek out those things which particularly belong to Our Excellency and, having found them, assign them to us.

3. But if the cities wish this inquiry to be dispensed with, we demand a tribute of two thousand marks of silver every year; though we will reduce this sum by a suitable amount if it seems to be excessive.

4. If anyone lodges with Our Majesty a complaint concerning these things which we have granted and permitted to you either inside or outside the city, we will not allow the complaint and will compel him to be silent.

5. We hold to be firm and valid any gifts or grants in any form made by us or by our predecessor as King or Emperor before the time of the war to bishops, churches, cities or any other persons clerical or lay, saving earlier grants; and they shall render us the usual services for this, but no tribute shall be levied.

6. We do not consider the dues, from sources inside or outside the cities, which are granted to the cities for the sake of peace to be among the *regalia* for which tribute must be paid.

7. All privileges, gifts and concessions which have been granted to the prejudice or detriment of the cities, places or persons of the League on the occasion of the wars, by us or by our representatives, to the injury of any of them shall be rescinded and annulled.

8. In those cities in which the bishop holds the office of count by privilege of the Emperor or King, if the consuls are accustomed to receive their consulate through the bishop, let them continue to do so. Otherwise each city shall receive the consulate from us. Hence when consuls are appointed in each city, they shall receive investiture from our representative in the city or diocese and so on for a period of up to five years. At the end of five years, each city shall send a representative to us in person to receive investiture, and so on in the future, so that at the end of every five years they shall receive it from us personally, and within the five year periods from our representative, unless we are in Lombardy ourselves. In that case they shall receive it from us. With our successor the same procedure shall be observed. And all these investitures shall be carried out without payment.

9. When we, the Emperor, depart this life at the summons of God, or grant the Kingdom to our son, you shall receive investiture in like manner from our son or his successor.

10. In case of appeals, if the sum involved exceeds twenty-five imperial pounds, the appeal shall be made to us, saving the rights and customs of the church of Brescia in appeals, though the parties shall not be forced to go to Germany. We will have our own representative in each city or diocese, who shall be judge of the appeal and shall swear that he will examine cases in good faith and determine them according to the laws and customs of the city, within two months of the opening of the suit or of notice of appeal being received, unless the case stands over because of some genuine obstacle or by consent of both parties.

11. The consuls who are appointed in the cities shall be men who have done or will do homage to us before they receive their consulate.

12. Our vassals shall receive investiture from us and do homage as

vassals; and all others aged between fifteen and seventy shall do it as citizens, unless they are persons who can and genuinely must be excused the oath.

13. Vassals who in time of war or truce have failed to ask for investiture or to perform the services due to us shall not on these grounds lose their fiefs.

14. Leasehold and precarial tenures shall remain as they are according to the customs of each city, notwithstanding our law, which is called the Emperor Frederick's Law.

15. We and our party freely forgive all damage, plunder and injury which we in person and our followers have sustained either from the League as a whole, or from any member of it, or from its supporters; and we bestow on them the fullness of our grace.

16. We will not spend unnecessary time in any city or diocese to the detriment of the city.

17. It shall be lawful to fortify the cities and to build outside defences for them.

18. Again, they shall be entitled to maintain the League which they now have and to renew it as many times as they wish.

.   .   .   .

27. All members of the League who swear fealty to us shall add to the oath of fealty a declaration that they will help us in good faith to maintain the estates and rights which we have and hold in Lombardy outside the League, if this is necessary and if they are called upon to do so by us or by our accredited representative; and, if we lose them, help us to recover them. The neighbouring cities shall be liable to do this first, and if necessary the others shall be bound to lend sufficient aid. The cities of the League which are outside Lombardy shall be obliged to do likewise within their own boundary.

28. If any of the cities fails to observe the things established on our behalf at the peace agreement, the other cities shall compel it to observe them in good faith, and the peace shall none the less remain in force.

29. When we enter Lombardy, they shall offer us the usual forage and *regale* which are due and customary at the proper and accustomed time. And on our outward and return journey they shall rebuild the roads and bridges adequately, in good faith and without deception. They shall offer to sell adequate supplies to us and to our men in good faith and without deception both on the outward and on the return journey.

30. Every tenth year they shall exact the oath of fealty from those

who have not sworn it to us, when we ask for this either in person or through our representative.

31. If anybody has been expelled from his lawful possessions by men on our side, they shall be restored without benefit or loss, unless the possessor can defend himself *in causa principali* or by right of ownership, saving earlier grants; and all offences shall be forgiven them. The same rule concerning restitution shall be observed towards those who belong to our party, unless the city is bound by oath not to make restitution; in which case we wish a good man to decide the matter instead.

32. Should any dispute over a fief arise between us and another person who is a member of the League, it shall be decided by the peers of the city or diocese in which the disagreement arises according to the custom of the city and within the same diocese, unless we are in Lombardy at the time; and then, if we so decide, the case shall be heard in our presence.

33. Further, we will refuse a hearing to those who wish to contravene agreements between two cities of the League or between a city and other persons which were not concluded by violence and have been confirmed by oath.

. . . .

35. We have therefore deemed that this peace shall be perpetually kept and confirmed in the form set out above, and as we have interpreted it with and through the negotiators of peace, William, Bishop of Asti, Henry, Margrave of Savona, Brother Theoderic of Silva Benedicta and Rudolf our Chamberlain, and in the form in which we had the peace sworn, and in the way in which the Lombards have interpreted it in good faith; and we have ordered our seal to be placed on the present charter, that it may stand firm and not be disturbed.

36. The names of the cities to which we have granted our grace and made the above concession or allowance are as follows: Vercelli, Novara, Milan, Lodi, Bergamo, Brescia, Mantua, Verona, Vicenza, Padua, Treviso, Bologna, Faenza, Modena, Reggio, Parma, Piacenza. We wish peace to be kept with those cities and places and have granted them our grace.

37. But we have not made the above concession or allowance to the following: Imola, the fortress of San Cassiano, Bobbio, the people of Gravedona, Feltre, Belluno and Ceneda. But we grant our grace to Ferrara and make the above concession or allowance if, within two months of the return of the Lombards from our court, the Ferrarese have reached an agreement with them about the above peace.

38. Both we and our son Henry, King of the Romans, have had this peace and agreement, as it is written above, sworn to upon our souls by our Chamberlain Rudolf.

39. The following are the princes and nobles of the court who have sworn that they will keep this peace: Hermann, Bishop of Munich; Henry, Bishop-elect of Chur; Thiethelm, Abbot of Reichenau; Godfrey, Chancellor of the Imperial Palace; Otto, Duke of Bavaria; Frederick, our son, Duke of Swabia; Bertold, Duke of Zähringen; Bertold, Margrave of Istria; Hermann, Margrave of Verona; Count Henry of Dietz; Count Diepold of Lechsgemünd; Count Ludwig of Helfenstein, brother of the Chancellor; Rudolf the Chamberlain; Wernher of Bolland; Cuno of Minzenberg; Conrad the Butler.

40. The following are the representatives who have accepted the above peace and agreement on behalf of the Lombards and have confirmed it by oaths in our presence:

[*The representatives of the Lombard cities mentioned in clause 36 are then listed*—ED.]

41. The following are the cities and places which have accepted this peace made under oath by the Lombards with us and have sworn the same things for themselves: Pavia, Cremona, Como, Tortona, Asti, Cesarea,[1] Genoa, Alba and other cities, places and persons who are and have been on our side.

42. The following are the names of the representatives who have received investiture with the consulate from us in the name of the city. . . .

The names follow.

The signature of the lord Frederick, invincible Emperor of the Romans.

I, Godfrey, Chancellor of the Imperial Palace, have witnessed this in the place of Christian, Archbishop of Mainz and Arch-chancellor of Germany.

These things were done in the year of Our Lord's incarnation 1183, indiction one, in the reign of the lord Frederick, most glorious Emperor of the Romans, in his thirty-second year as King and twenty-ninth as Emperor.

Given in a solemn court at Constance on June 25th. Happily amen.

---

1. The imperialist name for Alessandria.

CHAPTER IV

Innocent III and the Empire

§§ 25–9. These documents, which almost explain themselves, concern the dispute over the imperial election which arose in the early years of the pontificate of Innocent III. Among the principles at stake was the principle that the Empire should be hereditary, which the Emperor Henry VI had tried to establish in favour of his small son Frederick. On the other hand, the group of German princes which adhered to Frederick's uncle, Philip of Swabia, claimed (25 and 27) that they had the right to elect a King of the Romans whom the Pope must subsequently crown Emperor. Innocent III, however, held that should the princes elect an unsuitable candidate he would not be bound to consecrate and crown him. An enemy of the Swabian imperial house of Staufen, he opposed the choice of Philip and favoured his rival, Otto of Brunswick, who had been chosen by another party of princes led by Archbishop Adolf of Cologne. Extract 26, the so-called *Deliberatio*, throws light on the secret deliberations of Innocent III in consistory with his cardinals, late in the year 1200; on his reasons for rejecting both Frederick and Philip and supporting Otto; and on the legal grounds, including the doctrine of the 'transfer of Empire' [*translatio imperii*], on which Innocent claimed to intervene in the election. Some of the points already made in the *Deliberatio* and some additional ones were later published in the letter *Venerabilem* (28).

Although there were signs of a reconciliation between Philip and the Pope, Philip's murder by Otto of Wittelsbach in 1208 made it certain that Otto of Brunswick would succeed as Emperor. He was recognized by the princes at the Diet of Frankfurt in November 1208 and crowned Emperor in Rome in October 1209. Innocent's letter to Otto (29) was written between those two events. It describes the ideal relationship between Pope and Emperor; but Otto failed to fulfil Innocent's expectations.

See A. Luchaire, *Innocent III: la Papauté et l'Empire* (1906); Carlyle,

History of mediaeval political theory, II (Edinburgh-London 1909), 217–19, V (Edinburgh-London, 1928), 187 foll.; C. J. Hefele and H. Leclercq, *Histoire des Conciles*, V, ii (1913), 1179 foll.; M. Tangl, 'Die *Deliberatio* Innocenz' III', S.P.A.W. (1919); E. W. Meyer, *Staatstheorien Papst Innocenz' III* (Bonn, 1920), 29 foll.; E. F. Jacob and A. L. Poole in C.M.H., VI (1929); G. Martini, 'Traslazione dell' Impero e Donazione di Costantino nel pensiero e nella politica d'Innocenzo III', A.S.R.S.P., 56–7 (1933–1934); Jordan, *L'Allemagne et l'Italie*, 180 foll.; M. Maccarrone, *Chiesa e stato nella dottrina di papa Innocenzo III* (Rome, 1940), 82 foll., 131 foll.; H. Mitteis, *Die deutsche Königswahl* (Brno, 1944), 113 foll.; Barraclough, *Origins of modern Germany*, 193 foll.; C. C. Bayley, *The formation of the German college of electors in the mid-thirteenth century* (Toronto, 1949), 119 foll.; W. Ullmann, *Mediaeval papalism* (London, 1949), 168 foll.; S. Mochi Onory, *Fonti canonistiche dell' idea moderna dello stato* (Milan, 1951), 187 foll., 201 foll., 236–7, etc.; H. Tillmann, 'Zur Frage des Verhältnisses von Kirche und Staat in Lehre und Praxis Papst Innocenz' III', D.A.E.M., 9 (1951–1952); Folz, *L'idée d'empire*, 118 foll.; F. Kempf, *Papsttum und Kaisertum bei Innocenz III* (Rome, 1954—M.H.P., 19); H. Tillmann, *Papst Innocenz III* (Bonn, 1954), 83 foll.; P. A. van den Baar, *Die kirchliche Lehre der 'Translatio Imperii Romani'* (Rome, 1956—A.G., 78), 99 foll.; Pacaut, *La théocratie*, 148 foll.; W. Goez, *Translatio Imperii* (Tübingen, 1958), 157 foll.

On the source, see also F. Kempf, *Die Register Innocenz' III* (Rome, 1945—M.H.P., 9).

On the theory of the two swords in extract 29, cf. the literature cited above, Part II, no. 9.

§ 25

The letter of the German princes to Pope Innocent III, May 28th, 1199: *Regestum domni Innocentii tertii pape super negotio Romani imperii*, no. 14, ed. W. Holtzmann (Bonn, 1947), 24–6.

To the reverend father in Christ, the lord Innocent, Supreme Pontiff of the holy church of Rome, the princes and magnates of the Germanies, your sons in Christ . . . the Archbishop of Magdeburg, the Archbishop of Trier, the Archbishop of Besançon, the Bishop of Ratisbon, the Bishop of Freising, the Bishop of Augsburg, the Bishop of Constance, the Bishop of Eichstädt, the Bishop of Worms, the Bishop of Speier, the Bishop-elect of Brixen, the Bishop of Hildesheim, the Chancellor

of the Imperial Palace, the Abbot of Tegernsee, the Abbot of Ell-
wangen, and also the King of Bohemia, the Duke of Saxony, the
Duke of Bavaria, the Duke of Austria, the Duke of Meran, the Duke
of Lorraine, the Margrave of Meissen, the Margrave of Brandenburg,
the Margrave of Moravia, the Margrave of Ronsberg and other noblemen of all Germany, their due and ready allegiance with all loyalty and
obedience.

The fact that your blessed apostolic eminence has always been accustomed to treat pleasantly and kindly and to acquiesce in the pious
desires and wishes of petitioners makes the whole body of us fully confident that we shall find you, in your apostolic benevolence, ready to
listen to us and faithfully to do what we ask concerning those things
which we most justly demand of Your Holiness. Hence we have decided
to announce to Your Greatness that, on the death of our famous lord
Henry, Emperor Augustus of the Romans, a multitude of princes
gathered with a great number of nobles and servants of the Empire
present, and we duly and solemnly elected our illustrious lord Philip
to the Emperorship of the Roman dominion, for we could not find
anyone more loftily noble, more glittering with honour, or better
equipped to guide and to govern the Sacred Empire or to defend the
Church of God as is meet and expedient. Although we have not until
now assembled to deal profitably with the affairs of the Empire, on
account of a few princes who resisted justice, we have now, after
deliberating with our aforesaid lord King Philip, celebrated a solemn
court at Nuremberg to give him aid in unison (if our most high Lord
God so ordain) against those who trouble him, so that no one shall dare
to deny his lordship over the Empire and over the lands which his most
serene brother used to hold. Hence, we most earnestly beg the apostolic
office to be gracious so that, heeding the prayers of us who have always
cared for the welfare of the church of Rome, you will do nothing to
harm the rights of the Empire, carefully considering that we would not
allow the rights of the Church to be reduced or infringed by anyone.
Therefore may you fruitfully extend your favour and kindness towards
our most excellent lord and see fit to advance his honour and interests
wherever you can so that wickedness may not overcome justice, but
rather that falsehood may always be subdued by truth. Further, we
advise and pray you in the affairs of our lord to extend the apostolic
kindness and favour to our devoted and beloved friend and loyal
subject of our lord King Philip Markward, Margrave of Ancona, Duke
of Ravenna, regent of the Kingdom of Sicily and Seneschal in the

Imperial Palace; and not to offer aid to those who resist him, as we trust in Your Holiness—in the certain knowledge that in a short time, God willing, we shall come to Rome with our lord, with all the forces we can muster, to obtain for him the supreme dignity of the imperial coronation.

We have written all these things to you both for ourselves who are present here and on behalf of other princes from whom we have received representatives and letters, and who have also done fealty and homage to our lord.

Their names are as follows:

the Patriarchs of Aquileia; the Archbishop of Bremen; the Bishops of Verden, Halberstadt and Merseburg; the Bishops of Nuremberg, Munich, Osnabrück and Bamberg; the Bishops of Passau, Chur and Trent; the Bishops of Metz, Toul, Verdun and Liége; the Count Palatine of Burgundy; the Duke of Zähringen; the Duke of Carinthia; the Duke of Bitsch; the Margrave of Landsberg; the Margrave of Vohburg; the Count Palatine of Tübingen; the Count Palatine of Wittelsbach and numerous other counts and nobles, whose names we do not mention here.

Given at Speier, on May 28th.

§ 26

For Comment see Hallel Cp. 54.

The *Deliberatio Domni Pape Innocentii super facto imperii de tribus electis: Regestum . . . super negotio Romani imperii*, no. 29, ed. cit., 43–51.

In the name of the Father and of the Son and of the Holy Spirit.

It is the business of the Apostolic See to exercise care and prudence concerning the future of the Roman Empire, for it is acknowledged that the Empire is related to it both in the beginning and in the end [*principaliter et finaliter*]. In the beginning, because the Empire was transferred from Greece by and because of the Apostolic See, since the Apostolic See effected the transfer that it might itself be better defended. In the end, because the Emperor receives from the Supreme Pontiff the final or ultimate laying-on of hands by way of promotion: when he is blessed, crowned and invested with the Empire by him. Henry saw this very well when he received the crown from our predecessor Pope Celestinus of happy memory, withdrew for a time and then returned and requested the Pope to invest him with the Empire by means of the golden pall.

As three persons have recently been chosen for King, the boy [*i.e. Frederick, King of Sicily*—ED.], Philip and Otto, so there are three things to be considered with respect to each of them; what is lawful, what is seemly and what is politic.

As for the boy, the son of the Emperor Henry, it seems at first sight that it is not lawful to go against his election, which is upheld by the oath of the princes. For, even though the oath appears to have been extorted by violence, that is no reason for not keeping it: for although the oath which the children of Israel swore to the Gabaonites was obtained from them by a trick, none the less they decreed that it must be kept.[1] Moreover, although the oath was originally extorted by this means, Frederick's father, later realizing that he had acted wrongly, released the princes from the oath and parted with the letters concerning Frederick's election; and the princes subsequently elected the boy freely and in agreement in his father's absence, almost all of them swearing fealty and some of them doing him homage. Hence it does not appear lawful to go against lawful oaths. And it does not appear seemly that, when the boy has been entrusted to the guardianship of the Apostolic See and taken under its protection, he should be deprived of his Empire by the very thing that ought to uphold his rights, especially as it is written: 'You shall be a helper to an orphan.'[2] That it is not politic to oppose him undoubtedly appears from the argument that when this boy reaches years of discretion and realizes that he was deprived of the honour of the Empire by the church of Rome, he will not merely fail to show the church of Rome the customary reverence: rather will he assail it by all the means he can, withdraw the Kingdom of Sicily from loyalty to it, and refuse it the customary obedience.

But, on the other hand, there is evidence to the contrary: i.e. that it is really lawful, seemly and politic to oppose his election. That it is lawful, appears from the fact that the oaths were unlawful and the election undiscriminating. For they elected an unsuitable person, unfit to hold any office, let alone the Empire: a boy scarcely two years old and not yet reborn in the waters of holy baptism. Hence it does not appear that such unlawful and undiscriminating oaths ought to be kept. Nor is the objection about the Gabaonites valid here, for the oath sworn to them could be kept without harming the people of Israel: but these oaths can only be kept at a heavy cost, to the detriment not merely of a single nation but of the whole Church, and at the expense of the Christian people.

1. Joshua, ix.   2. Psalm x according to the Hebrews, 14.

Neither does the objection stand that these oaths appear lawful if we take into account the intention of those who swore them. They understood that, although they elected him to be Emperor at the time, he was not to rule immediately but when he lawfully came of age. But how could they judge his fitness? Could he not have been an imbecile, or perhaps so irresponsible as to be unsuitable even for a lesser office? Supposing they understood that he would eventually rule when he was fit to govern the Empire, but that meanwhile his father would look after the commonwealth. But something has since happened on account of which an oath of this kind cannot and must not be observed, something which the princes did not think about at all—the death of the boy's father. Hence, since the Empire cannot be taken over by a regent, and no temporary Emperor must be created, and the Church cannot and does not wish to be without an Emperor, it appears that it is lawful to provide another person for the Empire.

It is obvious to all that it is not seemly for the boy to rule. For how could he rule others, being in need of others to rule him? How could he guard the Christian people, being himself committed to the guardianship of another person? There can be no objection in the fact that he was committed to our guardianship, for he was not committed to us so that we might get him the Empire, but rather that we might defend the Kingdom of Sicily. That is clear from the word of Scripture, which says: 'Woe to the land whose King is a boy' and again 'whose princes eat in the morning'.[1] That it is not expedient that he should have the Empire appears from the fact that by this the Kingdom of Sicily would be united to the Empire, and the Church would be thrown into disorder by this union. For (not to mention the other dangers) he, on account of his imperial office, would refuse to do fealty and homage to the Church for the Kingdom of Sicily, as his father also refused. Nor is the objection valid that it is impolitic to oppose the boy's election lest he subsequently molest the Church, knowing that this caused him to lose the Empire. For he will never be able to say with truth that the Church has taken the imperial office away from him, since it is really his uncle who has invaded not only the Empire but also the boy's inheritance from his father, and who is intriguing to occupy his mother's possessions also through his minions; and the Roman church at great trouble and expense is striving to defend it with wisdom and power.

As for Philip, it seems likewise that it is not lawful to oppose his election. For since in elections one must consider the zeal, the worthi-

---

1. Ecclesiastes, x, 16.

ness and the number of the electors, and since it is difficult to estimate zeal, and since he was elected by the larger numbers and the worthier men, and since a greater number of the worthier princes has followed him up to now, he appears to have been rightfully chosen. Hence it does not appear legitimate to oppose his rightful and lawful election. It appears likewise that this would not be seemly,—it might look as though we were avenging the wrongs done to us by wishing to persecute him because his father and brother had persecuted the Church, and to exceed the duties of our office by punishing him for the offences of others, since the Lord orders us rather to 'Love your enemies, do good to those that hate you, and pray for those that persecute and slander you'.[1] It seems obvious that it is impolitic. For since Philip is mighty in land, wealth and subjects, it scarcely seems expedient for us to try to dam the flood, so opposing ourselves to the mighty that we make him the enemy of the Church and of ourselves. We might seem to be provoking still greater disagreement, and might make a new mistake worse than the first, whereas we ought rather to seek and pursue peace and tell the good news to others, and peace might easily follow if we supported him.

But, on the contrary, it does appear lawful for us to oppose Philip. For he was justly and solemnly bound by our predecessor with a sentence of excommunication: justly, because he had violently seized a part of the patrimony of St. Peter and damaged part of it with arson and plunder, and on being repeatedly admonished about this by our brothers he took no trouble to make amends; and solemnly, because it was done in the course of celebrating Mass in the church of St. Peter on an important feast-day. Philip subsequently acknowledged this when he sent a representative to the Apostolic See to get him absolution and when he eventually had himself absolved by our delegates after his election, contrary to the terms of our instructions to them. Hence it is clear that he was excommunicate at the time of his election.

And some people may think that he has not even now been freed from the fetters of excommunication, since the late . . . , Bishop of Sutri, did not in absolving him follow the instructions given him, for the instructions were these: that in exchange for the release of our venerable brother Nicholas, Archbishop of Salerno, whom we ordered Philip to release from imprisonment before he was himself absolved, the Bishop should relieve Philip of the trouble of making the journey to the Apostolic See; and that, having afterwards publicly received from Philip an oath according to the Church's instructions that

1. Matthew, v, 44.

he would obey our commands concerning the matters for which he had
been excommunicated, he should offer him the favour of absolution.
But the Bishop attempted to absolve Philip before the release of the
Archbishop, without receiving any oath from him, and not in public
but in private, in deed only because he could not rightfully do so. For
thus exceeding his authority, as, on his return, he recognized he had
done, he was removed from his bishopric and ended his days in a
monastery. Moreover, since we have often bound Markward and all
his supporters, both Germans and Italians, with the sentence of excommunication, and as Philip is not merely a supporter but is even the
very author of Markward's wickedness, it is clear that Philip lies under
sentence of excommunication. Further, since it is notorious that Philip
swore fealty to the boy but has now seized the Kingdom of Germany
and all parts of the Empire that lie therein, it is an established fact that
he is guilty of perjury.

But it is objected that if, as is set forth above, we regard that oath of
fealty as unlawful, how can we say that Philip is guilty of perjury, and
that he has violated an oath which it is said ought not to be observed?
But the answer is that, even though the oath was unlawful, Philip
should not have rashly repudiated it on his own initiative: he ought
first to have consulted our wishes—on the example of the oaths which
the children of Israel swore to the Gabaonites. Even though that was
obtained from them by a trick, still they did not repudiate it rashly on
their own initiative, but determined to consult the Lord God. Again,
since everything done against one's conscience leads to hell; and since,
according to the apostle, 'everything that is not of faith is sin',[1] and
since Philip excuses himself in this matter by saying that he would not
have accepted the Kingdom had he not known that others were planning to invade it, it is clear that he believed that that oath ought to have
been kept, and that his conscience was wounded by his so violating it. It
therefore appears that we must lawfully oppose this excommunicate
and perjuror and frustrate his endeavours.

That it is seemly for us to do so clearly appears from the fact that if,
as son previously succeeded father, brother now immediately succeeded brother, it would look as though the Empire was not conferred
on him by election but due to him by succession, and so a thing which
ought to be perfectly free would become hereditary, especially as not
only did Frederick put his son in his own place, but Henry [VI] also
wanted his own son to replace him; and perhaps by this means the

1. Romans, xiv, 23.

abuse would in future be turned into a custom. It is clear to everybody
that it is expedient for us to oppose Philip. For since he is a persecutor
and is descended from a race of persecutors, if we did not oppose him we
should appear to be arming a savage against us and giving him the
sword to cut off our heads.

[*This is followed by a description of the acts of persecution committed by the
Staufen against the Church*—ED.]

Philip, with whom we are now concerned, has begun by persecuting
the Church and persists in doing so to this day. For, when striving to
usurp the patrimony of the Church for himself, he used to sign himself Duke of Tuscany and Campagna, asserting that he had received
power up to the very gates of Rome and even that the part of the city
which is called 'Transtiber' had been handed over to his jurisdiction.
Even now he is persecuting the church of Rome and ourselves through
Markward, Diupold and their henchmen and attempting to take the
Kingdom of Sicily away from us. If he does this in the wilderness, how
much worse might he do in the green fields! If he persecutes us and the
church of Rome when not yet wet with blood, like one whose harvest
has yet to be reaped, then what would he do if (which God forbid!) he
obtained the Empire? Hence, with some reason, it seems admirable to
oppose his violence before it increases further. Holy Scripture bears
witness that, even among kings, sons have been punished for their
fathers. For surely the Lord said through Samuel, on account of the sin
of Saul: 'You have acted foolishly, and have not kept the commandments of the Lord your God which he enjoined upon you. Had you
not acted thus, the Lord would now have prepared you an everlasting
Kingdom of Israel; but now your Kingdom will not continue.'[1]

[*Further scriptural examples follow*—ED.]

As for Otto, it appears that it is not lawful to favour him, since he
was chosen by the lesser number; nor is it seemly, lest we appear to be
showing him the apostolic favour, not out of liking for him, but out
of hatred for another; nor is it expedient, because his party seems feeble
and weak compared with Philip's.

But it is known that, of those to whom the election of the Emperor
belongs in the first instance [*principaliter*], as many or even more
agreed upon Otto as agreed upon Philip. The fitness or worthiness of
the person elected is to be considered in such matters as much as, or
even more than, the number of electors. We must not look to the
numerical majority of the electors so much as to the soundness of their

---

1. 1 Kings, xiii, 13–14.

opinions. Otto is more suited to rule the Empire than Philip, since the Lord avenges the sins of the fathers upon the children even to the third and fourth generation of those who hate him[1] (that is, of those who repeat the sins of their fathers), and Philip is repeating the sins of his fathers in persecuting the Church. Although we must not return evil for evil, but do good to those who harm us, nevertheless we are not obliged to return honour for injury to those who persist in their usual misconduct, nor to arm savages against ourselves. We read that the Lord chose the humble to confound the strong, for he took David to be King from among the shepherds. It therefore appears that it is really lawful, seemly and expedient to extend the apostolic favour to Otto. For God forbid that we should give way to a man opposed to God or fear the countenance of the mighty, since, according to the apostle, we must abstain not only from evil itself but also from every semblance of it.[2] For it is written: 'Cursed be the man who puts his trust in man and makes flesh his arm.'[3]

We therefore, for the aforesaid reasons, do not see fit to insist on the boy's behalf that he should at present have the Empire. We utterly reject the person of Philip on account of manifest objections, and we declare that he must be prevented from usurping the Empire. Our legate must further urge the princes either to agree upon a suitable person or to submit themselves to our judgment or decision. But if they choose to do neither, we have waited a long time; we have admonished them to agree; we have instructed them by letter and through our representative; and we have seen fit to give them our advice. We must not seem to be fostering disagreement among them even while we say, like Hezekiah, 'Only let there be peace and truth in our time'.[4] Having followed from a distance that we may see the end, we must not be forced at last, like Peter, to deny the truth which is Christ. This matter brooks no delay. Otto is himself devoted to the Church and comes of devout people on either side, on his mother's from the house of the Kings of England, and on his father's of the family of the Dukes of Saxony, who were all loyal to the Church— especially his great-grandfather the Emperor Lothar, who twice entered Apulia for the honour of the Apostolic See and died obedient to the church of Rome. It is clear, therefore, that Otto must be favoured and accepted as King and summoned to the Imperial Crown, after carrying out all the due preliminaries for the honour of the church of Rome.

---

1. Deuteronomy, v, 9.   2. 1 Thessalonians, v, 22.
3. Jeremiah, xvii, 5.   4. Isaiah, xxxix, 8.

§ 27

The protest of the German princes against the Pope's intervention in the imperial election dispute, January 1202: *Regestum . . . super negotio Romani imperii*, no. 61, ed. cit., 90–2. Haller [p. 55]

The letter of certain princes favouring Philip's party.

To the most holy father and lord Innocent, Supreme and Universal Bishop of the Holy See of Rome, the Archbishops by the grace of God . . . of Magdeburg and Bremen, the Bishops of Worms, Passau, Ratisbon, Constance, Augsburg, Eichstädt, Havelberg, Brandenburg, Meissen and Nuremberg; the Bishop-elect of Bamberg; the Abbots of Fulda, Hersfeld and Kempten; the King of Bohemia, the Duke of Zähringen and ruler of Burgundy, the Duke of Saxony, the Duke of Austria and Styria, the Duke of Meran, the Landgrave of Thuringia, the Margraves of Moravia, the Ostmark, Meissen and Brandenburg, and the Counts of Orlamünde, Sommerschenburg, Brehna and Wettin, greeting and due reverence in Christ.

Reason cannot suppose nor raw simplicity believe that any disturbance of the law may originate from Rome, where law has hitherto stood firm and unshaken. For who would be so harsh or even wrongheaded as to think that ungodliness is spreading from the place where holiness ought to repose? For by the ordinance of God and not by any decision of man it was piously and wisely laid down that the capital of holiness should rest in the city of Rome, which was formerly the capital of godlessness. All must humbly pray that there be no reversion to the original state, lest it be said that omega has returned to alpha.

The holiness of the Sacred See of Rome and its fatherliness, which gives Christian support to all things, will therefore in no way allow us to suffer the unrighteous and dishonourable acts which have been, in a most unseemly fashion, perpetrated by the lord Bishop of Palestrina (who claims to be Your Holiness's legate) at the election of the King of the Romans. We cannot believe that Your Holiness, in your marvellous wisdom, was privy to them or that the holy assembly of cardinals connived at them. Whoever heard of such effrontery as this? Who can come forward to testify truly that anyone has been so bold in the past, since no legend bears witness to this, no history declares it and no document proves it? Where have you read, O Supreme Pontiffs, when have you heard, O holy fathers, cardinals of all the Church, that your predecessors or their representatives ever involved themselves in the elections of Kings of the Romans, so as either to play the part of electors or, like judges, to assess the validity of the election? We do not think you have any example with which to reply. On the contrary, in the election of Bishops of Rome, this right was formerly reserved to the Imperial Crown: that, unless the Roman imperial authority were agreeable, the election could not take place. But the Emperors in their generosity, always striving to extend the worship of God, and seeking to adorn his Church with special privileges, reverently surrendered this right to the Church of God. The decree of Henry I clearly explains this, for it runs as follows: 'We utterly forbid any of our representatives to presume to concoct any proof of an impediment to the election of a Bishop of Rome.' If a simple layman has reverently waived the right which he lawfully had, then how can His Holiness the Pope lay claim to a right which he has never possessed?

Since the reproaches of your holy court affect us like those of a dutiful mother, and since we are closely involved with the honour of the Roman Empire, we cannot keep silence about the wrong it has suffered. The whole body of the princes mentioned above therefore discloses with regret that the Bishop of Palestrina has interfered in the election of the King of the Romans in a manner wholly contrary to law, and we cannot see what role he can be assuming without committing offence. For he is acting either as an elector or as a judge [*cognitor*]. If as an elector, then why did he seek out this opportunity, in the absence of umpires, of exchanging truth for falsehood and virtue for crime? Why has the party of princes which is greater both in numbers and in dignity been so unjustly rejected? And the Bishop of Palestrina could not act as a judge. For if, in choosing a King of the Romans, a division should arise, there is no superior judge by whose sentence it must be healed: the spontaneous decision of the electors must patch it up. For the mediator between God and men, the man Jesus Christ, distinguished the duties of the two powers by appropriate functions and distinct titles: so that 'No soldier of God might involve himself in the affairs of this life',[1] and, conversely, no man who was involved in the affairs of this life might take charge of things divine.[2] But even if we recognize you as judge, the action of Palestrina cannot be justified. We can use your own argument against you: since, should either party be absent, the decision pronounced by the judge cannot be valid. How could the decision of the said Palestrina concerning Otto stand firm, since nothing had previously been done about it? What validity can there be in an act performed by the men whose

1. 2 Timothy, ii, 4.   2. Cf. above, Part II, no. 1B.

numbers are smaller and whose authority is less, an act invalidated by the absence of the other party? May you deal severely with the man who has done these unseemly things, and may he be disciplined with righteous anger.

For we have decided to inform you, most holy father, that we have given our votes to our most serene lord Philip, King of the Romans and always Augustus, with one voice and with common consent, vowing and stoutly promising that he will not withdraw from obedience to you and to the See of Rome; that his devoutness will render him acceptable to God and to you; that he will be full of filial respect; and that his vigour as a defender will commend him to you. Hence we beg that, at the right time and place, you will not deny him the benefit [*beneficium*] of anointing which is part of your function.

§ 28

Part of the letter 'Venerabilem fratrem nostrum' of Innocent III, expounding the papal version of electoral principles, March 26th, 1202: *Regestum . . . super negotio Romani imperii*, no. 62, ed. cit., 92–4.

To the noble [*Berthold*], Duke of Zähringen.

We have graciously received our venerable brother [Eberhard], Archbishop of Salzburg, our beloved son [Eberhard], Abbot of Salem, and the noble [Conrad], Margrave of the Ostmark, the representatives sent by certain princes to the Apostolic See, and have decided to grant them a gracious hearing. We have had the letters which certain princes sent us by their hands carefully perused, and have noted all their contents. The things which these princes have communicated to us by the same letters include one particular objection, for they say that our venerable brother [Guy], Bishop of Palestrina, legate of the Apostolic See, has assumed the role either of an elector or of a judge [*cognitor*]. If that of an elector, he has trespassed on other men's preserves and detracted from the dignity of the princes by interfering in the election. If that of a judge, he seems to have proceeded incorrectly in the absence of one of the parties, since that party was never summoned and therefore ought not to be judged contumacious.

Now we owe justice to every man in accordance with our duty to serve like an apostle, and just as we do not want others to usurp our rights, even so we have no desire to claim for ourselves rights which really belong to the princes. Hence we recognize, as we must, that these princes have the right and power to elect a King who may subsequently be promoted to be Emperor, for it is known that they have these by law and by ancient custom—especially as this right and power came to them from the Apostolic See, which transferred the Roman Empire from the Greeks to the Germans in the person of Charles the Great. But the princes ought to recognize, and in any case do recognize, as they have acknowledged in our presence, that the right and authority to examine the person chosen to be King and to be promoted to the Empire belongs to us who anoint, consecrate and crown him. For it is a regular and general convention that the man concerned with the laying-on of hands is also responsible for the examination of the person. For supposing the princes, even in full agreement (let alone in discord), elected to be King an excommunicate, a sacrilegist, a tyrant, an idiot, a heretic or a heathen, should we be obliged to anoint, consecrate and crown a man of that nature? God forbid such a thing!

Answering the princes' objection, then, we declare that our legate [Guy], Bishop of Palestrina, did not assume the role of an elector (as certain princes objected in their letters to us), for he neither elected anyone nor had him elected, and so he in no way interfered with the election. Nor did he act as a judge, since he did not think the election of either candidate, in so far as it was the deed of the electors, ought to be confirmed or declared void; and so he in no way usurped for himself any right of the princes, nor did he contravene any such right. But he did discharge the duty of a 'pronouncer' [denuntiator]. He pronounced the Duke personally unworthy and pronounced the King personally fit to have the Empire, on account of the merits of the persons chosen more than of the efforts of the electors; though it is also maintained that a greater number of those who by law and custom have the power of electing the King who may be promoted to be Emperor did agree upon King Otto. Again, since the supporters of Philip presumed to elect him in the absence of the others, whom they ignored, it is plain that they acted wrongly, since it is a well-tried point of law that the ignoring of one person serves more than the opposition of many to invalidate an election. Hence we can, with some reason, see that, as they deserved to lose their privilege for abusing the power allowed to them, their misconduct will not prevent others from making use of their rights.

And since the said Duke did not receive coronation or unction either in the proper place or from the proper person, but the said King received both these things in the right place, i.e. Aachen, and from the right person, i.e. our venerable brother [Adolf], Archbishop of Cologne, we therefore, as justice demands it, pronounce and nominate not Philip but Otto King. In rejecting the said Philip, Duke of Swabia, we needed to condemn, not merely to reprove him, on account of his obvious defects of character, for they require to be, not merely reproved, but openly condemned.

It is clear both by law and by precedent that, when in an election the votes of the princes are divided, we can, after admonishing them and waiting for a time, favour either of the parties, especially after we have been asked to anoint, consecrate and crown, which indeed both parties have many times asked us to do. For if the princes, having been admonished and given time, either cannot or will not agree, must the Apostolic See be left without an advocate and defender and suffer for their fault? The princes know, and you, noble lord, are aware that, when Lothar and Conrad were elected in conflict with one another, the Bishop of Rome crowned Lothar and after coronation he obtained the Empire, though Conrad subsequently came back into the Pope's favour.

We have therefore decided that the princes must be reminded by the said representatives that, just as we are abstaining from violating their rights, so must they abstain from violating ours, and must abandon the said Duke, who has been rejected by our just judgment, and must not refuse to support the said King Otto, save for some legitimate reason which they must bring forward and indicate.

§ 29

The papal version of the relationship between Pope and Emperor; an extract from Innocent III's letter to Otto IV on the position of Emperor, January 16th, 1209: *Regestum . . . super negotio Romani imperii*, no. 179, ed. cit., 226–7.

To the Same [i.e. To the illustrious King Otto, elected to be Emperor of the Romans].

Blessed be God, who by his ineffable mercy has for the most part fulfilled our desire concerning you and will, we are certain, never rest until he has fully carried it out, to the praise and glory of his own name and to the honour and advancement of the Church, the Empire and all the Christian people. As we have truly understood, you have marvellously increased both in worldly and in spiritual virtue, so that we can rejoice in you, saying, in the words of the Lord, that we have found a man after our own heart.

Behold, dearest son, our soul is so fused into yours and your heart is so bound up with ours that we are thought to feel and desire the same in everything, like one heart and one soul. The pen cannot write, nor the tongue describe, nor the mind grasp what immense advantages can be hoped for from this. For the government of this world was entrusted to the two of us in the beginning: for if we are of one mind and agreed upon good, then surely, as the prophet testifies, the sun and moon shall stand still in their places,[1] and the crooked shall become straight and the rough be made smooth.[2] For if the Lord be for us, nothing can stand in our way or resist us, since we have the two swords of which the apostles said to the Lord: 'Behold, here are two swords', and concerning which the Lord replied to the apostles: 'It is enough.'[3] For without doubt the authority of the bishop and the power of the king, which are symbolized by those two swords, and which both reach their highest point in us, are wholly sufficient in themselves to perform this function successfully if each of them is effectually aided by the other, until the state of the world, which has almost been ruined by an excess of evil, is restored by our solicitous endeavours, when vice has been cut down and virtue restored.

1. Cf. Habakkuk, iii, 11; also Joshua, x, 12–13.   2. Isaiah, xl, 4.
3. Luke, xxii, 38.

CHAPTER V

Frederick II as Emperor and as King of Sicily

THE GERMAN POLICY OF FREDERICK II AND HENRY VII

§§ 30–3. The first three of these documents show how the Emperor Frederick II and his son Henry VII made large concessions calculated to increase the independence of the ecclesiastical and lay princes of Germany and their power within their own territories at the expense of the developing cities.

The concessions in the privilege to the ecclesiastical princes (30) were made by Frederick in order to get his son Henry, previously crowned King of Sicily, chosen King of the Romans also. By this means, the Imperial and Sicilian Crowns could become united in the person of a member of the house of Staufen, in spite of papal opposition.

Henry VII's bold policy in favour of the cities provoked opposition among German princes to whom his father was at the time indebted for their service in Italy. There had been some hope of strengthening the territorial power of the Staufen Emperors in Germany through the cities, which were prepared to accept royal officials. But Henry was forced to reverse the policy and side with the princes. His concessions to them (31) were confirmed by Frederick in 1232 at the Diet of Friuli. The policy of attacking the autonomy of the towns was carried a stage further by an edict dissolving city communes (32)—although it proved impossible for Frederick to follow this line consistently. Already by 1235 he was treating certain cities more favourably.

Extracts 30–2 help to point the contrast between the diminution of imperial powers in Germany and the increasing royal autocracy in Sicily (see below, 36–9). In 1235, Frederick, at the Diet of Mainz, by appointing a permanent justiciar in Germany, showed some signs of repeating his Sicilian policy there (33).

See G. Blondel, *Étude sur la politique de l'empereur Frédéric II en*

Allemagne (1892); M. Stimming, 'Kaiser Friedrich II und der Abfall der deutschen Fürsten', H.Z., 120 (1919); A. L. Poole, 'Germany in the reign of Frederick II', C.M.H., VI (1929); E. Rosenstock, 'Über "Reich", "Staat" und "Stadt" in Deutschland von 1230–1235', M.I.Ö.G., 44 (1930); Barraclough in Barraclough, ed. *Mediaeval Germany*, I, 119 foll., with references; Mitteis, 'German feudalism', ibid., II, 260–1; Barraclough, *Origins of modern Germany*, 223, 235 foll., with further references; E. Sestan, 'Il significato storico della "Constitutio in favorem principum" di Federico II', *Atti del convegno internazionale di studi federiciani* (Palermo, 1952); J. D. Navack, 'L'expansion du *justiciarius* sicilien vers le nord et l'est européens', ibid.; E. Klingelhoefer, *Die Reichsgesetze von 1220, 1231/32 und 1235* (Weimar, 1955); E. Kantorowicz, *Frederick the Second* (London, 1957), 373 foll., 410–11.

§ 30

Frederick II's *Privilegium in favorem principum ecclesiasticorum*, Frankfurt, April 26th, 1220: ed. L. Weiland in M.G.H., Const., II (1896), 89–91.

In the name of the holy and indivisible Trinity. Frederick II, by the gracious favour of God King of the Romans, always Augustus and King of Sicily.

We duly recollect how loyally and effectually our beloved and loyal subjects the ecclesiastical princes have hitherto aided us by promoting us to the summit of the Empire, upholding us there after our promotion and later, graciously and in agreement, electing our son Henry to be their King and lord. We have therefore concluded that those by whom we were promoted ought always to be promoted themselves, and that those by whom we were supported should, together with their churches, always be defended by us, against any possible harm. Therefore, as certain customs or rather abuses burdensome to them have sprung up as a result of the long period of disorder in the Empire, which, by the grace of God, is now at peace, in the form of new tolls, of new coins which have ruined one another because of resemblances between the images upon them, of wars between advocates and of innumerable other evils: we have countered these abuses with certain statutes.

1. First we have promised that henceforth we will never on the death of any ecclesiastical prince claim for the fisc what he leaves. We forbid any layman to claim this for himself on any pretext: if the prince has died intestate, it shall pass to his successor; and if the prince has made any will, we wish this to be confirmed. If anyone, contrary to this decree, presumes to claim for himself what has been left, he shall be

proscribed and outlawed and be deprived of any fief or benefice he may have.

2. Item, we will not henceforth introduce new tolls or new coins into their territories or jurisdictions without consulting them or against their will; but will preserve and guard in their entirety the ancient tolls and coining rights granted to their churches. We will not ourselves infringe them or allow them in any way to be violated by others, since coinage is often upset and debased by imitating the image upon it, a practice which we utterly forbid.

3. Item, we will not, to their prejudice, receive in our cities men of any sort who are in the princes' service, no matter what their reason is for withdrawing from obedience to them. We wish them to observe the same rule among themselves, and we wish all laymen to observe it where they are concerned.

4. Item, we decree that no one shall damage the property of any church on the pretext of being the advocate of that property: if he does any damage, he shall make it good twice over and pay one hundred marks of silver to our treasury.

5. Item, if any of the princes by feudal right summons a vassal of his who has gravely offended him and thus recovers the fief, we will protect it for his use, and, if he wishes to confer the fief on us out of his own good and generous inclinations, we will receive it notwithstanding any personal feelings. If any fief falls vacant to an ecclesiastical prince by any means, including the death of the feudatory, we will on no account invade it upon our own authority (this would really be an act of violence) if we cannot obtain it by his good will and generous grant: but we will rather strive to defend it effectually for his use.

6. Item, we will (as is right) shun persons whom the ecclesiastical princes have excommunicated, so long as they have reported these to us by word of mouth, by letters, or through honourable and trustworthy representatives. Unless these persons are first absolved, we will not allow them to appear in court, always provided that excommunication shall not exempt them from answering persons who proceed against them, which they must do without advocates. But excommunication shall deprive them of the right and power to give judgment or give evidence in court and to proceed against others.

7. And, since the material sword was established to assist the spiritual, excommunication shall be followed by a sentence of outlawry from us if it is proved to us by any of the aforesaid means that they have remained under excommunication for a period of over six weeks; and

the sentence shall not be revoked unless the excommunication is first withdrawn.

8. We have firmly promised to rule and benefit them in this and in all other ways by just and effectual judgment; and they in turn have faithfully promised to help us effectually as far as they are able against every man who violently resists any such judgment of ours in their favour.

9. We further decree that no buildings, i.e. castles or cities, may be erected on the estates of churches on the pretext of advocacy or on any other pretext. If any of these have already been constructed contrary to the wishes of those to whom the estates belong, they shall be destroyed by the royal power.

10. Item, in imitation of our grandfather the Emperor Frederick of happy memory, we forbid any of our officials to claim for himself any jurisdiction over tolls or coins or in any other sphere in any city belonging to the same princes, save for a period of eight days before our court is publicly announced in that city and for eight days after it ends. On those days they must not presume in any way to infringe the jurisdiction of the prince and the customs of the city. And whenever we arrive in any of the princes' cities without announcing a public court, our officials shall have no rights in it, but the prince and lord of the city shall enjoy full power therein.

11. Knowing the great loyalty of the said princes towards us, we are the more anxious to further their interests. And since oblivion, the foe of memory, is accustomed to bury the deeds of men as long stretches of time unfold, we, exercising watchful care, wish these favours we have conferred upon the churches to be made perpetual ones. We decree that our heirs and successors in the Empire shall preserve and enforce them and cause them to be universally respected by laymen for the assistance of churches. And that they may be known to posterity and not escape the memory or knowledge of present generations, we have had them noted down upon this charter and had the charter inscribed with the names of those who were present, i.e. the princes, and authenticated by our seal.

The witnesses are as follows: Siegfried, Archbishop of Mainz; Theoderic, Archbishop of Trier; Engelbert, Archbishop of Cologne; Albert, Archbishop of Magdeburg; Hugh, Bishop of Liége; Otto, Bishop of Utrecht; Ecbert, Bishop of Bamberg; Conrad, Bishop of Ratisbon; Hartwig, Bishop of Eichstädt; Theoderic, Bishop of Munich; Henry, Bishop of Worms; Engelhard, Bishop of Naumburg; Henry, Bishop of Basel and many others.

The signature of the lord Frederick the Second, invincible King of the Romans and King of Sicily.

I, Conrad, Bishop of Metz and Speier, Chancellor of the Imperial Palace, have witnessed this in place of the lord Siegfried, Archbishop of Mainz, who is Arch-chancellor of all Germany.

These things were done in the year of Our Lord's incarnation 1220, indiction nine, under the rule of the lord Frederick II, most glorious King of the Romans and of Sicily, in the eighth year of his reign in Germany and the twenty-third of his reign in Sicily.

Given at Frankfurt on April 26th.

§ 31

Henry VII's *Constitutio in favorem Principum*, Worms, May 1st, 1231: ed. L. Weiland in M.G.H., Const., II, 418–20.

Henry, by the grace of God King of the Romans and always Augustus, his grace and every good wish to all his loyal subjects. We wish to maintain our ecclesiastical and lay princes and other loyal subjects of our realm in their liberty and to support them in every way. Hence, out of our royal generosity, we have granted them a privilege which we wish our cities to observe strictly.

1. First, we decree that we ought not to build any new castle or city to the prejudice of the princes.

2. Item, that new markets shall not in any way damage old ones.

3. Item, that no one may be forced to go to any market against his will.

4. Item, that ancient roads shall not be diverted except by the wish of travellers.

5. Item, that the jurisdiction of our cities outside their walls shall be abolished.

6. Item, that every prince shall peacefully enjoy the liberties, rights of justice, counties and hundreds, whether these hundreds are in his free possession or infeudated, according to the approved custom of his country.

7. Item, that the hundredmen shall receive their hundreds from the lord of the land or from the person enfeoffed by him.

8. Item, that no one shall change the meeting place of a hundred court without consent of the lord of the land.

9. Item, that no one of knightly rank [*synodalis*] shall be summoned to the meetings of the hundreds. (1).

1. *Synodales* were laymen of higher standing (such as nobles or *ministeriales*) who were directly answerable to the bishop and his synod for ecclesiastical transgressions, and were thus exempt from the jurisdiction of the archdeacons .

10. Item, that persons residing outside town walls [*pfalburgere*] may no longer be counted as citizens.

11. Item, that tributes of corn, wine and money and any others which the peasants have agreed to pay shall be remitted and no longer received.

12. Item, that bondmen belonging to princes, nobles, *ministeriales* and churches shall not be received in our cities.

13. Item, that properties and fiefs belonging to princes, nobles, *ministeriales* and churches which have been occupied by our cities shall be restored and not occupied in future.

14. Item, that we will not, either personally or through our own men, interfere with a safe conduct [*conductus*] issued by the princes through land which they hold of us in fee.

15. Item, that no one shall be compelled by our officials [*scultetos*] to restore the dues which, as of ancient custom, he received from his men before these men installed themselves in our cities.

16. Item, that no one who is harmful to the land or has been condemned or outlawed by a judge shall consciously be admitted to our cities; if any such are admitted they shall on conviction be expelled.

17. Item, that we will not cause any new coinage to be struck in the land of any prince to the detriment of that prince's coinage.

18. Item, that out cities shall not extend their jurisdiction beyond their own limits, except where we have some special jurisdiction.

19. Item, that in our cities a plaintiff shall bring suit in the court to which the defendant is subject, unless the defendant or chief debtor happens to be in the same place, in which case he shall answer in the same place.

20. Item, that no one in our cities may receive as security goods which form part of a fief, save with the consent of the overlord and from his hand.

21. Item, that nobody may be forced to perform municipal services unless he is bound to do so by law.

22. Item, that men under the protection of an advocate who reside in our cities shall pay in full the ancient and proper dues of the advocacy and shall not be molested with undue exactions.

23. Item, that bondmen, men under advocates and feudatories who wish to go to their lords shall not be detained by our officials.

Our Royal Majesty has decreed that our beloved and honourable princes shall enjoy these benefits, saving the privileges obtained from our father and those which may hereafter be obtained from him or from us; and we wish the vassals, *ministeriales*, men and cities belonging to us and to the Empire to enjoy the same right.

The witnesses are as follows: Siegfried, Archbishop-elect of Mainz; the Archbishops Theoderic of Trier, Albert of Magdeburg and Henry of Cologne; the Bishops Hermann of Würzburg, Henry of Worms, [Berthold] of Strassburg, [Berengar] of Speier, [Sibot] of Augsburg, [Berthold] of Chur; the Abbots of St. Gall, Weissenburg and Prüm; the Dukes of Meran, Lorraine and Brabant, and as many others.

Given in a solemn court at Worms, in the year of Our Lord 1231, on the first of May, indiction four.

§ 32

Frederick II's *Edictum contra communia civitatum*, Aquileia, December 1231–May 1232: ed. L. Weiland in M.G.H., Const., II, 192–4.

In the name of the holy and indivisible Trinity. Frederick II, by the gracious favour of God Emperor of the Romans, always Augustus, and King of Jerusalem and Sicily.

We hold the monarchy with the title 'Roman' primarily of the Maker by whom kings reign and princes hold their princedoms, and who has set our throne above the peoples and kingdoms; and we are established in the wholeness of power. It therefore befits Our Imperial Majesty not only to guard and maintain in their ancient rights those by whom we obtained our supreme glory and those in whom it consists, for they were summoned with us to part of the care, and receive honour and glory from our supremacy: but also, so far as equity allows and reason permits, to adorn them honourably and fittingly with new and honourable gifts both of right and of grace. By the failure and neglect of law, in the regions of Germany, certain detestable practices have become so much a matter of custom that those who keep up the appearance of good will be able to cloak their wicked acts under false covering; and this detracts from the honour and rights of the princes of the Empire and consequently enfeebles the Emperor's authority. It therefore falls to us to ensure that customs of this nature, which we consider rather to be corrupt practices, are not continued any further.

Therefore, desiring a most generous interpretation for the liberties and gifts which our beloved princes of the Empire now possess and are to hold for the time being by gift of our supremacy, and wishing them to be held by the princes in every way in peaceful freedom, by this our edictal decree, in every city and town in Germany we dissolve the communes and councils and depose the masters or governors of the citizens and any other officials who have been appointed by the whole body of citizens without the consent of the archbishops or bishops, no matter by what name they are known in the different places.

We likewise annul and dissolve the confraternities and associations of every craft, no matter by what name they are commonly called.

Again, we have seen fit to ordain by this our edictal decree that in every city or town where it is lawful to coin money, neither victuals nor merchandise may be bought or sold for any unit of silver other than the moneys which are common to every city or town.

For as in bygone days the archbishops and bishops used to be responsible for the government of cities and of all property which was dispensed by the supreme Emperor, even so do we wish them and their officials whom they have specially appointed to remain perpetually in charge of this government, notwithstanding any abuse which has arisen by anyone acting to the contrary in any city—for we consider this to have been done in deed but not of right.

Therefore, that these monstrous abuses may be totally uprooted, and not cloaked under any cover of authority, from this day forward we revoke and annul and declare null and valueless all privileges and letters patent and close which we or our predecessors or any archbishops and bishops have benevolently given to any private person or city, and which concern associations, communes or councils contrary to the interests of the princes and the Empire.

We declare that this carefully formulated statute and decree has been issued in the form of a judgment by deliberation of the princes and with our certain knowledge. We therefore ordain and decree by imperial edict that no person whatsoever, be he great or humble, clerk or layman, shall at any time in the future or in any way presume to oppose or obstruct this our statute and decree. And if anyone does so presume, let him know that, as well as incurring our displeasure, he will, by way of penalty, be fined forty pounds of pure gold, which we wish to go to our fisc. To record this our statute and decree and perpetually enforce it, we have ordered the present divine charter to be drawn up and to be authenticated by the impress of the golden bull with the seal of Our Majesty.

The witnesses of this deed are as follows: Berthold, Patriarch of Aquileia; the Archbishops Albert of Magdeburg, Theoderic of Ravenna and Berardus of Palermo; the Bishops [Ecbert] of Bamberg, Siegfried of Ratisbon, Chancellor of the Imperial Palace, and Henry of Worms; and the Bishops of Brixen, Osnabrück, Chur, Reggio, Imola, Modena and Faenza; the Dukes Albert of Saxony, Otto of Meran and Bernard of Carinthia; the Counts Henry of Ortenberg, Henry of Nassau, Conrad of Hohenlohe, Simon of Spanheim and H . . . his brother, and Lothar of Hohenstadt; G . . . of Arnstein, legate of the Sacred Empire in Italy; G . . . of Bolland; Gunzelin; Richard, Chamberlain of the Imperial Palace, and many others.

The signature of the lord Frederick the Second, by the grace of God invincible Emperor of the Romans and King of Jerusalem and Sicily.

I, Siegfried, Bishop of Ratisbon, Chancellor of the Imperial Palace, have witnessed this in the place of the lord Siegfried, Archbishop of Mainz and Arch-chancellor in Germany.

These things were done in the year of Our Lord's incarnation 1232, in the month of April, indiction five, under the imperial rule of our lord Frederick the Second, by the grace of God invincible Emperor of the Romans and always Augustus, King of Jerusalem and Sicily, in his twelfth year as Roman Emperor, his seventh as King of Jerusalem and his thirty-fourth as King of Sicily; happily Amen.

Given at Aquileia, in the year, month and indiction stated above.

§ 33

The establishment of a royal court or *Hofgericht*: chapter 28 of the Peace of Mainz, August 1235: ed. L. Weiland in M.G.H., Const., II, 246-7.

The government of the Empire and the affairs of various lands and provinces demand attention. As it is always advisable for us to deal with these by our own personal care, we wish lawsuits over which we cannot preside in person to be determined by a man of proved loyalty and honourable reputation who shall be in charge of judgments in our place. His judgment shall be final, save in those matters which we have specially reserved to be decided by us in person.

We therefore decree that our court shall have a justiciar, a man of free condition who shall remain in that office for at least one year, provided he bears himself righteously and well. He shall preside here in court every day, save on Sundays and other great festivals, dispensing justice to all who complain save in cases affecting the persons, rights, honour, fiefs, property or inheritance of princes and other persons of the

P

highest rank, and except for cases of the greatest importance; for we reserve these to be examined and judged by our own Supreme Highness. This judge shall not fix dates or appointed times for difficult cases which are his responsibility and which involve such persons without special orders from us. He shall not outlaw condemned men or free them from outlawry, for we reserve these powers to the authority of Our Excellency. And the judge shall swear that he will not accept anything for his judgment, and that he will not, out of love or hatred, fear or favour, in response to bribes or entreaties or for any other reason, make a decision other than one that he knows or conscientiously believes to be right, in good faith and entirely without deceit or trickery. We remit and assign to the judge the dues which are derived from releasing men from outlawry and are commonly called *Wette*—that is, those paid by men whose cases have come before him—so that he may be a kinder judge and may not take gifts from anyone. He shall not release anyone from this penalty, so that men may be more afraid of outlawry.

LETTERS OF GREGORY IX AND INNOCENT IV

§§ 34–5. These extracts are taken from letters issued in the name of Gregory IX and Innocent IV during the prolonged struggle between Empire and Papacy in the reign of Frederick II. Both letters were answers to imperial recriminations and accusations. *Aeger, cui levia* (35) was designed to refute the imperial arguments put forward after Innocent IV had excommunicated Frederick II at Lyons in 1245. Both letters are important for their interpretation of the Donation of Constantine (above, Part I, no. 4), and for the use which they make of it to affirm, in a sense, the temporal power of the Papacy. *Si memoriam beneficiorum* (34) also makes use of the theory of the transfer of Empire (cf. Part III, nos. 26 and 28 above). To define the relationship between clerical and lay power, *Aeger, cui levia* invokes the figure of Melchisedech (cf. above, Part II, no. 1B) and makes further use of the allegory of the two swords (cf. above, Part II, no. 9B; Part III, nos. 10, 20A).

See G. Laehr, *Die Konstantinische Schenkung in der abendländischen Literatur des Mittelalters bis zur Mitte des 14. Jahrhunderts* (Berlin, 1926), 89 foll.; Ullmann, *Mediaeval papalism*, 151 foll.; W. Ullmann, 'Frederick II's opponent, Innocent IV, as Melchisedech', *Atti del convegno internazionale di studi federiciani*; Folz, *L'idée d'empire*, 99; van den Baar,

Translatio Imperii, 133 foll.; Pacaut, *La théocratie*, 155 foll.; Goez, *Translatio Imperii*, 167 foll.; M. Pacaut, 'L'autorité pontificale selon Innocent IV', M.A. (1960); W. Ullmann, 'Some reflexions on the opposition of Frederick II to the Papacy', A.S.P., 12 (1962).

§ 34

The papal version of the relationship between Pope and Emperor: an extract from the letter 'Si memoriam beneficiorum' of Gregory IX to Frederick II, October 23rd, 1236: ed. G. H. Pertz and C. Rodenberg in M.G.H., *Epistolae saeculi XIII e regestis pontificum romanorum*, I (Berlin, 1883), 604–5.

... We cannot pass by a matter which has been publicly revealed to the entire world: i.e. that Constantine, who held the sole monarchy over all regions of the world, with the unanimous consent of all the Senate and people established not only over the City but over the whole Roman Empire, decided it was fitting that, as the vicar of the Chief of the Apostles ruled the Empire of souls and of the priesthood throughout the entire world, even so should he become the chief governor of things and bodies throughout the entire world. Thinking that the man to whom he knew the Lord had committed the government of heavenly things on earth ought with the bridle of justice to govern things earthly, Constantine deprived himself by his own vow and handed over in perpetuity to the care of the Bishop of Rome the imperial emblems and sceptres and the City and all its subject region, where you have lavished money in your efforts to trouble us, like Behemoth, who thinks nothing of drinking up a river and hopes that Jordan will flow into his mouth.[1] Constantine even handed over the Empire itself. He thought it most undesirable that a terrestrial Emperor should wield any power in the very place where the head of the whole Christian religion has been established by the heavenly Emperor, and so, leaving Italy to the apostolic government, he chose himself a new dwelling in Greece. Thence the Apostolic See later, without in any way reducing the substance of its own jurisdiction, transferred the supreme court of the Empire to the Germans in the person of Charles the Great, who showed that the almost insupportable yoke laid upon him by the church of Rome ought to be borne dutifully and devoutly; it placed this upon your predecessors by the grant of consecration and anointing and con-

1. Job, xl, 18.

ceded them the power of the sword at the subsequent coronation. You recall that this was done to your own person. Hence, so long as you fail to recognize your own maker, you are convicted of detracting from the rights of the Apostolic See and to an equal extent from your own loyalty and honour. . . .

§ 35

The papal version of the relationship between Pope and Emperor: extract from the Bull 'Aeger, cui levia' issued by Pope Innocent IV at Lyons, 1245: E. Winkelmann, *Acta Imperii inedita seculi XIII et XIV*, II (Innsbruck, 1885), 698.

. . . It is imperceptive to suppose, not knowing how to seek out the origins of things, that the Apostolic See first obtained its rulership of the Empire from Prince Constantine, for this rulership is known to have lain with it both naturally and potentially at an earlier time. For the Lord Jesus Christ, the Son of God, as true man and true God, was true king and true priest after the order of Melchisedech, as he plainly showed by sometimes using for men's sake the honourable title of Royal Majesty and sometimes on their behalf performing the office of priest with his father. He therefore established not only a pontifical but also a royal monarchy in the Apostolic See, handing the reins at once of heavenly and of earthly Empire to St. Peter and his successors. This is sufficiently symbolized by there being more than one key, that it may be understood that the Vicar of Christ has received the power of judgment through the first key which we have received in temporal matters upon earth and through the other in spiritual matters in heaven. The same Constantine, being joined to the Catholic Church by the Christian faith, humbly resigned to the Church the unbounded despotism which he had unlawfully exercised abroad. As a monument to his resignation, a token and a sign full of mystical meaning, we, in reverend imitation of earlier fathers, retain the emblems of the princely status which he left. And Constantine received from the Vicar of Christ, the successor of Peter, the divinely regulated power of the Empire, that he might henceforth use it legitimately to punish the wicked and praise the good, and that, though he had previously abused the power allowed him, he might now be satisfied with the authority he was granted.

For the two swords of the two governments are contained within the bosom of the faithful Church, as the declaration of the apostle shows, in accordance with the authority of God; and hence no one who is not in the Church can have either sword. Peter is believed to have a right to both, since of the material sword the Lord did not say to him 'throw away your sword', but 'put it away in the sheath'—meaning, 'you are no longer to wield it personally'. He distinctly said '*your* sword' and '*your* sheath',[1] so as to give a sign that his vicar, the head of the Church militant, although the actual use of this sword was forbidden him by divine prohibition, should have the authority by which the sword is used for the service of law, the punishment of evil and the protection of good. The power of this material sword is enfolded within the Church, but is unfolded through the Emperor, who receives it from the Church; and, being only latent and confined whilst in the bosom of the Church, it becomes real when it is transferred to the Prince. This is plainly demonstrated by the ritual in which the Supreme Pontiff presents the sword contained in its sheath to the Emperor whom he crowns, and the Prince receives and draws it and by brandishing it gives the sign that he has received power to wield it. . . .

SICILIAN LAWS OF FREDERICK II

§§ 36-9. These are taken from the *Liber Augustalis*, the Constitutions issued for the Kingdom of Sicily by the Emperor Frederick II at Melfi in August 1231. They record his attempt to restore order and establish a strong centralized regime on the basis of a code of laws some of which were issued by the Emperor himself and some of which had stemmed from his Norman predecessors in Sicily. Extracts 36A and B are statements of Frederick's official view of the origins and purpose of the royal authority and of the Prince's mission to dispense justice. Extracts 37A to E are mainly concerned with the mechanism by which justice was to be impartially and uncorruptly administered. Extracts 38A and B concern the preservation of royal demesne and regalian rights. The series of extracts under 39 tells something of the nature of feudalism in the Kingdom of Sicily and of the control which the Emperor claimed to exercise over fiefs and feudatories.

See W. Cohn, *Das Zeitalter der Hohenstaufen in Sizilien* (Breslau, 1925), 113 foll.; G. Pepe, *Lo stato ghibellino di Federico II* (Bari, 1951), 36 foll., 127 foll.; A. De Stefano, *L'idea imperiale di Federico II* (Bologna, 1952),

1. John, xviii, 10-11; Matthew, xxvi, 51-2.

9 foll., 124 foll.; A. Marongiu, 'Concezione della sovranità ed asso-
lutismo di Giustiniano e di Federico II', F. Calasso, 'Rileggendo il
"Liber Augustalis" ' and Navack, 'L'expansion du *justiciarius*', all in
Atti del convegno internazionale di studi federiciani; Kantorowicz, *Frederick
II*, 222 foll.; E. H. Kantorowicz, *The King's two bodies: a study in
mediaeval political theology* (Princeton, 1957), 97 foll.; T. Buyken, *Das
römische Recht in den Constitutionen von Melfi* (Cologne, 1960).

§ 36

Extracts from the Constitutions of Melfi or *Liber Augustalis*, the codifica-
tion of law issued for the Kingdom of Sicily by the Emperor Frederick
II in 1231, incorporating some legislation of his Norman predecessors:
all in J. L. A. Huillard-Bréholles, *Historia Diplomatica Friderici Secundi*,
IV (1854).
The Prince and his position as lawgiver.
A. Preamble: Huillard-Bréholles, IV, 3–5.

THE EMPEROR FREDERICK II, CAESAR OF THE ROMANS ALWAYS AUGUSTUS,
OF ITALY, SICILY, JERUSALEM, AND ARLES, HAPPY, VICTORIOUS AND
TRIUMPHANT.

Here begins the first book of the imperial constitutions.

PREAMBLE

When the structure of the world had been shaped by Divine Providence and the primary material of nature of the better sort duly assigned
to the models of things, he who had planned the creation, pondering his
work and seeing that it was good, determined on profound deliberation
to place before his other creatures Man, as the most worthy of creatures
from the globe beneath the orbit of the moon, created in his own
image and likeness, whom he had set a little lower than the angels.[1]
Transforming him from the mud of the earth he made him alive in the
spirit, and, crowning him with a diadem of honour and glory,[1] he
added to him a part of his own body for wife and companion; and he
conferred on them a great privilege in that he originally made them
both immortal. He placed them, however, under a law of his commanding, and, because they failed to observe it strictly, as the penalty
of their transgression he deprived them of the immortality which he
had previously bestowed upon them. But that God in his mercy might
not so suddenly and ruinously undo completely what he had made,

1. Psalms, viii, 5–6; Hebrews, ii, 7.

and lest from the destruction of the human form might result the destruction of others, since they would lack direction and serve no useful purpose, God sowed the earth with mortals of the seed of both and subjected it to them.

These mortals were not ignorant of their ancestor's crime, the taint of his transgression was extended to them through their fathers, and they conceived mutual hatreds and divided into lordships the property which is by natural law common; and man, whom God created simple and righteous, did not hesitate to involve himself in disputes. And so, under the stress of very necessity, and likewise at the instigation of Divine Providence, the heads of nations were created, that criminal licence might be disciplined by them; that they, being judges of life and death in the nations, might, being in a way like executors of Divine Providence, establish what each man's fortune, lot and condition should be. These are the things especially required at their hands by the King of kings and Prince of princes, so that they can say they have discharged the stewardship entrusted to them:[1] they must protect the Holy Church, the mother of the Christian religion, from being defiled by the secret treachery of the detractors of the faith, and must guard her by the power of the material sword from the attacks of open enemies, and as far as possible they must preserve peace for the people, and after peace justice, for these embrace one another like two sisters.

And therefore we, whom the right hand of God alone raised beyond human expectation to the summit of the Roman Empire and the crowns of other kingdoms, wishing to return to the living God double the talents entrusted to us,[2] in reverence for Jesus Christ, from whom we received all we have, have determined to 'render the calf of our lips'[3] by promoting justice and establishing laws, first providing for that part of our dominions which is known to stand most in need of an immediate provision for justice from us. Therefore, since the Kingdom of Sicily, the precious inheritance of Our Majesty, has, mainly because of our childhood weakness and our absence, been shaken by the onslaughts of disturbance in the past, we have determined to provide for its peace and justice with the greatest industry, for we have always found it loyal and ready to obey Our Serenity, though some people who did not belong to the Sicilian or to our own fold did resist us. We therefore wish the present decrees issued in our name to prevail only in our Kingdom of Sicily; rescinding as obsolete the laws and customs in this Kingdom that conflict with these our statutes, we order the statutes to be strictly

1. Cf. Luke, xvi, 2.　　2. Cf. Matthew, xxv, 14–30.　　3. Hosea, xiv, 3.

observed by all men in future. We have ordered all earlier decrees of the Kings of Sicily and ourselves whose retention we have commanded to be transferred to the aforesaid statutes, that those which are not included in the present corpus of statutes may not have any force or authority in courts or outside them.

B. Book I, *titulus* xxxi: Huillard-Bréholles, IV, 33–4.
  Of the observance of justice.
  THE SAME AUGUSTUS [*i.e. the Emperor Frederick*].

It was not without great consultation and profound deliberation that the Roman citizens transferred to the Roman Prince by the royal law [*lex regia*] the right to establish law and also the sovereign power [*imperium*],[1] so that the source of justice might flow from the man who was defending justice,—from him who, from the summit of the imperial estate assigned to him, governed peoples by his might. And so we can see that it was not merely a useful but even a necessary provision that, with these two things, i.e. the source of law and the protection of law, side by side in the person of the same man, justice should never lack force, nor force be applied without justice. Caesar must therefore be father and son, master and servant of justice—he must be father and master in spreading justice abroad and in maintaining it when he has done so; and he must be a son in respecting justice and a servant in ministering to its plenty.

Therefore, bearing this consideration in mind, we, who have received from the hand of the Lord the sceptre of the Empire and the government of the Kingdom of Sicily (among other kingdoms), announce to all our loyal subjects in this Kingdom the resolution on which we are determined: we are minded to dispense justice to every man among them with ready zeal and without any exception of persons, so that in every place they may, by means of our officials, to whom we have committed its administration, be able to find abundance of it. We wish the officials' duties to be distinct, and we place some of them in charge of civil suits and others in charge of criminal prosecutions.

C. Book I, *titulus* iv: Huillard-Bréholles, IV, 9.
  That no man may meddle with the acts or resolutions of Kings.
  KING ROGER

There must be no dispute about judgments, resolutions or dispositions made by the King; for it is a form of sacrilege to dispute about his

---

1. Justinian, *Institutes*, Bk. I, *titulus* ii, section 6.

judgments and acts or his statutes and resolutions, or about the fitness of one chosen and appointed by the King.

§ 37

The preservation of peace and administration of justice.
A. Book I, *titulus* viii: Huillard-Bréholles, IV, 12–13.
   Of respect for peace, and of the general peace to be observed in the Kingdom.
      THE SAME AUGUSTUS [*i.e. the Emperor Frederick*]
   We command that peace, which is inseparable from justice as justice is from peace, be respected throughout each and every portion of this Kingdom, so that no man may in future avenge himself on his own authority for excesses and injuries that have been or may be committed; nor may he seize goods or persons or take reprisals or start a war within the Kingdom. He must conduct his case according to legal form before the master justiciar and district justiciars, or before the local chamberlains, bailiffs or lords, whichever of them has jurisdiction over the case. But if it happens that anyone is provoked by violent injury into putting up a defence for the safety of his person or his property, of urgent necessity, we do not forbid him instant defence,—that is, before he turns to other acts or other persons,—though he must be moderate if his defence is to be lawful. He may defend himself with weapons similar and equivalent to those with which he is attacked: so that if he is attacked with sharp weapons, he may lawfully defend himself with sharp weapons. If his adversary attacks him without sharp weapons, or with any other kind of weapons, he may defend himself by the same form of combat, so long as he does so, as has been said, instantaneously.

B. Book I, *titulus* xliv: Huillard-Bréholles, IV, 47–8.
   Of the office of justiciar.
      THE SAME AUGUSTUS
   Law and justice have conferred the name and rule of justiciar on those who, being so closely related to law and justice in name, must freely and diligently respect them. Hence it is that cases of supreme importance are reserved to their judgment and that they must take nothing for their office and that this cannot be sold to anyone at a price.
   Therefore we publicly declare what things comprised in the Assises of

our predecessors shall be under their jurisdiction: i.e., brigandage; 'great theft'; damage to houses; deliberate assaults; arson; cutting down fruit trees and vines; violence towards women; duels; crimes of treason; cases involving sharp weapons; the disregard of enclosures or reserves, whether personally or through agents; and, in general, all offences for which on conviction men would have to suffer corporal penalties or mutilation of their limbs. We regard as a 'great theft' one of more than twenty *augustales*, if a civil action for theft is being brought; whilst a criminal prosecution leading to corporal punishment may be laid before the justiciar even if it involves a smaller sum.

Justiciars shall know that they are responsible for judging civil cases also if chamberlains and bailiffs default. Chamberlains and bailiffs are regarded as defaulting if, two months after the day of its being announced to them that cases had been committed to them by a superior, they have not given due and proper satisfaction to the plaintiffs in their affairs,—unless the chamberlains and bailiffs have asked for instructions and are forced to take longer. The same rule must always be applied to lords who refuse to do full justice to their men within the aforesaid time at the requirement of a superior or on orders from us. They may have jurisdiction over fiefs and feudal affairs, with the exception of suits involving castles, baronies and great fiefs which are inscribed on the registers of our treasury: each and all of these we reserve to the jurisdiction of our court.

Book I, *titulus* xl, *pars* ii; Huillard-Bréholles, IV, 49–50.
THE SAME AUGUSTUS
We wish the master justiciar of our great court, placed like a mirror of justice in the courts of our jurisdiction, to be an authority to other justiciars by his example as well as by virtue of his title: that the inferior ranks may see in him the rule they should keep themselves. Certain cases are so particularly reserved to his court that no one else may presume to judge them without special authority from us—they concern counties, baronies, cities, castles and great fiefs which are inscribed on the registers of our barons' treasury. The master justiciar shall examine and determine lawsuits involving, as plaintiffs or defendants, courtiers who cannot depart at will from our court without an order from us or our delegates, but who are directly assisting us or our officials —so long as they are in our service and not in that of the officials (for they might, perhaps, be appointed to some office by the officials). Courtiers shall enjoy the special privilege of being able to summon

their opponents to the great court in civil and criminal cases. Whilst the master justiciar is with us in our court, he shall assert his jurisdiction over appeals and requests for advice from inferior judges or from our representatives which have been submitted to be heard by Our Supremacy, to hear and duly determine them.

Book I, *titulus* xlix: Huillard-Bréholles, IV, 53.
That no prelate, count or baron may exercise the office of justiciar.
THE SAME AUGUSTUS

We wish nobody by unlawful presumption to usurp the things which are known to belong to the peculiar splendour and pure sovereignty of Our Highness. Therefore, by this edict of Our Pious Majesty, which is to prevail forever, we strictly forbid prelates of churches, counts, barons, knights and local corporations to be so bold as to exercise the function of justiciar upon their lands or to delegate it to anyone: they must look to the master justiciar and justiciars appointed by Our Excellency. Those who infringe this prohibition of Our Highness by appointing or being appointed justiciars shall be penalized by confiscation of their lands.

c. Book I, *titulus* lxxix: Huillard-Bréholles, IV, 54–5.
Of judges and notaries and their number.
THE SAME AUGUSTUS

We do not wish more than three judges and six notaries to be appointed in places of our demesne anywhere in the Kingdom, excepting only the cities of Naples, Salerno and Capua, in which we wish five judges and eight notaries to be appointed, for here almost all agreements are concluded in the presence of judges and notaries. We decree that they are not to be appointed, as formerly, by master justiciars and chamberlains, but only by us, except the judge and notary for plaintiffs, who, as it has been laid down, can be appointed by the master chamberlains. We ordain that they are all to be appointed with the precaution that no judge or notary public may be installed unless he belongs to the demesne and is a man of the demesne, so that he may be subject to no service or condition and to no other person, lay or ecclesiastic, but be bound directly to us alone. The aforesaid judges and notaries shall appear, with testimonials from the men of the place to which they are to be appointed, before us or before the man who acts as our regent throughout the Kingdom in our absence. These letters must bear witness to the loyalty and good conduct of the judge or notary to be appointed and to his being learned in the customs of that place. We reserve to our court the examination in letters and in written law.

D. Book I, *titulus* 1; Huillard-Bréholles, IV, 53–4.
The penalty to which corporations shall be subject if they create mayors and other officials.

THE SAME AUGUSTUS

Since there are officials enough and to spare appointed by Our Supremacy so that every man can find justice in civil and criminal cases, we abolish the unlawful practice which has arisen in certain portions of our Kingdom, and order that no mayors [*potestates*], consuls or rectors are to be created in any place, nor may any man usurp an office or jurisdiction for himself on the strength of any custom or of appointment by the people. It is our will, rather, that in every part of the Kingdom there shall be only officials appointed by Our Majesty or on our orders, i.e. master justiciars, justiciars, chamberlains, bailiffs and judges—and that they shall uphold both our rights and those of our loyal subjects. If in future any corporation does make such appointments, it shall be perpetually dissolved and all the men of that city shall be perpetually regarded as villeins. We sentence anyone who accepts any of the aforesaid offices to capital punishment.

E. The abolition of personal law and of some special privileges before the law.
Book II, *titulus* xvii: Huillard-Bréholles, IV, 89.
Of the abolition of the law of the Franks in the courts.

THE SAME AUGUSTUS

Wishing to abolish the special law or rather lawlessness of the Franks which has hitherto obtained both in civil and in criminal courts, we would have it known to all loyal subjects of our Kingdom through the issue of our present decree that we, who consider that everyone has an unbiased right to justice, do not want any distinction of persons in the courts. Rather do we wish justice to be administered to everyone on an equal footing, whether the plaintiff or defendant be Frank, Roman or Lombard. . . .

Book I, *titulus* cvi: Huillard-Bréholles, IV, 72.
Of the privileges of those who did not respond if summoned outside their own city, and of the invalidation of these privileges.

THE SAME AUGUSTUS

By the present constitution we declare null and void the privileges conceded to certain places by us or by our predecessors and also the customs maintained in those places, such as Messina, Naples, Aversa, Salerno or any others, whereby men summoned by our court or by district justiciars in cases recognized as belonging to their jurisdiction have hitherto been protected from the obligation to go outside these places for justice to be done—on this account, although they disregarded summonses, they escaped the penalty for contumacy and so had greater freedom to commit evil deeds. Now, however, if anyone from any place, there being absolutely no distinction left, has been summoned by a competent judge and is contumacious, either in civil or in criminal cases, he shall be subject to the penalties introduced by our statutes.

§ 38

Protection of demesne lands and regalian rights.

A. Book III, *titulus* i: Huillard-Bréholles, IV, 119.
  Of regalian rights.

KING ROGER

We wish our princes, counts, barons, archbishops and all bishops and abbots to know that no one who holds any portion, large or small, of our *regalia*, may by any means or contrivance give away, sell, alienate or reduce the whole or any part of it, so that our regalian rights are reduced, taken away or damaged.

B. Book III, *titulus* iv: Huillard-Bréholles, IV, 121.
  Of observing rights of his court.

THE EMPEROR FREDERICK

We believe it to be fitting and reasonable that we, who occupy the throne of justice and perpetually and constantly maintain everybody's rights, should not forget our own rights, and should recall them to our lordship and demesne when they have been withheld by the temerity or (to speak more plainly) by the unlawful presumption of others. Therefore, by the issue of this law, which is to be strictly observed, we proclaim to all loyal subjects of our Kingdom of Sicily that they must wholly resign into our hands all cities, castles, fortifications, townships and manors and anything inside or outside them which has customarily been royal demesne or of the royal demesne. We forbid rents and services owed to us to be withheld or suppressed by anyone in any way.

All loyal subjects of our Kingdom, no matter what their status is, shall surely know that if any persons are in possession of any of the aforesaid things for which they have no privilege from the divine Kings Roger and William I and II our predecessors, and no special rescript from Our Highness either obtained from us with our certain knowledge or granted by our predecessors our divine and august forebears and confirmed with our certain knowledge, and have still not surrendered these things into our hands or those of our delegates without being requested to do so by next Christmas, they shall without a doubt pay to our court fully four times the yield, rent or any profit they have received from the property so wrongfully withheld.

§ 39

Feudal legislation.
Book III, *titulus* v: Huillard-Bréholles, IV, 122–3.
  Of the revocation of fiefs and feudal goods.

THE SAME AUGUSTUS

Extending the statute of our grandfather King Roger of divine memory, which prohibits the diminution of fiefs and feudal goods, we decree that no alienations or contracts of any kind for the diminution or exchange of fiefs and feudal goods may have any validity whatsoever unless they are confirmed by special licence of Our Highness. We decree that no contracts, oaths or penal clauses concerning fiefs and feudal goods which have been drawn up or imposed without an order from our court may have any force. To those who thus contract and alienate we grant the power to revoke all these things of their own right. We pronounce void all decisions made by compromise concerning these matters, since by our statute jurisdiction over them is reserved to specific persons, i.e. the master justiciar and justiciars only. However, we permit barons and knights to let lands which fall to them [*excadentias locare*], provided they are let for the same annual service and revenue as they used to be of old, so that the service and revenue may in no way be reduced.

  On the same matter.

THE SAME AUGUSTUS

By this edictal law which shall prevail for ever we warn all loyal subjects of our Kingdom that no count, baron or knight and no cleric or other person may presume by any form of alienation between living persons, or by means of a last will, to transfer to another, or to exchange in whole or in part, any goods which are tied to services and on which revenues and services are due to our court, so that our court loses the service or revenues.

Book III, *tituli* xviii–xx, Huillard-Bréholles, IV, 131–2.
Of the guaranteeing of lords by vassals.

THE EMPEROR FREDERICK

Lords must be guaranteed by their vassals in their lives and limbs, against the capture of their persons and in their worldly honour. Vassals shall not reveal any plan which has been confided to them, and if they hear of any misfortune threatening their lords which they cannot prevent either personally or through another man they must take care to inform their lords or some other persons on behalf of their lords as quickly as possible, either personally or through other men. Vassals shall not take part in any trick, plan or conspiracy whereby their lords lose the land which they have—they must, rather, take care to defend it for their lords as far as they are able against every man, though respecting in all things their fealty to us and our orders and instructions and those of our heirs.

Of vassals standing surety for their lords.

THE SAME AUGUSTUS

If a vassal refuses to stand surety for his lord on being publicly required to do so by him, or commits a felony against him, his sons or his wife, or fails even after three admonitions to perform the service which he owes him, or refuses to give an account on the lord's behalf to those who bring suit in his court of what belongs to the lord by sentence of the judge, then the lord can dispossess him of what he holds of the lord after obtaining a judgment [*per exguardium*].

On the other hand, if a lord will not stand surety for a vassal of his who is facing a criminal charge in court concerning a matter which is not the concern of Our Royal Majesty, or if the lord beats his vassal without just cause, or commits adultery with his wife or deflowers his daughter against her will, he shall lose the vassal's homage, and the said vassal shall be directly attached to our court.

Of the aids to be demanded from vassals.

KING WILLIAM

Numerous loyal subjects of our realm have complained to us that prelates of churches, counts, barons and knights in their needs demand and extort aids from their vassals just as they please. Wishing, therefore, to take merciful measures against this harsh oppression of our subjects, we decree that lords must not seek aid from their vassals, save only in the following cases: i.e. for redeeming the person of the lord, if he happens to be captured by our enemies when engaged in our service; for making his son a knight; for marrying his daughter or sister; and for the purchase of land—but only when he is buying it in our service or in that of our army. Also, aid may be sought in moderation in providing the things given for our entertainment. Concerning the prelates of churches, we decree that they may seek aid from their vassals only in the following cases: i.e., for their consecration; when they are summoned to a council by the lord Pope; for the service of our army, if they form part of it; if we summon them or send them on our service; or for our entertainment, when we are accommodated on their lands or are receiving entertainment from them. In all the above cases the lords shall demand and require aid from their vassals in moderation.

Book III, *tituli* xxiii–xxv: Huillard-Bréholles, IV, 134–6.
Of not marrying a wife without permission of the court.
THE EMPEROR FREDERICK
Maintaining the honour due to our crown, we decree by the present statute that no count, baron or knight and no other person who holds baronies, castles or fiefs immediately of us or of another person which are noted down in the registers of our treasury may dare without our permission to take a wife or to give in marriage daughters, sisters, nieces or any other persons whom he can or must give in marriage, nor may he dare to provide his sons with a wife who has personal or real property without our permission. The custom which is said to have obtained in some parts of the Kingdom shall not impede this law.
Of the succession of noblemen to fiefs.
THE SAME AUGUSTUS
When a count or baron has gone the way of all flesh, his sons or grandsons shall not dare to receive the oaths from the vassals, unless, as the custom is, they have first obtained permission and instructions from Our Excellency to receive the oaths. If anyone acts to the contrary, he shall know that the said barony and fief and the rest of his goods, both moveable and immovable, will be confiscated.
Of announcing the death of a baron to the Emperor.
THE SAME AUGUSTUS
After the death of a baron or knight who holds of a count or of another baron a barony or fief which is noted down on the registers of

our treasury, we wish the deceased's death to be announced to Our Excellency by the count or baron of whom he held the aforesaid things, who must say what and how much the deceased used to hold of him. We wish a list of the personal possessions of the deceased to be written out and all these things to be drawn up on public documents and sent to our court, so that we may order to whom they must be assigned. When a barony or fief which we are responsible for granting is to be granted by us, then, as the custom is, we will take care to send letters to the man from whom the fief is held informing him that he must consign whatever is held of him, be it castle or level ground, to the man to whom we have granted it. Having received our instructions, the count or baron concerned shall without delay see that this is done. He may receive a relief, as is the custom, for handing over possession of the land granted, but it must not exceed the sum of ten ounces of gold.

Q

PART FOUR

France and Flanders

CHAPTER I

Feudal Problems in France and Flanders

ASPECTS OF FEUDALISM

§§ 1–7. The documents in this section concern the Kingdom of France and some of the great fiefs on the periphery of France, though not necessarily those which always depended on the King of France. Several points contained in these documents are used as examples by Professor F. L. Ganshof in his book *Feudalism* (New York, 1961), on which the section is mainly based.

Extract 1 describes the pressure to which royal vassals were subject from lords more powerful locally than the King during the anarchic years at the end of the ninth and the beginning of the tenth century. This excerpt is taken from a life written by Odo (who became the second Abbot of Cluny in 927) of the pious Count Gerald (855–909), founder of a monastery at Aurillac in Auvergne. The founder of Cluny, William the Pious, Count of Auvergne, assumed the title of Duke of Aquitaine in the late ninth century.

See Ganshof, *Feudalism*, 59 foll., 102.

Extract 2 is a rare (and hence a celebrated) example of a general theoretical statement of the mutual obligations of vassal and lord. The letter in which it appears was sent by Fulbert, Bishop of Chartres from 1006 to 1028, to William V, Duke of Aquitaine.

See H. Johnstone, 'Fulbert, Bishop of Chartres', C.Q.R., 102 (1926), 57 foll.; H. Mitteis, *Lehnrecht und Staatsgewalt* (Weimar, 1933), 312 foll.; M. Bloch, *Feudal Society* (London, 1961), 219, 228; Ganshof, *Feudalism*, 83 foll.

Extracts 3, 5 and 6A are taken from the official chronicle of Hainault, compiled in 1195–1196 by Gislebert of Mons, a clerk and favoured civil servant in the employ of Count Baldwin V of Hainault.

Although the chronicle is mainly concerned with the reign of Baldwin V (1171–1195), Gislebert's description (extract 3) of the terms on which an earlier Count of Hainault was enfeoffed to the Bishop of Liége may have been extracted from a contemporary document which was available to him. Count Baldwin II of Hainault and his mother the Countess Richilda passed under the direct lordship of the Bishop of Liége in 1076. This is a useful concrete example of a particular agreement between a liege lord and vassal.

See F. L. Ganshof, 'Note sur le rattachement féodal du Comté de Hainaut à l'Église de Liége', *Miscellanea J. Gessler*, I (Antwerp, 1948); Ganshof, *Feudalism*, 80, 94–5, 97, 122.

Extract 4 raises the question of the right of the vassal to alienate fiefs and of the lord's power to control such alienations. It also shows some of the difficulties which arose when land was given to churches.

See Ganshof, *Feudalism*, 148.

Extract 5 shows the process by which a lord could apply sanctions against a rebellious or disobedient vassal.

See Ganshof, *Feudalism*, 99 foll.

Extract 6 concerns 'reliefs' or dues payable to the lord when a fief changed hands, and the regulations governing such payments in France. Reliefs were an important source of revenue to feudal suzerains.

See C. Petit-Dutaillis, *The feudal monarchy in France and England from the tenth to the thirteenth century* (London, 1936), 187, 251; Bloch, *Feudal Society*, 206 foll.; Ganshof, *Feudalism*, 136 foll.

Extract 7 embodies some regulations governing the division of fiefs, introduced in France in 1209. These were directed against the custom known as *parage*, whereby, if a man left several sons, all of them obtained a share in the estate, but the eldest brother alone did homage to the lord for it and the younger brothers held their portions from the eldest. The ordinance was designed to preserve a direct relationship between the lord and all the brothers concerned.

See Petit-Dutaillis, *The feudal monarchy*, 303, 307; Bloch, *Feudal Society*, 205, 208; Ganshof, *Feudalism*, 139 foll.

§ 1

The mediatization of benefices: Odo of Cluny, *De vita sancti Geraldi Auriliacensis Comitis*, ch. xxxii, in Migne, P.L., 133, 660–1.

As the state of the commonwealth had been exceedingly disturbed, the margraves in their insolence had subjected the royal vassals to themselves. It had already been proved, as a result of many tests, that—

as it is written—the Almighty was against the enemies of Gerald. It seemed impossible for them to vanquish him—the Evil which they attempted to throw in his path recoiled upon them instead, as it is written: 'If a man digs a pit for his neighbour, he shall himself be the first to fall into it.'[1] William, Duke of Aquitaine, a good man who deserved praise for many reasons, having in time strikingly increased in power, tried, not with threats but with entreaties, to persuade Gerald to withdraw from the royal service and commend himself to him. But Gerald, who had recently obtained the grant of a county, refused to agree to this. However, he commended his nephew Rainald to William together with a vast number of vassals. Yet William felt no resentment because he remembered that his own father Bernard had out of affection commended him in his youth to the lord Gerald. He had therefore always treated him in a spirit of pleasant companionship and with great reverence. When there was some question pending, William would come to confer with Gerald. Sometimes William, delighted by the charm of this pleasant man, would entreat him to stay with him longer. And often, when they went upon a progress, William would make him go with him further.

§ 2

Obligations created by the contract of vassalage: Fulbert of Chartres, *Fulberti Episcopi Carnotensis Epistolae*, no. xxxviii, in M. Bouquet, *Recueil des historiens des Gaules et de la France*, X (1760), 463.

The mutual obligations of lord and dependant.

To William, the most glorious Duke of the Aquitainians, Bishop Fulbert offers the aid of his prayers.

Having been told to write something about the nature of fealty, I have briefly noted the following points for you on the authority of the books. A man who swears fealty to his lord ought always to remember these six words: unharmed, safe, honourable, profitable, easy, possible. Unharmed, because he must not do his lord any physical injury. Safe, because he must not betray his secrets or damage the defences by which his lord can be safe. Honourable, because he must not detract from the lord's jurisdiction or from anything else which pertains to his rank. Profitable, because he must not cause the loss of any of his property. Easy and possible, lest he make it difficult to do the good deed which

1. Cf. Proverbs, xxvi, 27.

his lord could otherwise easily perform, or make impossible what
would otherwise have been possible. It is right that the vassal [*fidelis*]
should beware of doing harm in this way: but he does not earn
his fief merely by so restraining himself. It is not enough merely to
abstain from evil, if he does nothing that is good. He must still therefore
loyally aid and advise his lord on the above six points, if he wishes to
appear worthy of his benefice and to keep the fealty which he has sworn.
The lord ought in all these things to do the same for his vassal. And if
he does not do so, he will deserve to be considered a man of bad faith
and the vassal will be thought a traitor and a perjurer if he is found to be
at fault, whether in what he actually does or in what he consents to, on
any of these points.

I would have written to you at greater length had I not been occupied
with many other matters, even with the restoration of our city and of
our church, all of which was burnt down recently in a terrible fire. Although we cannot fail to be somewhat affected by this loss, nevertheless
we breathe again in the hope of consolation from God and from you.

§ 3

Agreement between the Count of Hainault and the Bishop of Liége,
1076: Gislebert of Mons, *Chronicon Hanoniense*, ed. L. Vanderkindere
(Brussels, 1904), 13–14.

In assigning all these allods and fiefs to the church of Liége, and in the
liege homage of this great man the Count of Hainault, it was laid down
that the Count of Hainault owed his lord the Bishop of Liége service
and aid for all purposes and against all men with all the forces of
his vassals [*homines*], both infantry and cavalry, and that once the
Count was outside the County of Hainault these forces should be
maintained at the Bishop's expense. If the lord Count came to the
lord Bishop for the purpose of receiving his land, the lord Bishop
had to pay him any expenses he had incurred after leaving the
County of Hainault. If the lord Bishop summoned the Count of
Hainault to his court or to any conference, he had likewise to pay
him his expenses. If the lord Emperor of the Romans summoned
the Count of Hainault to his court for any reason, the Bishop of
Liége ought at his own expense to bring him safely to and from
the court and appear on his behalf and answer for him in the court.
Furthermore, if anyone should for wicked ends attack the land of

Hainault, the Bishop of Liége had to provide the Count of Hainault with army for army at the expense of the Bishop. Should the Count of Hainault lay siege to any fortress which belonged to his own honour or should siege be laid to him, the Bishop must at his own expense assist the Count with five hundred soldiers, whilst the Count must provide the Bishop with means to buy victuals at a fair price. If there were grass or other fodder necessary to horses in the fields, the Bishop and his men might take this at the Bishop's choice. The Bishop of Liége owed this assistance to the Count of Hainault over three periods in a year, each consisting of forty days. With the Count, three castellans of Hainault, i.e. those of Mons, Beaumont and Valenciennes, did homage to the Bishop of Liége. The Bishop of Liége had to give the Count of Hainault three pairs of garments at Christmas, each garment to be worth six marks of silver (Liége weight), and he was to give garments also to each of the castellans, again each garment to be worth six marks. Should any allod anywhere in the whole county be given to the Count of Hainault and subsequently received back from him as a fief, or should he acquire as his property any allod, any serfs or any serving women within the boundaries of his county, he would at once hold them, with the rest of his fief, of the Bishop of Liége. And although many eminent men, such as dukes, barons and counts, and other noblemen and their men of peace had to answer and make amends to the law court of Liége, the Counts of Hainault and their men of peace were in no way bound to answer to this court.

§ 4

Agreement between the Bishop of Thérouanne and the Count of Flanders, 1150: T. Duchet and A. Giry, *Cartulaires de l'eglise de Terouane* (Saint-Omer, 1881), 22-3.

Since one generation passes away and another takes its place, but written testimony greatly helps to recall past events, I, Milo, by the grace of God Bishop of Thérouanne, and I, Thierry, by the grace of God Count of Flanders, wish to make known to present and future how in our time doubt and controversy over distinguishing our rights was resolved and determined on the advice and consideration of ecclesiastical persons and barons of our land.

. . . .

. . . It was added that clerks, widows and orphans and any other persons under the tutelage of the Church who come from fiefs and hereditary lands which are subject to secular law shall not transfer from secular to ecclesiastical law unless they have first suffered violence or oppression or unless their rights have been taken away or denied them openly enough for them to be able to prove this by the testimony of reputable Christians.

And we must not omit another point established by the same agreement: i.e. that it is not lawful for anyone to make to the Church a gift of fiefs or of any other lands subject to secular law save with the consent of the lords and in the presence of the *échevins* [*scabini*]; but that gifts which are made in this way cannot be annulled or taken away from the churches.

It is further stipulated that the lords shall in no way be able to prevent the gifts unless they adduce some good reason against making them.

Finally, if the gift has been made with the consent of the lords and in the presence of the *échevins*, the rights of the lord shall be preserved in all respects.

And since an evil custom has sprung up that certain people, for the purpose of diminishing the rights of the lords, transfer themselves and the things they have built to the lands of churches, it is established: that the rights of the lords in the matter of dues and in all customs must remain intact (provided, however, that the peace of the church is preserved, and that it shall not be lawful for the lords to seize anyone on ecclesiastical estates).

§ 5

The Count of Hainault proceeds against a rebellious vassal, 1176: Gislebert of Mons, *Chronicon Hanoniense*, ed. Vanderkindere, 119–20.

That same year, disputes arose between the Count of Hainault and his vassal and kinsman Jacques d'Avesnes over certain wrongs which Jacques was doing to the lord Count. Hence the lord Count summoned Jacques to his court and required him to restore him the castle of Condé, as he had pledged himself to do. Jacques, after resorting to many frauds and to useless chicanery, eventually refused outright to restore the castle. The lord Count called upon his vassals—i.e. the peers of Jacques and other noblemen—to decide what was to be done about this. Hence it was judged that Jacques had no further rights in his castle, unless he should succeed in retaining it by the goodwill and favour of the lord Count. After being persuaded many times to hold back by Philip,

Count of Flanders, who had frequently interceded with the Count of Hainault with prayers on behalf of Jacques, the Count of Hainault mobilized his army and at Easter 1176 launched a fierce attack not against the castle mentioned above, but against the greater and better part of Jacques's land, i.e. against Avesnes itself. And so that his army could more easily cross the wood which was called l'Aie d'Avesnes, he caused it to be cut down by his forces, so that a hundred men could cross it abreast without hindrance. Jacques, who was on the opposing side with his forces, which consisted of many soldiers assembled together from many places in France and in his own land and of other infantry and cavalry, saw this and did not dare to join battle with the lord Count of Hainault. Indeed, since Jacques could not withstand the forces of his lord the Count, he begged for mercy, prostrated himself at the foot of the armed Count and restored the castle of Condé to his authority. The lord Count took pity on his vassal and received his castle and razed it to the ground, but he restored the manor to him and granted him peace. In this army with the Count of Hainault were his uncle Henry, Count of Namur, and Ralph, Count of Clermont in France.

§ 6

A. The feudal relief: the agreement of Philip Augustus with Count Baldwin VIII of Flanders (Baldwin V of Hainault), 1192. Gislebert of Mons, *Chronicon Hanoniense*, ed. Vanderkindere, 274–5.

The King, changing his former evil intentions towards the Count of Flanders and Hainault and Marquis of Namur, instructed him by letter that he would have a safe conduct in order to approach the King. He concluded a treaty with him at Peronne in Vermandois, whereby the Count promised to pay the lord King five thousand marks of pure silver (Troy weight) in two instalments within a year as a relief for the land of Flanders, since it is a matter of law, not of friendly arrangement, in France that every vassal as a relief for his liege fief shall give his lord a sum equivalent to the annual value of the fief. For the homage of the Count and of his wife, the Countess Margaret, the rightful heir to the land of Flanders, the lord King decided upon Remembrance Sunday in Lent [i.e. *March 1st*] at Arras.

B. The feudal relief: an ordinance of Louis IX, May 1235. E. J. De

Laurière, *Ordonnances des roys de France de la troisième race*, I (1723), 55–6.

It was ordained for the purpose of abolishing malpractices that when a fief passes from father to son or in some other way, if the man who must pay the relief on it cannot do so, the lord shall keep that man's estate for one year, if there is arable land there which is under cultivation. The lord shall take one-half of the yield of any vines grown there, and if none are grown there, the lord may grow them and take the fruits.

If there are fishponds there, they shall be valued upon oath by two knights, vassals of the lord, if he has any—if not, he must ask the overlord for them. They shall inquire how much these fishponds could be worth over a period of five years, and the lord shall have a fifth part of this for the year he holds the fief. With game reserves, the same procedure shall be followed.

As for woods, the lord shall have one-seventh part of what they would be worth if they were kept for seven years.

If there are men who owe *taille* or aid, the lord may not levy it.

When rear-fiefs change hands, the lord shall have the relief within a year and at the end of the year he shall for every rear-fief receive dues consisting of four Parisian pounds, which the person taking up the rear-fief shall be bound to pay to the lord.

If any fief which is being taken up forms part of a dowry, compensation shall be paid according to the value of the dowry.

After the lord has held the land for one year, he shall receive homage from the heir, in such a way that the heir must first pay the lord for the fishponds, game reserves and woods, and for the dowries and dues, or else give him sufficient security. This he shall be bound to do within 80 days.

And whilst the lord is holding fishponds, game reserves or woods, he must look after them in good faith.

§ 7

Regulations on the division of fiefs: an ordinance of Philip Augustus and some of his barons, May 1st, 1209: De Laurière, *Ordonnances des roys de France de la troisième race*, I, 29–30.

Philip, by the grace of God King of the French, Eudes, Duke of Burgundy, Hervé, Count of Nevers, Renaud, Count of Boulogne, Gaucher, Count of St. Pol, Guy de Dampierre and many other magnates of the realm of France have unanimously agreed and established by public agreement that from the first day of May onwards the following regulations shall be observed concerning feudal tenures.

1. If it happens that by heirs succeeding or by any other means there is a division in a fief held of a lord as a liege fief or in any other way, no matter how the division arises everyone who holds a part of that fief shall hold it in chief from its lord without any intermediary, just as the one man held it before the division was made.

2. Whenever service is due to the lord for the whole fief, each of the feudatories shall be bound to render service to the lord in proportion to the amount of the fief that he holds, and to serve the lord and to pay the relief and all dues.

3. Any contrary custom and anything previously done in a conflicting manner, before the first day of May, shall stand without alteration; but henceforth the procedure shall be as stated above.

So that this cannot be obliterated by forgetfulness and so in future rendered void we have confirmed the present writing with our seals. Done on the first of May in the year of Our Lord 1209, at Villeneuve-le-Roi, near Sens.

CHAPTER II

The French King as Suzerain

THE KING MUST BE NO ONE'S VASSAL

§ 8. This document, concerning the County of Amiens, which Philip Augustus had acquired in 1184, illustrates the important principle that the King, as head of the feudal hierarchy, could not become anybody's vassal.

See L. Halphen, 'La place de la royauté dans le système féodal', R.H., 172 (1933); Petit-Dutaillis, *The feudal monarchy*, 201; F. Lot and R. Fawtier, *Histoire des institutions françaises au moyen âge, II: Institutions royales* (1958), 19 foll.

§ 8

The principle that the King must hold of no man. A decree issued by Philip Augustus at Compiègne, between April 21st and October 31st, 1185: E. Berger and M. H. F. Delaborde, *Recueil des Actes de Philippe-Auguste, Roi de France*, I (1916), 169–70.

In the name of the Holy Trinity. Amen. Philip, by the grace of God King of the French.

It is appropriate to the royal office that the King should confer favours on those who are loyal to him; so that, when we reward some men as they deserve, others may be inspired by these examples to imitate them. Therefore, all men present and future shall know that when we received the land and County of Amiens from Philip, Count of Flanders, who relinquished it to us, we clearly recognized the loyalty and devotion which the church of Amiens showed us. Not only did this church display much devotion to us in this matter but—although the fief and County of Amiens belonged to it because it has it by our royal grant and it ought to have received homage for it—the church of Amiens wished us to hold its fief without doing homage and graciously granted that we might do so, since we cannot and must not do homage to anyone. Bearing in mind the loyalty of this church, we release it and its Bishop from any obligation to provide hospitality to us or to our servitors and we order church and Bishop to be left in peace so long as we and our successors as Kings of the French hold the land and County of Amiens. However, if anyone who can do homage to the church of Amiens subsequently holds that land, he shall do homage to the Bishop for the fief, and the Bishop from that time onwards shall extend hospitality to us and to our successors as Kings of the French and to our servitors, as other Bishops of Amiens used to do in the past.

That all these things may be firmly established, we have ordered this charter to be authenticated by our seal and by the addition of the royal signature below.

Done at Compiègne, in the year of the Lord's incarnation 1185, in the sixth year of our reign, with those whose names and signatures are appended below present in our palace. The signature of Count Thibaut, our Seneschal. The signature of Guy the Butler. The signature of Matthew the Chamberlain. The signature of Ralph the Constable. Given by the hand of Hugh the Chancellor.

THE DEPRIVATION OF JOHN, KING OF ENGLAND

§§ 9–10. These are two contemporary accounts of the process by which John, King of England, was evicted from his Duchy of Normandy, and of the justification for his removal. The first is taken from the chronicle of the English Cistercian abbey of Coggeshall. The second, a letter of Innocent III to John, evidently contains the French King's official account of the affair. Immediately before the train of events described in these documents, by the Treaty of Le Goulet in May 1200, John had recognized that he held certain fiefs of Philip Augustus. In August 1200, John had married Isabella, daughter of Audemar, Count of Angoulême, although she was already betrothed to Hugh Le Brun of Lusignan, Count of La Marche.

See K. Norgate, 'The alleged condemnation of King John by the court of France in 1202', T.R.H.S. (1900); A. Luchaire in E. Lavisse, *Histoire de France*, III, i (1901), 122 foll.; K. Norgate, *John Lackland* (London, 1902), 75 foll.; L. W. V. Harcourt, *His Grace the Steward and trial of peers* (London, 1907), 246 foll.; C. Petit-Dutaillis, *Le déshéritement de Jean Sans Terre et le meurtre d'Arthur de Bretagne* (1925), 4 foll.; H. Mitteis, *Politische prozesse des früheren Mittelalters in Deutschland und*

Frankreich (Heidelberg, 1927), 84 foll.; Petit-Dutaillis, *The feudal monarchy*, 216 foll.; Lot and Fawtier, *Histoire des institutions*, II, 38–9; R. Fawtier, *The Capetian Kings of France* (London, 1960), 145 foll.; F. M. Powicke, *The loss of Normandy* (Manchester, 1961), 127 foll.

§ 9

The condemnation of John, King of England, as vassal to Philip Augustus, 1202: a monk of Coggeshall, *Chronicon Anglicanum*, ed. J. Stevenson (London, 1875), 135–6.

In the year 1202 an agreement had been reached between Philip, King of France, and John, King of England, in the absence of the Count of Boulogne, who had bound himself in friendship to the King of England as he had previously done to King Richard, together with the Count of Flanders. But King John at once began a fierce attack on the Count of La Marche, Hugh Le Brun, and his brother the Count of Eu, because they had rebelled against him because of the daughter of the Count of Angoulême, to whom Hugh Le Brun had previously betrothed himself. But since the Counts could bear the King's assault no longer, they complained to King Philip, as the overlord, of the excessive violence of their lord, the King of England. King Philip many times ordered the King of England to refrain from attacking them, and he concluded a peace treaty with the vassals of the King of England.

But since the King of England utterly refused to yield to the commands or entreaties of the King of France, he was, in his capacity of Count of Aquitaine and Anjou, summoned by the chief nobles of the Kingdom of France, to come to the court of his lord the King of France at Paris and submit to the judgment of the court, to answer to his lord for the wrongs he had done and to obey the law which his peers decreed. But the King of England answered that he was Duke of the Normans and alleged that he had no obligation to attend any conference [*colloquium*] at Paris, but only to appear at a conference held by the King of France within the boundaries both of the Kingdom and of the Duchy; for a decree to this effect had been made of old between the King and the Duke, and it had been confirmed by authentic charters. But King Philip asserted that it was utterly unjust that he should lose his rights over the County of Aquitaine supposing the same man were Duke of Normandy and Count of Aquitaine. Discussion on the resolution of this dispute and of numerous others which arose from day to day was further prolonged, and in a short time the anger of both Kings began to kindle and savage threats were uttered. Eventually the court of the King of France assembled and gave judgment that the King of England should be deprived of all the land which he and his ancestors had hitherto held of the Kings of France, because they had for a long time almost completely refused to render any of the services which were due on account of these lands, and they were willing to obey their lord in scarcely anything. King Philip, therefore, gladly accepting and approving this sentence of his court, assembled his army, promptly attacked the castle of Boutavant in Normandy, which King Richard had built, and razed it to the ground. Then he took all the land of Hugh de Gournai and all the castles around it. He also invaded the castle and County of Albemarle and the County of Eu and all that land as far as Arques, without meeting resistance. Count Renaud of Boulogne, wholly abandoning his friendship with King John, for he had previously made a separate peace with the King of France, was reconciled with his lord, and acted as standard bearer in every battle and was distinguished among the whole army for his honourable conduct. The King assigned to Renaud's care Albemarle and several other castles which he took.

§ 10

The letter 'Quid tuis meritis' of Innocent III to John, King of England, October 31st, 1203, concerning the authority of Philip Augustus as suzerain: *Delectus epistolarum Innocentii III Papae*, in Bouquet, *Recueil des historiens des Gaules et de la France*, XIX (1833), 444–5.

To John, King of England.

Let your royal conscience teach you what you deserve of us, for you are fully aware that in many respects you have shown yourself ungrateful for our favours, and you have neither reciprocated them nor exerted yourself like your ancestors and predecessors to honour the church of Rome as you ought. But we are concerned, not with what you do, but with what we ought to do, and we do not give you your deserts, but rather carry out the duties of our pastoral office; and we believe that as a result you will try harder to show yourself obedient and loyal to us and to the church of Rome. We have, therefore, in the dispute which is in progress between you and our dearest son in Christ,

Philip, illustrious King of the French, done as much as we decently
could (more, indeed, than some people might believe), as our nuncio,
our beloved son the Abbot of Casamari, who is fully informed of the
truth of the matter, will be able to tell Your Serenity.

But we wish you to know that the King of the French says that you,
not he, are guilty of provoking this quarrel, and that you provided, not
only the occasion, but also the cause of the disagreement. For he has
recently informed us, by letters and by envoys, that you inflicted many
injuries and no slight damage upon the church of St. Martin of Tours,
which acknowledges that all its temporal possessions are held of him,
and that your vassals killed a vassal of St. Martin's. Although you were
frequently called upon to make amends, you successively asked for and
accepted three or four different dates for doing this, and the King
always sent you his representatives on the day appointed, but he was
unable to obtain any damages from you—indeed, you have put him
off for more than a year by delays of this sort.

Moreover, when you had without good reason and solely of your
own free will deprived vassals enfeoffed to the King of the French of
their castles and lands, he, as the overlord, struck by the complaints of
the plundered, ordered you, not only once, but repeatedly to make
amends for this. You promised to do it, but did not do so; you only
laid heavier burdens on the oppressed. He tolerated this for more than a
year, demanding and awaiting satisfaction. And when he had ex-
changed advice with his barons and vassals, and appointed a definite
date for you to appear in his presence to do without backsliding what
the law enjoined, although you were his liege vassal, you did not go on
the day appointed, and did not send any representative, but completely ignored his commandment. Subsequently, he personally met
you and reminded you verbally of these matters, since he had no
desire to make war upon you if you showed that you would conduct
yourself towards him as your duty bound you to do. But since you had
no wish to make amends in this way either, and although on the advice
of his barons and vassals he had broken off the contract with you
[*diffidare*], having made war upon you, he sent you four of his
knights, wishing to ascertain through them whether you were willing to
make amends for what you had done against him. Further, he wished
it to be known to you that he would henceforth conclude a treaty
against you with your own vassals wherever possible. But you hid
yourself from those who were seeking you and chose to absent yourself,
so that they were completely unable to see you. But your men met

them, and said that they already knew the instructions the King of the French had given them, and that they could not speak with you.

The King of the French further added that at that time he had not formed a pact with any of your vassals and had not received homage from them: but subsequently he did make pacts with some of them, and he says that he received homage from some of them. He maintains that the cause of this was your contumacy,—though he is still prepared to do you full justice in his court if you ask for it and if he receives a sufficient guarantee that you will abide by the judgment of the court. We therefore advise Your Royal Serenity and exhort you in the Lord to work devotedly for peace, and not only to accept a peace or truce, supposing you are offered one, but also not to be in the least ashamed to offer one yourself. Take great care lest, even while you assert that the King of France is doing you wrong, you are really wronging him and detracting from the honour and respect which is his due. When the truth is known, we are just as much bound to uphold his rights as we are to support your rightful claims.

We readily command to Your Serenity our beloved son Stephen of Fossanova, canon of York, your nuncio, since he has conducted your business with us both earnestly and diligently.

Given at Anagni, on October 31st in the sixth year of our pontificate.

PHILIP AUGUSTUS AND RAYMOND OF TOULOUSE

§ 11. This letter addressed to Pope Innocent III by Philip Augustus concerns his relations with Raymond VI of St. Gilles, Count of Toulouse: Toulouse was the last great fief to be absorbed by the French crown. The letter explains the cautious and qualified attitude of Philip Augustus towards the crusade against the Albigensian heretics (or Cathars) organized by Innocent III. The Count of Toulouse was, in the eyes of the Pope, implicated in the recent murder of the Cistercian legate Peter of Castelnau, and was believed to be a supporter of the heretics. For the time being it was left to Simon de Montfort, a minor lord of the Parisian region, to lead the attack on the County of Toulouse.

See Luchaire in Lavisse, *Histoire de France*, III, i, 259 foll.; A. Luchaire, *Innocent III: la croisade des albigeois* (1905), 115 foll.; Petit-Dutaillis, *The feudal monarchy*, 276 foll.; P. Belperron, *La croisade contre les albigeois et l'union du Languedoc à la France 1209-1249* (1942), 140 foll.; Fawtier, *The Capetian Kings of France*, 118 foll.

§ 11

Philip Augustus's letter to Innocent III on the confiscation of Toulouse from Count Raymond, 1208: L. Delisle, *Catalogue des Actes de Philippe-Auguste* (1856), 512–13.

THE SECOND ANSWER WHICH THE KING MADE TO THE LORD
POPE CONCERNING THE ALBIGENSIANS

As for your orders to us concerning the death of Peter of Castelnau, to which the Count of St. Gilles was a party, you shall know that we deeply regret his death, for he was a very upright man who did very good works. And if you have some reason to complain of the Count, we have much cause for complaining of him also. You shall know that in the great war which we fought against Richard, King of England, by way of opposing us he took to wife King Richard's sister, although we and our father of Christian memory had incurred great expense in defending the Count and his father and his land. And when we were fighting King John for the wrongs he had done, we found the Count's vassals opposing us in the fortress of Falaise. And you shall know that in none of the wars we have fought have we had any assistance from the Count, either from himself or from his men, although he holds of us one of the largest baronies in our Kingdom.

As you advised us to proceed as we saw fit concerning this matter, you shall know that when your letters reached us, we were on the march with our army to meet the forces of the King of England, which had violated a truce and refused to make amends to us or to our vassals. You shall know that to the bishops who spoke with us on this matter we answered that, if the clergy and barons supplied sufficient aid which we deemed capable of doing some good to the land, and if we obtained a truce which seemed to us to be well guaranteed and maintained, we would readily send some of our vassals and our money to assist.

On the question of your laying the Count's lands open to seizure, you shall know that we have learnt from learned and distinguished men that you have no right to do this until he has been condemned for heresy. When he has been condemned for it, only then ought you to give notice of this and instruct us to lay his land open, as it is a fief of ours. For you have not yet informed us that you regard the Count as condemned. We are not saying this to excuse him, since we wish to *accuse* rather than *excuse*, as, God willing, we shall prove by our actions when the opportunity presents itself.

GUARANTEES TO THE KING

§ 12. These three agreements help to show how the Capetian Kings strengthened feudal loyalties by a system of guarantees and securities.
See Petit-Dutaillis, *The feudal monarchy*, 303 foll.

§ 12

Guarantees and securities given to the King for the loyal service of his vassals.

A. Security given to the lord King by the commune of Hesdin on behalf of Prince Louis, his eldest son (February 1211 old style, February 1212 new style): A. Teulet, *Layettes du Trésor des Chartes*, I (1863), 375.

G . . . the mayor, the *échevins*, the sworn men and the whole commune of Hesdin, to all whom the present letters reach, greeting.

You shall know that we have sworn and promised in good faith to Philip, our lord King of France, that if our lord Louis, his son, should fail to render him good and loyal service at a time when the King was willing to do him justice in his court, we would assist the lord King against him every time that our lord Louis failed him in this respect, until amends had been made to the lord King either at the King's pleasure or at the judgment of his court.

We have sworn and promised in good faith that, should our aforesaid lord Louis die, we will cleave to the lord King until the heirs of our lord Louis have come of full legal age.

Done in the year of Our Lord 1211, in the month of February.

B. Security given to the lord King by Robert, Count of Alençon, on behalf of Amaury of Craon, concerning the fortress of Chantocé (February 1211 old style, February 1212 new style): ibid., 375–6.

Robert, Count of Alençon, to all who shall examine these present letters, greeting in the Lord.

You shall know that I am debtor and pledge for 1000 Parisian pounds to my lord Philip, illustrious King of the French, that he shall be able to avail himself of the fortress of Chantocé against his enemies whether he enters with a large or with a small following. If he cannot avail himself and a large or a small following of this fortress against his enemies, whenever he needs to do so, I will pay him 1000 Parisian pounds within forty days of being required to do so.

And should I fail to do this, the lord King would be entitled to seize all my land without being guilty of aggression and hold it until this entire sum of money had been made good to him.

Done at Le Mans, in the year of Our Lord 1211, in the month of February.

c. Duke Hugh IV of Burgundy makes amends to Louis IX for his refusal to act as guarantor for Count Thibaut of Champagne, April 1st–7th, 1234–1235: A. Teulet, *Layettes du Trésor des Chartes*, II (1866), 287.

I, Hugh, Duke of Burgundy, make known to all who examine these present letters that I have, in obedience to the wishes of my dearest lord Louis, illustrious King of the French, paid amends of 5000 marks of silver because I refused at his command to stand surety for the noble Thibaut, Count of Champagne.

And I am bound, during the month in which Easter occurs, to give the King sufficient guarantors for these 5000 marks: i.e. my dearest mother, the Duchess of Burgundy, for 2000 marks; and, for 600 marks each, the Count of Mâcon, the lord of Le Puiset, the lord of Montréal, William of Mont-Saint-Jean and the lord of Montaigu.

And if it turns out that I cannot have anyone or more than one of these as security, I am bound to give other sufficient guarantors by the aforesaid date.

And be it known that if I or my guarantors should fail to pay this money, in obedience to the lord King, then he, two months from the time of this demand being made of us on his behalf, could, without committing any offence, seize the entire fief which I hold of him and keep it in his hands until full amends were made to him according to his wishes, unless I myself in person were held hostage at Paris to my lord the King for the sum which was lacking.

I have sworn to the lord King upon holy relics that all these stipulations will be well and strictly observed by me. I have also sworn to be loyal to him and his heirs, and to serve him and them well and loyally against all other peoples, and to obey him as my liege lord.

To bear witness to this, I have decided to affix my seal to these present letters.

Done in the month of April, in the year of Our Lord 1234.

CHAPTER III

Royal Administration and Justice under Philip Augustus and Louis IX

ROYAL CENTRALIZATION

§§ 13–15. These documents illustrate certain aspects of the progress of centralizing monarchy in France under Philip Augustus and Louis IX. They deal, especially, with the appointment of bailiffs, who were set over the local provosts on the royal demesne, as direct representatives of the royal authority whose office was renewable at the King's pleasure. Philip Augustus's ordinance of 1190 (13), sometimes known as the Testament, was designed to provide for the government of the realm during his absence on the Crusade. Bailiffs evidently existed before this ordinance was issued, but it offers precise and valuable evidence about their functions. The duties of bailiffs, seneschals, provosts and other royal officials as they were in the mid-thirteenth century are set out in Louis IX's great ordinance of 1256 (14). Louis IX appointed the first *enquêteurs* to act as a check on the activities of the bailiffs on the eve of his departure for the Crusade in 1247. Guillaume de Saint Pathus, who compiled the biography of Louis IX from which the description of the *enquêteurs* (15) is taken, was confessor to Queen Margaret of Provence, Louis IX's widow—probably from 1277 to 1295.

See Luchaire in Lavisse, *Histoire de France*, III, i, 102 foll., 235 foll.; C. V. Langlois, ibid., III, ii (1901), 339 foll.; C. V. Langlois, 'Doléances recueillies par les enquêteurs de Saint Louis et des derniers capétiens directs', R.H., 92 (1906), 100 (1909); J. R. Strayer, *The administration of Normandy under Saint Louis* (Cambridge, Mass., 1932); Petit-Dutaillis, *The feudal monarchy*, 185 foll., 298 foll.; C. Petit-Dutaillis, *L'essor des états d'occident* (1937), 271 foll.; Lot and Fawtier, *Histoire des institutions*, II, 144 foll., 194–5, 315; Fawtier, *The Capetian Kings*, 176 foll.

In general, on the nature of royal power in thirteenth-century France, see W. Ullmann, *Principles of government and politics in the middle ages* (London, 1961), 193 foll.

§ 13

The ordinance of Philip Augustus of June 1190, providing for the government of France during the King's absence on the Crusade: E. Berger and M. H. F. Delaborde, *Recueil des actes de Philippe-Auguste, Roi de France*, I (1916), 416–20.

In the name of the holy and indivisible Trinity. Amen. Philip, by the grace of God King of the French.

It is the duty of a King to look after the interests of his subjects by all possible means and to place the public welfare before his own private advantage. Since we are most eagerly and with all our strength fulfilling our vow to make a journey to aid the Holy Land, on the advice of the Most High we have determined to ordain how to deal with the business of the kingdom that must be transacted and how to dispose of our last mortal possessions if we should die upon the journey.

First, therefore, we ordain that our bailiffs shall in each provostship on our estates appoint four wise and law-abiding men who will bear honest witness, and the business of the village shall be transacted only with their advice or with that of at least two of them. At Paris, however, we appoint six honest and law-abiding men whose names are T[hibaud le Riche], A[thon de la Grève], E[brouin le Changeur], R[obert of Chartres], B[audouin Bruneau?] and N[icolas Boisseau?].

In lands of ours which have been specified by name, we have appointed our bailiffs, who shall each month fix one day called the assize, on which all who make a complaint shall receive justice and their rights without delay through the bailiffs, and we shall likewise receive justice and our rights; and a record shall be kept there of all fines which are due to us.

Further, it is our will and command that our dearest mother Queen Adèle, with our dearest uncle and vassal William, Archbishop of Reims, shall every four months fix one day on which they shall hear at Paris the complaints of the men of our Kingdom, and there deal with them to the honour of God and the profit of the realm.

We further ordain that on that day representatives of each of our villages and also our bailiffs who hold assizes shall appear before them to describe in their presence the affairs of our land.

If any of our bailiffs has committed a crime, other than murder, robbery, homicide or treason, and if the Archbishop, the Queen and others who attend to hear of the offences committed by our bailiffs are agreed upon this, we order them to inform us, three times in every year, by letters written on the aforesaid days, which bailiff has offended, and what he has done, and from whom he has received money, gifts or services for causing us or our vassals to lose their rights.

Our bailiffs shall in a similar fashion send us information about our provosts.

The Queen and Archbishop shall not be empowered to remove our bailiffs from their bailiwicks save for murder, robbery, homicide or treason; nor shall bailiffs have the power to remove provosts, save for one of these crimes. We, on God's advice, once these persons have informed us of the facts of the case, will inflict a punishment which will serve as a fitting deterrent to others.

Likewise, the Queen and Archbishop shall report to us three times a year concerning the state of our realm and its affairs.

If it happens that an episcopal see or the headship of a royal abbey falls vacant, we wish the canons of the church or the monks of the monastery which is vacant to come before the Queen and Archbishop, as they would come before us, and ask them for freedom to elect; and we wish the Queen and Archbishop to grant this to them without opposition. We advise the canons and monks to elect a pastor who will be pleasing to God and useful to the realm. The Queen and Archbishop shall keep the *regalia* in their hands until the chosen candidate has been consecrated and blessed, and then the *regalia* shall be handed to him without opposition.

We further ordain that if a prebend or ecclesiastical benefice falls vacant, when the *regalia* come into our hands, the Queen and Archbishop shall confer them in the best and most honourable fashion possible upon honourable and learned men, taking the advice of Brother Bernard. Our donations, which we have made by letters patent, shall be excepted from this.

We forbid all prelates of churches and vassals of ours to pay *taille* or other taxes whilst we are on God's service. If the Lord God's will be done and death befalls us, we strictly forbid all men of our land, both clergy and laity, to pay *taille* until our son—may God keep him safe and sound for his service—reaches the age at which, by the grace of the Holy Spirit, he can rule the Kingdom.

Should anyone wish to make war upon our son, and the revenues that he has be not sufficient, then all our vassals must assist him with their persons and their property, and the churches shall extend to him the aid which they are accustomed to render to us.

We forbid our provosts and bailiffs to arrest any man or seize his property, whilst he is willing to give good guarantors that he will appear for trial in our court, except in cases of homicide, murder, robbery or treason.

We further ordain that all our revenues, dues and emoluments shall be brought to Paris at three dates: firstly on the Feast of St. Remigius, secondly at the Purification of the Blessed Virgin and thirdly on Ascension Day; and they shall be handed over to our aforesaid burghers, and to Pierre le Maréchal. Should any of these happen to die, Guy de Garlande shall appoint another in his place.

When our revenues are received, Adam, our clerk, shall be present and record the receipts; and each of the burghers shall have a key to each of the coffers in the Temple in which our treasure is stored, and the Temple itself shall have one. We will give instructions in our letters as to how much of this treasure shall be sent to us.

We ordain that, should we happen to die on the journey we are making, the Queen and Archbishop and the Bishop of Paris, and the Abbots of St. Victor and St. Denis, and Brother Bernard shall divide our treasure into two parts. They shall distribute one-half as they choose in order to repair churches which have been destroyed as a result of our wars, so that the worship of God can take place within them. They shall give some of the same half to those who have been ruined by our taxes; and the rest of the same half to those whom they choose and whom they believe to be most in need, for the salvation of our soul and that of our father King Louis and those of our ancestors. We order the guardians of our treasure and all the men of Paris to keep the other half of the treasure for the needs of our son until he reaches an age at which he can rule the Kingdom with the advice of God and by his own intellect.

If death should befall both us and our son, we order the aforesaid seven men to distribute our treasure as they choose for the sake of our soul and his. As soon as the news of our death arrives, we wish our treasure, wherever it is, to be taken to the house of the Bishop of Paris, and there kept under guard, and afterwards it shall be disposed of as we have ordained.

We instruct the Queen and Archbishop to keep in their own hands as many as they decently can of the honours, such as abbeys, deaneries and certain other offices, which are in our gift when they fall vacant until we return from serving God; and those that they cannot retain, they shall give and assign in a godly fashion on the advice of Brother Bernard and they shall do this to the honour of God and the profit of the realm. But should we die on the journey, we wish them to give the honours and offices in the churches to those whom they perceive to be most worthy of them.

That this may be firmly established, we order this charter to be authenticated by our seal and by the addition of the royal signature below.

Done at Paris, in the year of the Incarnate Word 1190, in the eleventh year of our reign, with those whose names and signatures are appended below present in our palace. The signature of Count Thibaut, our Seneschal. The signature of Guy the Butler. The signature of Matthew the Chamberlain. The signature of Ralph the Constable. Given at a time when the Chancery was vacant.

§ 14

Ordinance of Louis IX on the duties of seneschals, provosts and bailiffs, 1256: De Laurière, *Ordonnances des roys de France*, I, 78–81.

We ordain that all our seneschals, bailiffs and others, no matter what office they hold, shall take an oath that when they perform these offices they will do right to everyone without exception of persons, to the poor as to the rich and to the stranger as well as to the familiar person, and that they will observe the good and well-tried customs and usages of the various places. Should it happen that they transgress their oath and are convicted of doing so, we wish them to be punished both in their property and in their persons, if their fault demands it.

Again, the above-mentioned seneschals and bailiffs shall swear to preserve faithfully both our rights and our rents, and swear that they will not knowingly allow them to be taken away, removed, withheld or reduced.

Again, they shall swear that they will not, either themselves or through other persons, accept any gift of gold or silver or any personal or spiritual benefits or anything else other than fruit or wine or some other present which shall not in value exceed ten sous in any one week.

Again, they shall swear that they will not cause these things to be taken by their wives or children, or by other relatives and kinsfolk or by members of their household or by those who keep the accounts or by any investigator or visitor whom we send to make inquiries about them in the places where they have held office in our name.

Again, all our officials shall swear that they will not sell or barter away any part of our rents, our provostships, our bailiwicks, our waters, our forests, our coining rights and our other dues, or indeed of anything which belongs to us, and that they will in good faith receive and hand over to us the profit from coining rights which they receive on our behalf. If they do sell any of our rents or lease out any of our other revenues and dues, they must sell and lease them at the best possible rate and in good faith, and in the manner most profitable to us.

Again, they shall swear that if they find any official or serjeant subordinate to them who is disloyal, a robber, a usurer or full of other vices for which he ought to be dismissed from our service, they will not support him in return for any gift or promise, in response to entreaties from friends or for any other reason, but will correct his faults in good faith.

Again, our other officials who hold lesser offices, such as provosts, vicars, viscounts, mayors, foresters, serjeants and other such officials, shall swear that they will not give any gift to their superiors or to their wives or children or to other friends or to anyone belonging to them.

And so that this oath may be more strictly kept we wish it to be taken at a full session of the court in front of all the clergy and laity, even though they have already taken it before us, so that they may doubly dread the sin of perjury not only from the fear of God and ourselves, but out of shame before the people.

We further desire and ordain that all our seneschals, bailiffs and other officials and servants, no matter to what estate or condition they belong, shall restrain themselves from saying any words disrespectful to God, to our Holy Lady Mary, or to any of the saints, and shall abstain from playing dice or entering brothels and taverns.

Further, the making of dice shall be prohibited in every part of our Kingdom, and any man who is commonly found dicing or commonly reported to be doing so, or frequenting a tavern or a brothel, shall be accounted discreditable and shall be disqualified from giving any testimony as to facts.

Again, that all harlots and common prostitutes shall be expelled from and put outside all our cities and towns, and especially that they shall be removed from the streets which lie at the centre of these towns, and put outside the walls and far away from all holy places, such as churches and burial grounds. And if anyone lets any house in these cities and towns, or lets any place not specially designed for the purpose, to common harlots, or receives them in his house, he shall yield and pay to those appointed to see to this on our behalf a sum equivalent to the rent of the house for one year.

No one shall go to drink in a tavern unless he is on a journey or unless he has no house in the town.

We forbid all our seneschals, bailiffs and other high officials to buy or cause to buy or to acquire personally or through others any lands or estates which are situated in their own seneschalcies, bailiwicks or administrative districts, or to buy up any debt which we owe or anything else of the kind within their administrative districts, without special leave from us. And should it happen that any such purchases or acquisitions are made, we wish them to be annulled and we ordain that if it pleases us the said estates and debts which have been purchased in this way shall fall into our hands.

Again, we forbid any of the aforesaid officials in our service to marry any of their daughters or sons or any person belonging to them to the people of their seneschalcies or bailiwicks or other administrative districts without special leave from us: nor may they place them in the cloister or obtain for them any benefice of the holy Church or any estate, nor may they take any food-rent or hospitality-taxes [*procurations*] levied on religious houses or levied near to them at the expense of religious orders, nor take any property or pensions from anyone who has to do with us.

We do not wish these restrictions on marriage and on acquisitions to be extended to other minor officials mentioned above, nor to petty provosts nor to others who purchase our revenues.

Further, we command that no seneschal, bailiff or other official that we have may keep too great an abundance of serjeants or beadles, but they must manage with as few as possible in order to carry out our commands and those of our courts, and we wish the beadle and serjeant to be named at a full assize; otherwise they shall not be recognized as beadle or serjeant. And should it happen that our beadles or serjeants are sent to some strange or distant place, we do not wish them to be accredited unless they have letters from their superiors, and if they do otherwise this shall be reported to their local superiors, whom we order to punish them adequately.

Again, we forbid any seneschal, bailiff or other official placed in or appointed to our service to oppress our subjects in an unjust manner. Our subjects may not be imprisoned for any debt which they owe unless they owe it to us.

Again, we ordain that none of our seneschals, bailiffs, provosts or other officials may impose any fine for debt or for any misdemeanour on the part of our subjects unless they do so after a full session of the court, where the fine has been judged or assessed on the advice of good men, even though security has already been exacted for it in their presence. And if he who is accused of any fault does not wish to wait for the judgment of the court which has been offered him, but instead offers it a certain sum of money, if this sum is suitable it shall be accepted. If not, we wish the fine to be assessed according to what is stated above, even though the culprit is willing to carry out the wishes of the court.

Moreover, it is our desire that those who hold our provostships, vicariates, viscounties, mayoralties, bailiwicks or other posts may not sell their office to others without our leave. And if several persons together buy the above-named offices, or any one of them, we wish one of the purchasers to perform the duties on behalf of all the others, and to enjoy the liberty and immunity from military service and from *tailles*, taxes and common charges, as is the custom.

Again, we forbid selling the said offices to relatives, brothers, nephews or cousins, or to familiars of cousins, or to friends, or to any gentlemen. The officers must not use their position to exact payment of any debts owed to them unless these debts are owed to them on account of their official duties. They must seek payment of their personal debts by virtue of the authority of the seneschal and bailiff or other superior judge in the neighbourhood, just as if they were not in our service.

Moreover, we forbid bailiffs, seneschals and the other above-named officials to force our subjects to pay fines by means of threats or terror or of any form of chicanery, whether secretly or openly. Nor may they bring charges against them without reasonable cause.

Again, we forbid our above-mentioned officers to trouble our subjects in cases which they have before them by changing the place of the hearing without reasonable cause. On the contrary, they must transact the business which comes before them in the places where it has been customary to deal with it, so that our subjects do not abandon the pursuit of their rights because of the trouble and expense involved.

Again, we forbid them to dispossess any person of anything that he holds without passing judgment in his case or without a special mandate from us. Nor may they oppress our subjects by imposing new *tailles* or new customs. Nor may they order, for the purpose of making money, that military service must be performed, for we wish no one who owes military service to be forced to go to the host in his own person, without reasonable and necessary cause, and no one who is willing to come to the host shall be forced to pay money to buy his way out.

Again, we forbid any of our officials to prohibit the transport of wine, corn or other merchandise through our Kingdom or out of our Kingdom save for some urgent reason, and when it is appropriate that some prohibition should be imposed we wish this to be done on the advice of trustworthy persons [*prudeshomes*], without any hint of deceit or trickery. And, such a measure having been taken upon advice, they must not rescind it on their own initiative; nor, whilst the measure is in force, may they issue any special dispensations therefrom.

Again, we desire that all our seneschals, bailiffs and other officials, after they give up their offices, shall for a period of forty days attend, either in their own persons or through deputies, at the place where they have been in charge of the administration so that they can, before the new seneschals, bailiffs or other superior official investigators, answer those whom they have wronged and who wish to complain of them.

We reserve to Our Majesty power to make declarations, adjustments, corrections and deletions as we are advised in all these matters which we have ordained for the peace and tranquillity of the subjects of our realm.

Given at Paris in the year 1256.

§ 15

The inquests of Louis IX: Guillaume de Saint-Pathus, *Vie de Saint Louis*, ed. H. F. Delaborde (1899), 150–1.

The saintly King sometimes heard that his bailiffs and provosts were injuring the people of his land either by judging corruptly or by unjustly taking away their property. Hence he was accustomed to appoint certain investigators [*enquesteurs*], who were sometimes Friars Minor and Friars Preachers, sometimes secular clergy and sometimes even knights. Sometimes he did this once a year and sometimes several times a year, and they were to make inquiries concerning the bailiffs, provosts and other serjeants here and there about the realm and throughout the realm. He gave these investigators power that, if they found anything that the said bailiffs or other officials had by wicked acts removed or taken away from any person, they should cause it to be restored without delay. They were also empowered to remove from office any corrupt provosts or other lesser serjeants whom they found deserving of dismissal. Then it happened that one who had been bailiff of Amiens, because he had turned out badly, was removed from the bailiwick and put in prison, where he remained for a long period, and he was sentenced to sell his houses and estates before he left the King's prison, so that he might restore what he had corruptly taken away. As a result, he was so poor that he could scarcely have a draught-horse to ride, even though he had previously been very rich.

JUDGMENT BY PEERS

§ 16. This is a possible illustration of how the great vassals of the French King, when they were in the early thirteenth century being effectively made subject to the justice of the King's court, tried to defend themselves by claiming to be judged by their peers.

For this, and for bibliographies on the so-called 'peers of France', see Petit-Dutaillis, *The feudal monarchy*, 235–6, 240–1; also Lot and Fawtier, *Histoire des institutions*, II, 297.

§ 16

Summons and judgment by peers: the case of Jean de Néelle and Countess Joanna of Flanders, 1224: C. V. Langlois, *Textes relatifs à l'histoire du Parlement depuis les origines jusqu'en 1314* (1888), 35–6.

When a dispute arose between Joanna, Countess of Flanders, on the one hand, and Jean de Néelle on the other, Jean summoned the Countess for default of justice before the court of the lord King. The lord King had the Countess summoned before him by two knights.

The Countess appeared on the day and claimed that it was not sufficient to summon her by means of two knights, because she ought to be summoned by her peers. Both parties submitting to judgment on this point, it was decided in the lord King's court that the Countess had been sufficiently and adequately summoned by the two knights and that the summoning of the Countess by them held good and was valid.

Again, the Countess claimed that Jean de Néelle had peers in Flanders, by whom he ought to be judged in the court of the Countess, and that she was prepared to do him right in her court by means of his peers, and Jean was not saying that the Countess had failed to do him right by means of his peers by whom he ought to be judged in the Countess's court: and so the Countess required of Jean de Néelle that he should attend her court. Jean de Néelle, on the other hand, answered that he had no wish to return to the Countess's court, because she had failed to do him right and he had cited her for default of justice before the court of the lord King, where he was prepared to convict her of defaults of justice in the judgment of the lord King's court. On this question it was decided that Jean de Néelle had no obligation to return to the Countess's court and that the Countess must answer him in the court of the lord King, before which he had cited her for default of justice.

Furthermore, since the peers of France said that the Chancellor, Butler, Chamberlain and Constable of France, as officials in the lord King's household, ought not to take part with them in pronouncing judgment upon the peers of France; and since these officials in the lord King's household on the other hand said that according to the uses and customs observed in France they ought to take part with the peers of France in judging peers: it was decided in the lord King's court that these officials in the lord King's household ought to take part with the peers of France in judging peers; and then these officials pronounced judgment on the Countess of Flanders at Paris, together with the peers of France, in the year of Our Lord 1224.

LOUIS IX DISPENSES JUSTICE

§ 17. Here Louis IX appears as the ideally accessible King, ensuring that justice was dispensed with the utmost rapidity. Jean, lord of Joinville (1224/5-1317), the author of the now-famous life of Louis, was Seneschal to the Court of Champagne and a close personal friend of the King.

The *Life of St. Louis* has been translated into English recently by Joan Evans (1937, 1938), by R. Hague (1955) and by M. R. B. Shaw (1963) in *Chronicles of the Crusades*.

§ 17

St. Louis dispenses justice: Jean, Sire de Joinville, *Histoire de Saint Louis*, ed. N. de Wailly (1874), 34.

It happened many a time in summer that the King after Mass would go to sit in the wood at Vincennes, and would lean against an oak tree and make us sit round about him. And all who had some business came to speak with him, and were not stopped by ushers or other persons.

Then he would personally ask them: 'Is there anyone here who has a lawsuit?' And those who had suits would rise. Then he would say: 'Keep silence, all of you, and you will be dealt with, one after another.' Then he would call my lord Pierre de Fontaines and my lord Geoffroi de Villette, and say to one of them: 'Deal with this case for me.'

And when he saw that there was any correction to be made in the words of those who were speaking on his behalf, or in those of men speaking for somebody else, he would personally make the correction. I sometimes in summer saw that to deal with his people he would come into the garden in Paris, dressed in a tunic of camlet, a surcoat of linsey-woolsey without sleeves, a mantle of black taffeta about his neck, without a hood but with his hair well combed, and a hat of white peacock's feathers upon his head. And he had carpets laid out in order to seat us round him, and all the people who had business before him would stay round about. Then he would deal with them in the way that I previously described him doing in the wood at Vincennes.

THE KING AND THE COMMUNES

§§ 18–19. These documents are offered here to provide some illustration of the nature of communes in France in the twelfth and thirteenth centuries, of the privileges accorded to them, and of the degree of control which the monarchy in the days of Louis IX claimed to exercise over them.

See Luchaire in Lavisse, *Histoire de France*, III, i, 227 foll.; A. Luchaire, *Les communes françaises à l'époque des capétiens directs* (1911); cf. Strayer, *Administration of Normandy*, 81 foll.; Petit-Dutaillis, *The feudal monarchy*, 196 foll., 314 foll.; C. Petit-Dutaillis, *Les communes françaises: caractères et évolution des origines au XVIIIe siècle* (1947), with bibliography; cf. A. R. Lewis, 'The development of town government in twelfth century Montpellier', *Spec.*, 22 (1947); Lot and Fawtier, *Histoire des institutions*, II, 199; Fawtier, *The Capetian Kings*, 206 foll.

§ 18

Philip Augustus establishes a commune at Pontoise, 1188: E. Berger and M. H. F. Delaborde, *Recueil des Actes de Philippe-Auguste, Roi de France*, I (1916), 283–5.

In the name of the holy and indivisible Trinity. Amen. Philip, by the grace of God King of the French.

All men, present and future, shall know that we have established a commune at Pontoise, reserving fealty to us and our successors and saving all customs, in this wise:

That all who dwell in the parishes of Pontoise and Saint-Martin shall by perpetual right be free and immune from every unjust tallage, from unjustified arrest, from unfair use of the right to purchase their goods, and from all unreasonable exactions, no matter whose vassals they are. If any retainer of a knight commits an offence against his master, then the knight his lord shall summon him to his house (if it is in Pontoise) and he shall make full satisfaction. But if the retainer refuses to do what is right, the knight shall seize any of the retainer's goods that he can find on his own land, though he must leave them all on the spot and take nothing away. Then the knight shall show the mayor and peers of the community that for lack of satisfaction he has seized the property of his retainer. The mayor, having (if he wishes to do so) summoned the peers of the community to him, shall force the knight's retainer to make amends to the knight according to the law by which he (the retainer) lives because he has refused to behave justly, and any reasonable action shall be taken against him in full for the original offence.

If anyone brings within the walls [ad castrum] somebody who has unwittingly done wrong to a member of this community, and if that person can prove upon oath that he did this in ignorance, he shall, this once only, be allowed to go free and in peace; otherwise we decree that he must be arrested.

Anyone who comes to market within the walls shall be allowed to come and go in peace, so that he may never, whether he is coming or going, be molested by anyone, unless he is a debtor or a guarantor or commits or has committed an offence for which he ought to be detained.

Traders who are in transit or who dwell in Pontoise shall at all times be left in peace.

If anyone living outside the walls has committed any offence against the community, and has refused to make amends on being summoned to do so, the community may punish him for it in whatever way it can.

If one man has assaulted another, the assailant, having been brought to trial by the mayor and peers of the community, shall be called upon to make amends, and if he refuses to do this he shall be forced to, whether he likes it or not.

All the men shall as a community provide for common needs, such as the watch, the prisons and the moats and all things pertaining to the defence and security of the village. Care must be taken to ensure that smaller burdens are imposed upon persons of smaller means, in proportion to their means, and that more is exacted of persons of greater means. The burden of any other needs which may arise shall likewise be distributed among all men of that place in common and suitably adjusted (as was said above) to each man's means.

They shall likewise perform in common all tasks which pertain to our service, each man in proportion to his ability to undertake them; and if anyone commits an offence against the peers of the community who have to decide how this is to be done, he shall make suitable amends to them.

No one other than the men themselves may guard the vineyards of the men of this community, and if any one says that he has a right to guard them, he must prove this in our presence.

We further grant that they and their heirs may always hold in peace and quiet any property that they have rightfully and lawfully bought or received as security, and which they have subsequently held for a year and a day in peace without committing fraud and without denying anybody his rights therein, purchases as purchases, securities as securities.

We likewise grant that they may always hold everything which they have obtained by right of inheritance and anything they have acquired in a just and reasonable fashion and which they subsequently hold in the manner specified above. But out of regard for equity we have also decreed that if any interested party is out of the country at the time, but subsequently returns and makes a complaint, they must give him his rights in full.

We further grant to the men of this community the privilege that they shall not, for military or host service or upon any summons of ours, be obliged to go beyond the Seine or the Isère.

We have also granted to them the privilege that no cart shall pass through the Auvers gate.

Again, we have granted to the commune our provostship and the grain taxes of Pontoise upon condition that they pay us five hundred pounds a year and our seneschal thirty pounds a year for our provostship. But we will pay the other dues and gratuities out of our own property. For the grain taxes they shall pay us fifteen measures of grain, i.e. ten of wheat and five of oats.

We have made all the grants listed above, saving the rights of churches, and, that they may be established for ever, we order this charter to be authenticated by our seal and by the addition of the royal signature below.

Done at Mantes in the year of Our Lord's Incarnation 1188, in the ninth year of our reign, with those whose names and signatures are appended below present in our palace. The signature of Count Thibaut, our Seneschal. The signature of Guy the Butler. The signature of Matthew the Chamberlain. The signature of Ralph the Constable. Given at a time when the Chancery was vacant.

§ 19

Louis IX's ordinance on the communes of Normandy, *circa* 1256: A. Giry, *Documents sur les relations de la royauté avec les villes en France de 1180 à 1314* (1885), 85–6.

THE ORDINANCE MADE BY THE KING CONCERNING
THE VILLAGES IN NORMANDY AND THE ELECTION OF MAYORS

We ordain concerning our communes in Normandy that on the morrow of the festival of the blessed apostles Simon and Jude[1] the mayor for the current year together with other reputable men of the village shall elect three reputable men, and these three men shall be presented to us at Paris during the octave of St. Martin following.[2] We will give the village one of these three men as mayor.

It is our will that every year upon that day, that is, on the morrow of the festival of the apostles Simon and Jude, a statement of all the affairs of the village may be drawn up in the presence of these three reputable men; and the mayor and the aforesaid three reputable men shall bring this statement or account to our servants who are placed in charge of our accounts, during the octave of St. Martin in the winter.

Again, we forbid our communes and villages, on pain of proceedings against their persons and their property in every place, to presume to enter into any loan agreement with anyone or to attempt to make any form of gift, other than presents of wine in pots or jars, without leave from us.

Again, we ordain that no one from any village or commune may go or return to the court or to any other place to transact the business of the village save only the mayor or somebody deputizing for him; and he may not take with him more than two companions and a clerk from

1. i.e. on October 29th.   2. Around November 18th.

the village, together with an advocate if they need one. The mayor and his companions may not take a great number of people or horses with them on the business of the village, nor may they spend more than they would if they were going on their own business.

Again, we ordain that no one whatsoever, other than the man who is paying the expenses, may keep the money of the village by him. And this man cannot have more than twenty pounds at a time. The money of the village must be kept in the common chest.

Any commune which in any year by the aforesaid date pays the tallage which has been assessed by our servants shall be entirely free of debts and interest charges.

CHAPTER IV

Royal and Clerical Power

§§ 20-3. These documents concern the major problem of the relationship between royal and ecclesiastical authorities in France in the thirteenth century. They indicate some of the points at which collision between the two powers was liable to arise—over their respective jurisdictions, over the question of excommunication, over the levying of taxes, and so forth.

The agreement between Philip Augustus and his barons (20), attempting to check the extension of clerical jurisdiction, was to some extent observed and enforced in Normandy, if not in other parts of the Kingdom.

Extract 21 provides an example of collaboration between a great ecclesiastical authority and the royal power.

Extract 22, concerning excommunication, is again taken from Joinville's *History of St. Louis* (see no. 17 above). The events it describes may be dated in the year 1263.

Extract 23 forms part of a document which was copied by Matthew Paris (d. 1259), a monk of St. Albans in a position to be well informed about European events. This document complains of the heavy taxation levied by the Papacy upon the French clergy and of the extent to which the French church was being exploited in the interests of foreigners. Probably it was genuinely a document drawn up by a royal official on behalf of Louis IX. It does not necessarily represent the King's views with perfect accuracy; but it is certainly important as a reflection of the anti-clericalism which was becoming widespread in France at the time of the conflict between Innocent IV and Frederick II.

See Luchaire in Lavisse, *Histoire de France*, III, i, 216 foll.; Petit-Dutaillis, *The feudal monarchy*, 262 foll.; G. J. Campbell, 'The attitude of the monarchy toward the use of ecclesiastical censures in the reign of Saint Louis', *Spec.*, 35 (1960); Fawtier, *The Capetian Kings*, 211 foll.; Lot and Fawtier, *Histoire des institutions*, III (1962), 264 foll.

On extract 23 in particular, see E. Berger, *Saint Louis et Innocent IV: étude sur les rapports de la France et du Saint-Siège* (1893), 267 foll.; Langlois in Lavisse, *Histoire de France*, III, ii, 60 foll.; G. Barraclough, *Papal provisions* (Oxford, 1935), 11 foll.; L. Buisson, *König Ludwig IX, der Heilige, und das Recht* (Freiburg, 1954), ch. 4; R. Vaughan, *Matthew Paris* (Cambridge, 1958), 78 foll.; G. J. Campbell, 'The protest of Saint Louis', T., 15 (1959).

§ 20

Articles defining the extent of clerical jurisdiction drawn up by Philip Augustus and his barons, 1205–1206: C. Brunel, H. F. Delaborde, C. Petit-Dutaillis and J. Monicat, *Recueil des Actes de Philippe-Auguste, Roi de France*, II, 489–91.

The agreement which was made at Paris between the clergy and the barons.

The first point is that the clergy bring cases concerning fiefs into the courts of the Church, because they say that there was an oath or promise between the parties to the dispute, and on these grounds the lords lose their jurisdiction over their fiefs. The answer is that the King and barons agree that they are willing for the clergy to have jurisdiction over perjury and over the breaking of faith, but they do not want the clergy to have jurisdiction over the fief. If a man be convicted of perjury or of breaking faith, let the clergy impose a penance on him, but the lord shall not on account of this lose his jurisdiction over the fief, nor shall the clergy seize the fief because of it. Further, the King and barons wish a widow to be able, if she wishes, to complain either to the King or to the Church concerning her dowry, if it does not form part of a fief; and if she complains to the Church, and the man from whom she is demanding the dowry says that he will answer before the lord from whom the fief originates, the Church can force him to answer and can rightfully decide the disputes between them.

The second point is that when a clerk is arrested for a crime for which a man ought to lose life or limb, and is handed over to the clergy to be degraded, the clergy wish him, after being degraded, to be set completely at liberty.

The answer to this is that the clergy need not actually hand him over to the royal court when he has been degraded, but they must not on the other hand free him or put him in some place where he cannot be arrested, but the justiciars may arrest him outside the church or church-yard and do justice upon him, and they cannot be sued for doing so.

On the third point it is established that tithes shall be paid as they have hitherto been paid and as they ought to be paid.

Fourthly: that no burgher or villein, if he has one or more sons, may give to any son who is a clerk as much as half or more than half his land; and if he gives him a portion of the land which is less than half of it, the clerk must render the service and assistance which was due on the land to the lords to whom it was due, but on the other hand he may not be tallaged unless he trades or lends money at interest; and after his death the land shall return to his closest relatives; and no clerk may buy land unless he performs for his lord the service which is due on the land.

The fifth point: that archbishops and bishops must not require burghers or others to swear that they have never lent at interest and never will do so.

If a clerk is convicted of robbery, he shall be handed over to the Church to be degraded, and after the degradation the King or justiciar may arrest him outside the church or hall and do justice upon him, and they may not be sued for doing so.

If a clerk sues anyone who is not a clerk concerning any property of which he has never been in possession, he must bring the defendant, not into the Church court, but into the court of the lord to whom juris-diction belongs, unless the Church has jurisdiction because the land belongs to it.

Again, clerks must not excommunicate those who sell corn or other merchandise on Sundays, or those who buy from or sell to the Jews or do their work, but the King and barons are willing that women em-ployed as nurses by Jews should be excommunicated.

Again: supposing anyone voluntarily puts himself in the prison of the King or of another man, where the King or another has the right to a heriot,[1] so that he may be ransomed without losing life or limb; or supposing the King or any other arrests someone so that he may be ransomed without losing life or limb: and this person escapes from prison and flees to the Church, the Church wishes to free him and to deprive the lord of the ransom.

The King and barons answer that if a man voluntarily puts himself in anyone's prison so that he may be ransomed, or if a man is arrested for the sake of a heriot without the possibility of losing life or limb, the

1. *Habet capitale*: this may mean the right to take the best beast or some other chattel of a deceased tenant.

Church ought not to deprive the lord of the heriot or of his ransom or free the man if he flees to the Church. On the contrary, the man may be taken into custody outside the church or hall, and the guards who do so may not lawfully be sued for this.

Again, the clergy may not lawfully excommunicate any person for a crime committed by his servant, nor lay his land under interdict, until he (the lord) or his bailiff, if the lord is out of the country, has been approached about the matter.

Again, if anyone either knowingly or inadvertently commits a crime against the Church, he must not be excommunicated nor may his land be laid under interdict until he, or his bailiff if he is out of the country, has been questioned about it.

Again, suppose a man is summoned to an ecclesiastical court and the judges compel him at the first summons to swear that he will abide by their sentence, although he is not guilty of default of justice and has not been excommunicated: the King and barons answer that this ought not to be done.

Again, when the clergy sue anyone over some question involving serfdom and the defendant says that he is another man's serf, the clergy wish him to answer in their own court, although he says that he is the serf of another man, and they force him to answer before them on pain of excommunication and excommunicate those who support him. To this the King and barons reply that the defendant ought to answer in the court of the man whose serf he claims to be.

§ 21

The Archbishop of Rouen prepares the way for the royal bailiffs: extract from a letter of March 27th, 1217: L. Délisle, *Cartulaire Normand de Philippe-Auguste, Louis VIII, Saint Louis et Philippe-le-Hardi* (Caen, 1852), 39.

To all the faithful of Christ whom the present letters reach, Robert, by the grace of God Archbishop of Rouen, greeting in the Lord.

You shall know that we have made this grant to our lord Philip, illustrious King of the French: that whenever his chief bailiffs call upon our deans to come, each of them with four priests, to make inquiries concerning churches about which there is some doubt to whom the right of presentation belongs, and to remove fugitives from churches according to the uses and customs of Normandy, it is our will and command that these deans and priests, as it is set out above, shall neither delay nor resist and shall come upon the day appointed by the lord King's bailiffs for them to do this. But should they fail to do this, we desire and grant that each of these deans shall for every time he defaults pay a fine of nine pounds, which shall invariably be given to the house of lepers in Rouen, so that the nine pounds cannot be paid to us or to any deputy of ours save for the purpose of aiding the said lepers.

And, for love of King Philip, we have granted, for as long as we are pleased to do so, that we and our officials will not excommunicate the chief bailiffs of the lord King without first approaching the lord King about the matter, and giving them fifteen days' grace, unless the bailiffs are holding a tonsured clerk or keeping his chattels and refusing to give them up to us or to our officials; and we have granted that we will, at the next session of the high court at Easter, hold and pay attention to an inquiry into this point through bishops and barons and other trust-worthy persons.

§ 22

The King and excommunication: Jean, Sire de Joinville, *Histoire de Saint Louis*, ed. N. de Wailly (1874), 368, 370.

I will tell you of the King's wisdom. Sometimes people would declare that there was no one in his council as wise as he was. This was apparent because, when they spoke to him about certain things, he would not say 'I will take advice on this', but when he saw clearly and unmistakably what was right, he would give an immediate reply without taking advice. I heard that he gave such an answer to all the prelates of the realm of France concerning a request which they made of him, and which ran as follows.

Bishop Guy of Auxerre spoke to the King on behalf of all the prelates. 'Sire', he said, 'these archbishops and bishops here present have instructed me to tell you that Christianity is in your hands decaying and disappearing, and that it will decay still further if you do not take heed, because nowadays nobody is afraid of being excommunicated. We therefore request you, Sire, to order your bailiffs and serjeants to force excommunicated persons who have been under sentence for a year and a day to make amends to the Church.' And the King, without taking advice, answered them that he would willingly order his bailiffs and serjeants to put pressure on excommunicated persons just as the prelates asked, so long as he was allowed to judge whether the sentence was just or not.

Then the prelates conferred and answered the King that they would not give him jurisdiction over anything that really belonged to the Church courts. But the King replied in his turn that he would not give them jurisdiction over what belonged to him, and would not order his serjeants to force excommunicated persons to get themselves absolved, without inquiring whether this was right or wrong. 'For if I did that, I should be going against God and the right. I will give you an example —the bishops of Brittany kept the Count of Brittany excommunicate for seven years, and then he received absolution through the Roman curia. Had I put pressure on him from the first year onwards, I should have been in the wrong.'

§ 23

The King's claim to use the treasure of the Church for the good of the realm—extract from an address presented to Pope Innocent IV on behalf of the King of France, 1247: Matthew Paris, *Chronica Majora*, VI, *Additamenta*, ed. H. R. Luard (London, 1882), 110–12.

The lord King's ancestors founded the churches of the realm and endowed them out of their own property, especially for the performance of divine worship, and in this honourable act retained and always kept a special right of their own for themselves and their heirs in those churches which hold their temporal goods of them, since the temporalities of churches are held by human, that is by royal right—and apart from their spiritual duties they have many other great services to render the lord King. Hence the lord King has the right to take as his own all the treasure and temporalities of churches to meet his own needs and those of his Kingdom.

But if anyone objects that a secular or lay prince cannot claim for himself this right in the property of churches to canonical services, we answer that much greater and more special was the right which Charles the Great and many Kings of the Franks after him enjoyed, as the canons expressly declare—for this was the power of choosing the Supreme Bishop and disposing of the Apostolic See and of granting investiture to all archbishops and bishops. It is not very long since the Kings of France in their own chambers conferred all bishoprics on those whom they chose; and if some of them have waived certain rights for God's sake, nevertheless the Kings of France have never actually waived many other rights over churches which they do not now enjoy, as do the princes and other patrons of churches, but which were once conferred on them by the general consent of the Church and also granted to them by ancient custom and prolonged usage.

We therefore feel that burdening the churches afresh in such an insupportable fashion causes great loss and manifold injury to the King and his realm, and it seems that his successors will suffer great inconvenience if the property of churches is converted to uses other than those for which it was originally given to them. Moreover, as a result of this, there has been less divine worship in the churches of the realm, and this is in danger of further shrinking and dying out, although the lord King does not want it to diminish in his time but rather to increase. By the impoverishment of churches the realm is made poorer, for when the property of churches is thus exported from the realm, the realm is plundered and foreigners grow rich on the spoils. Moreover, this manner of demanding money is new to our own times, and because it might be made into a precedent and develop into a most injurious custom, the King does not want this obligation to be imposed in his own time on the churches of the realm and hence on the realm itself. Again, burdens of this sort may weigh upon the churches, which are now heavily taxed and have become habitually poor, so heavily that they cannot render to the Kings the many great services which they are obliged to perform for them. When the temporalities of churches are thus carried off, the Kingdom is harmed no less than it would be if they were being removed from the lord King's own treasury; since in case of need the treasure of churches belongs to him and he can then use it as his own. Again, as the lord King has taken the cross and is about to set out for the Holy Land, he wishes—as, indeed, he ought to wish—the churches of the realm to assist him, as their patron, generously on his pilgrimage, and he wishes them none the less to have some means of bearing the cost of the defence of his kingdom as they ought if the need arise.

The lord King reminds you of what you undoubtedly know already, that he has a sincere affection for you and greatly sympathizes with you in your needs. But, however much he loves you, he cannot fail to maintain, as far as he is able, the wellbeing, liberties and customs of the Kingdom entrusted to him by the Lord God, where the Church has always enjoyed great honour and great liberty and peace until his own time, in his own time and down to the present day.

TABLE OF SOURCES

Throughout this table, part numbers are set in roman numerals, section numbers in arabic figures.